Transplantation Gothic

MANCHESTER
1824

Manchester University Press

Transplantation Gothic

Tissue transfer in literature, film, and medicine

SARA WASSON

Manchester University Press

Published by Manchester University Press
Altrincham Street, Manchester M1 7JA

www.manchesteruniversitypress.co.uk

British Library Cataloguing-in-Publication Data
A catalogue record for this book is available from the British Library

ISBN   978 1 5261 3286 4   hardback

First published 2020

The publisher has no responsibility for the persistence or accuracy of URLs for any external or third-party internet websites referred to in this book, and does not guarantee that any content on such websites is, or will remain, accurate or appropriate.

Typeset by
Servis Filmsetting Ltd, Stockport, Cheshire

In memory of my father, Stuart Alan Clark

Contents

Figures

Cover image. Andrew Carnie, *Gold Elysium* (2017). Gold watercolour on stitched canvas. © Image courtesy of Andrew Carnie.

Preface

I would like to thank Lancaster University for the Fiftieth Anniversary scheme that made this research possible, and the intellectually adventurous and delightful colleagues and PhD students who make working here such a joy. Special thanks to Catherine Spooner, Brian Baker, Jen Ashworth, Zoe Lambert, and Liz Oakley-Brown, Sally Bushell, Hilary Hinds, Sharon Ruston, Rebecca Gibson, Kerry Dodd, and Neal Kirk. I also want to thank the many formidable and generous scholars working in the field of transplantation, for inspiration and fellowship, particularly Donna McCormack, Margrit Shildrick, Gill Haddow, Megan Crowley-Matoka, and Ciara Kierans. Fond thanks also to Naomi Salman for translations of French.

I would also like to thank the UK Arts and Humanities Research Council (AHRC) for funding the *Translating Chronic Pain* research network, the findings from which have deeply informed this book. The project includes an online anthology of flash writing about pain and a Creative Manifesto, available at www.lancaster.ac.uk/translating-pain, and I continue to invite submissions. Finally, if I were to list all the members of the wider Gothic Studies community to whom I am indebted this would cause the inevitable metaphors of monstrosity to become applicable in the acknowledgements page before even reaching the text itself, so I will refrain and send only fervent, spectral, affection.

Acknowledgements

The author and publisher wish to thank the following for permission to reproduce copyright material. Every effort has been made to identify copyright holders. If any have been overlooked please contact us.

Routledge for permission to include sections from the book chapter 'Recalcitrant tissue: organ transfer and the struggle for narrative control', which previously appeared in J. Edwards (ed.), *Technologies of the Gothic in Literature and Culture* (New York: Routledge, 2015), pp. 99–112, and which appears here as a subsection of Chapter 4.

Manchester University Press for permission to reprint portions of 'Scalpel and metaphor: the ceremony of organ harvest in Gothic science fiction', which appeared in *Gothic Studies*, 17:1 (2015), 104–23, and which appears here as a subsection of Chapter 5.

Andrew Carnie, *Gold Elysium* (2017). Gold watercolour on stitched canvas, and *Commonality in Liquidity* (2007). Digital drawing (2007). © Images courtesy of Andrew Carnie.

Isidro de Villoldo, *Milagro de San Cosme y San Damián* (c. 1547), © Museo Nacional de Escultura, Valladolid. Photo: Javier Muñoz y Paz Pastor CE0362.

Taylor Guest, Poster for *Harvest*, dir. by Shelby Hibbs. University of Texas at Dallas Theatrical Production, 2018. © Taylor Guest.

Excerpt from Natasha Trethewey's poem 'Miracle of the black leg', from *Thrall: Poems* by Natasha Trethewey. Copyright © 2012 by Natasha Trethewey. Reprinted by permission of Houghton Mifflin Harcourt Publishing Company. All rights reserved.

Excerpt from J.D. Reed's poem 'Organ transplant', *The New Yorker* (26 September 1970), 126. Copyright © The New Yorker. Reprinted by permission of Condé Nast.

Introduction

Bodies dis(re)membered: Gothic and the transplant imaginary

'My blood has adopted a child / who shuffles through my chest / carrying a doll'.[1] J.D. Reed's poem describes a particular recipient's experience of living with a transplanted heart. Simultaneously compassionate and sinister, this poem captures some of the ambivalence that may gather around the received tissue – the possibility of a tender coexistence, yet also haunting and strangeness. The image also confronts us with the human reality of the organ's origin – not a mechanical replacement but organic tissue with a *history*, its transfer mediated by a network of technology, institutions, financial interests, and legislation.

This book is a shadow cultural history of transplantation, as mediated through medical writing, science fiction, life writing, and visual arts in a Gothic mode from the nineteenth century to the present. Tissue transfer is a boundary practice in multiple senses, unsettling conventional distinctions between self and other and between life and death, and challenging the limits of the body's capacity to transform and the ethical limits of scientific practice. As such, it is unsurprising that Gothic tropes and intertextualities have characterised imaginings and representations of the processes ever since the Gothic emerged as a distinctive genre and mode. This book identifies a variety of texts and cultural artefacts that draw on a Gothic mode to reflect on – and, in turn, to shape – the mutable discourses of transplantation science. In the context of tissue transfer and related illness, Gothic representation can correlate with the way subjects may experience their bodies as uncanny, once familiar but now strange, may feel helpless and physically vulnerable, and may strive to decipher the cryptic signs of medical record and bodily symptoms, may endure carceral hospital sites and the strange temporalities of waiting list and aftermath. They may be subjected to rituals of medical monitoring, and may become supplicants to powerful figures with mysterious knowledge. Yet literary and cinematic medical Gothic does more than represent patient–clinician encounters, for it can also comment on wider social dimensions of illness. The book takes up contemporary debates around the management of chronic illness, the changing economics of healthcare, and the global biopolitics of organ procurement and transplantation – in sum, the strange times and weird spaces of tissue mobilities.

I will usually speak of 'tissue transfer' rather than 'organ transplantation'. 'Tissue' is more accurate, since, beyond whole organs, other human tissues and cells are increasingly transferred and profitable. I also avoid the term 'deceased donor', despite it being preferred by transplantation professionals, because it disguises the degree to which death is a process and the ambiguities of categories of death, which continue to be legally and physiologically complex (see Chapter 1). Instead, following Margaret Lock, I find the term 'cadaveric donor' – in wide use from the 1960s until recently – to be a usefully liminal term for a liminal state. I avoid the term 'organ retrieval' because it inaccurately naturalises the process, implying that tissue is being restored to its original site and masking surgical realities of extraction. I do use the term 'procurement' since that is overwhelmingly the term in circulation in medical contexts, but I regularly alternate it with 'surgical extraction'. I generally use the term 'supplier' rather than 'seller' since, as Martin Gunnarson and Susanna Lundin note, suppliers may not receive promised payment and the ideologically charged term 'seller' implies both a certain agency and a product separate from a self.[2] I speak of 'transfer tissue' rather than 'graft' for the same reason I speak of 'transfer' rather than 'transplantation': following Lesley Sharp's point that while 'transplantation' emphasises surgical grafting into recipient, 'transfer' includes the donor as well as the meditating practices and parties.[3] Using 'transplantation' as shorthand for this whole process, as customary in popular parlance, foregrounds the surgical moment while the donor, their kin, the procurement apparatus, and the recipient's post-transplant condition fade from view.[4] It is particularly at these sites that a Gothic mode and intertextualities tend to emerge: in a sense, 'transplantation Gothic' describes suffering attendant on the zones that the shorthand of 'transplantation' hides.

As such, this project is about seeking out literature that restores particular suffering to the field of vision: donor bodies opened for organs to be taken, recipient bodies opened for organs to be inserted, and practitioners with their own affective burdens. Yet no representation can give stable, comprehensive access into the experience of these plights: at times all that can be shown is the invisibility of distress – a scar, an imagining, a trace. Furthermore, work in a Gothic mode may also work to exacerbate such erasure and marginalisation.

Popular Gothic and horror fictions of transplantation are so abundant that they have, unsurprisingly, drawn comment from historians and social scientists studying transfer.[5] Such comments tend to dismiss these fictions as titillating sensation, and Gothic representations of medicine can indeed sensationalise and foster distrust of medical practitioners. Evidence suggests that, for example, Robin Cook's transplantation horror thriller *Coma* (1977) influenced decreases in donor kin consent to cadaveric donation.[6] In a related vein, the transplant surgeon and historian David Hamilton identifies such fictions as symptomatic of periods when practice was not scientifically rigorous or well-managed:

> This genre blossomed as a result of the anarchy in the transplant world of the 1920s ... The inventive authors had licence to transfer much else with the tissue – hands donated from dead murderers could prove murderous, brain grafts might be malevolent, and simian characteristics could appear after monkey testis transplants. *With good science restored* in mid-twentieth century, transplant themes were temporarily absent from the fiction of the day, but the controversies of the heart transplants and brain death in the 1970s encouraged publishers and writers to return to these genres. These novels fed on the new fears of the times, featuring sleazy doctors and organ-snatching gangs, but in the more settled periods that followed, popular nonfiction accounts found success, and positive personal stories of successful organ grafts sold well.[7]

In Hamilton's telling, fantastical and horror fictions are symptoms of errors in the management or communication of transplantation practice, and are contrasted with the decorum of 'positive' 'nonfiction accounts', which emerge when 'good science [is] restored'. Transplantation Gothic certainly flourishes at moments when practices become controversial, but also emerges in periods characterised by scientific and popular consensus over ethical practice. As I will show, Gothic is not solely an 'anxious' mode.

Social scientists are rightly wary of the way that popular media can reduce transplantation to a glib dichotomy. Megan Crowley-Matoka and Margaret Lock, for example, observe that popular media abound in 'celebratory images of scientific progress and lives saved through transplantation, to nightmare visions of the international black market in human organs'.[8] I suggest that, whilst these texts may well reinforce such a dichotomy, they can also complicate it. The Gothic fictions of this book resist the salvific registers which dominate transplantation discourse in the UK and US, while simultaneously resisting the exoticisation of predatorial tissue economies as alien to post-industrial regions. To that end, this book primarily addresses Gothic representations of transfer suffering *within* post-industrial economies of the US and UK in particular, considers intra-national as well as transnational predation and explores how predatorial harvest is not only a function of illegal markets but also a product and symbol of complex networks of structural ruination.

The juxtaposition of 'transplantation' and 'Gothic' may seem inappropriate, even grotesque. Transplantation surgery is, after all, astounding and lifesaving – as Sharp admits, it 'may well be viewed as the quintessential example of millennial medicine, for we have remained in awe of its accomplishments since the mid-twentieth century and into the twenty-first'.[9] The Chair of the UK Donation Ethics Committee, Sir Peter Simpson, recently declared that 'everything about it can be seen in a positive light', in that it benefits recipients,

donors, kin, and wider society.[10] Surgeons, recipients, and grateful loved ones
invoke the language of 'miracle' to describe the work.[11] Is this practice, then,
better described solely in terms of celebration?

Notwithstanding the life-saving achievements of transplantation, suffering
is still part of transfer in multiple ways. Recipients and recipients-in-waiting
occupy complex affective positions that can include ambivalence, both before
and after transplantation. Donation and procurement may involve physical or
emotional suffering for a range of parties. There may be inequalities in terms of
what demographics tend to comprise recipient and donor pools. Particularly in
contexts of organ sale, living donors may be impelled by desperate straits and
may incur long-term physical, emotional, financial, and social consequences.[12]
Donor kin may feel distress if procurement processes are handled in ways
which clash with cultural norms for grieving, or at post-transplant protocols of
donor anonymity.[13] Within certain milieux, some practitioners, too, have felt
pressured by particular protocols, particularly in environments where financial
incentives impact the process. Finally, controversies exist around heroic state
efforts to prevent particular deaths while neglecting other causes.

Despite these very real issues, a celebratory register is virtually mandatory
around donation and transplantation science, and, as Lesley Sharp warns, com-
pulsory celebration

> can effectively silence competing or subversive sentiments, including shared
> desires among recipients and the kin of deceased organ donors to seek out one
> another; the all-too-frequent lifetime suffering of patients who struggle with the
> physiological effects and financial burdens associated with daily doses of exor-
> bitantly expensive and potentially toxic immunosuppressants; and widespread
> social ambivalence regarding clinically orchestrated forms of death, the surgi-
> cal violation of the integrity of donors' bodies, and the eerie sense that trans-
> plant survivors' lives have been saved, extended, or enhanced with fleshy parts
> acquired from the dead.[14]

These are controversial things to say. In Britain and in the US, the two countries I explore in most detail, there is a profound imperative to speak of transplantation and its precursors in positive terms. Without doubt, organ donation
is a praiseworthy practice that saves lives. Yet, as with any social practice, there
are ambiguities, and, in a practice that rests on the wounding or death of another
body it is astonishing that voicing this ambiguity is so taboo. *Celebrating transplantation does not require denying the suffering that can be part of these complex
processes*, and such denial is ethically problematic when it can lead to erasing
the sacrifice of donors or donor kin, or the suffering of donors and recipients.
Ethnographic research has nuanced the mandatory positivity of this discourse
for numerous contexts, and this present book seeks to complement that body of
work from within the discipline of literary study.[15]

In focusing on suffering I am not, however, implying an idealised or nostalgic view of the pre-transplantation body as uniquely intact, or suggesting that either tissue extraction or transplant is intrinsically a violation. Some critics have done this: Leslie Fiedler, for example, reads Mary Shelley's *Frankenstein* (1818, 1823), Bram Stoker's *Dracula* (1897), H.G. Wells's *Island of Doctor Moreau* (1896), and Robert Louis Stevenson's *Strange Case of Dr Jekyll and Mr Hyde* (1886) as 'iatrophobic nightmares' symptomatic of a universal, transhistorical resistance to medical or pharmacological extensions of life.[16] I have significant concerns about naturalising any particular conception of an idealised, 'intact' body; embodiment is culturally constructed and 'the body' is not a prediscursive given.[17] There is nothing intrinsically, universally negative about transfer. I also, however, take representations of distress seriously, including expressions of the affective complexity of experience of recipients, donors or suppliers, kin and practitioners, and symbolic expressions of precarity within particular social contexts. *The wounds that most concern me are not surgical, but social and emotional*, and such injuries are not inevitable in transfer.

But – why 'Gothic'? Many of the texts I am examining are marketed as horror or science fiction, so why not call this book *Transplantation Fantastic?* Science fiction, Gothic, and horror are, after all, overlapping forms of Fantastika, to use John Clute's term.[18] Why employ the more abstruse 'Gothic' which, despite its thriving critical field, is more cryptic for a wider readership? Firstly, I suggest that the concept of a Gothic 'mode' is valuable shorthand for a specific combination of disturbed emotion, claustrophobic space, and disjointed temporality, a constellation of characteristics which can be especially useful in describing challenging transfer-related experience. Secondly, 'Gothic' denotes an influential literary tradition which continues to serve intertextually as resource within popular culture, deployed in sometimes surprising ways by patients, clinicians, social scientists, and medical historians. Gothic fictions such as Mary Shelley's *Frankenstein* (1818) and H.G. Wells's *Island of Doctor Moreau* (1896) have influenced works beyond their nineteenth-century manifestations, icons continually repurposed to make sense of and challenge discourses around transfer. As Catherine Spooner observes, 'Gothic narratives have escaped the confines of literature', like a virus, 'to infect all kinds of media'.[19] My third answer, proceeding from the preceding two, is that my interest is not only in texts classified as 'horror', 'science fiction', or 'fantastic' but also in life writing and indeed scientific prose, composed in a Gothic mode or informed by Gothic intertextualities. In other words, using the critical category of Gothic allows me both to broaden my discussion beyond the bounds of arbitrary publishing categories and to be more specific about elements of the texts I am examining.

'Gothic' emerged as a term of art criticism during the second half of the eighteenth century to describe architecture, fiction, drama, and poetry, becoming, as Robert Miles says, 'a vibrant dialect in the Western cultural imagination'.[20]

Within this broad field of cultural production, literary Gothic – and, later, cinematic Gothic – has a particular concern with the threat of bodily torment. Corporeal vulnerability is at the heart of Edmund Burke's *Philosophical Inquiry into the Origin of Our Ideas of the Sublime and Beautiful* (1757), an early and influential theorisation of the appeal of extremity and fear. Instead of seeing the sublime as a state evoked by the experience of beauty or grandeur, Burke argues it is most intensely evoked by a sense of mortal fragility: 'Whatever is fitted in any sort to excite the ideas of pain and danger ... is productive of the strongest emotion which the mind is capable of feeling'.[21] As David Punter says, Gothic offers 'an image language for bodies and their terrors'.[22]

Bodies are violated, threatened, and transformed in these works, and the intuition of corporeal vulnerability shapes representation in three characteristic ways. Since the eighteenth century, the Gothic increasingly functions less as a genre than as a mode which occupies other literary forms.[23] In defining this Gothic mode, criticism tends to identify a triad of disturbance in affect, space, or time: distressing emotion, claustrophobic spaces, and anachronistic temporalities. The emotions and affects described in these texts typically include horror, terror, paranoia, melancholy, fear, dread, and a sense of the uncanny; they 'substantively refer to a world of horror', in which '[i]magination and emotional effects exceed reason', to quote Andrew Smith and Fred Botting.[24] The intradiegetic affects and emotions are not generalisable to readers and viewers, who are more likely to feel pleasure.[25] Protagonists, however, suffer in body, mind, or both, and their turmoil is reflected in the disorientation of the narration. As Smith and Jeff Wallace say, Gothic consistently expresses the sense 'that the subject is not in possession of itself', and Robert Miles observes that Gothic describes subjects in states of 'rupture, disjunction, fragmentation'.[26] That emotional vulnerability colours the apprehension of space and time. Sites are rendered in terms claustrophobic or agoraphobic, spaces too vast or small, settings 'swell[ing] with nightmarish presence', or an 'oppressiveness ... the ego's sense of being under it as if underground or under water'.[27] Within these sites, time behaves as strangely as space: the past threatens to return as hidden knowledge, atavistic entities, or cursed repetition.[28] As Sue Zlosnik says, 'Time too presents itself as disturbingly unstable, with a primitive past all too likely to irrupt into a present that is also haunted by intimations of a menacing future'.[29] Gothic is characterised by an abiding tension between anachronism and modernity, and a sense that modernity's progress is frail. Through this triad of characteristic disturbance of affect, space, and temporality, Gothic texts fulfil, as Angela Carter writes, 'a most singular moral function ... that of provoking unease'.[30]

Gothic is, moreover, highly intertextual, its iconic figures adapting with each new era. The most famous nineteenth-century Gothic fictions of tissue transfer are *Frankenstein* and *Moreau*. In Shelley's novel, the medical student

Victor Frankenstein tries to discover the secret of life by gathering fragments of human remains, stitching them together to create a new body, 'collect[ing] bones from charnel houses … [t]he dissecting room and the slaughter-house', and applying 'the instruments of life' to animate the result.[31] Later in the century, Wells's *Moreau* imagines a Pacific island under the control of a London surgeon exiled after public outrage at animal vivisection. Moreau tortures animals in his 'House of Pain' to make them seem and identify as human, striving to 'alter … chemical reactions and methods of growth, to modify the articulation of [a creature's] limbs, and … change it in its most intimate structure'; in the process, he reduces them to 'something bound painfully upon a framework, scarred and bandaged'.[32] Both novels describe lone experimenters breaking taboos in the service of solitary ambition, unchecked by bonds of human companionship. Yet these texts – and particularly *Frankenstein* in its 1818 form – can also be read as marking the exciting possibilities of science, and the nineteenth century saw an abundance of such possibilities.[33] Nineteenth-century texts are informed by scientific explorations that became fundamental to the emergence of tissue transfer, including developments in dissection, blood transfusion, extracorporeal tissue storage, anaesthesia, resuscitation, and mesmeric trance. Equally salient to the social prehistory of tissue transfer are fictions of live burial, notably Edgar Allan Poe's 'The premature burial' (1844), and vampire fictions of blood transfer, notably Bram Stoker's *Dracula* (1897) and Mary Elizabeth Braddon's 'Good Lady Ducayne' (1896).[34] As it emerged in the late twentieth century, transplantation came to revisit, in sometimes surprising ways, many of the strangest and most vivid elements of these nineteenth-century medical investigations and fictions, notably the question of technologically mediated reanimation (from cardiac and pulmonary stimulation, both manual and electric) and strange states of sleep (including mesmerism, near-death experience, and anaesthesia). Nineteenth-century Gothic continues to influence representations of exploitative harvest and ambiguous deathlike states.

Iconic Gothic texts serve intertextually as resources within popular culture, deployed by patients, clinicians, social scientists, and medical historians, to make sense of and challenge discourses around tissue transfer. A patient invokes vampire imagery to describe trauma in dialysis treatment,[35] a medical historian draws on *Moreau* to communicate changing attitudes towards transplantation and transfusion,[36] social scientists quote Poe to communicate the difficulty of diagnosing death,[37] and *Frankenstein* is invoked repeatedly to describe everything from ethical issues with advanced biotechnology, through to tissue recipient experience and the ethical value of representations of hybrid being.[38] A Gothic mode and intertextuality can be identified in clinical writing itself (Chapter 1), within horror and science fiction fantasies of donor precarity (Chapters 2, 3, and 5), and within both fictional and autobiographical

representations of recipient experience (Chapter 4). Rather than a neatly deter-
ministic relation between the biomedical context and these texts, I read both the
fictions and the transplantation milieu as responding to particular sociocultural
moments.

As such, this book engages a question that regularly recurs in Gothic studies:
the degree to which fictional representations may be informed by real suffering.
A profitable commercial enterprise since its inception, Gothic primarily elicits
reader or viewer pleasure, but the affective responses are not always straightforward and can include discomfort and dread.[39] Readers or viewers are in
spectator positions, responding to the intradiegetic agony with a 'complex relationship of sympathy and abjection', as Steven Bruhm says.[40] As Xavier Aldana
Reyes observes, without implying that all such work 'constitutes an enlighten-
ing piece of social critique', there is legitimacy both to consuming these texts
for pleasure and/or for analysing them in terms of their emergence from – and
shaping of – wider cultural issues, and Gothic can often be deployed to imagine
and communicate suffering of historical record.[41] Maisha Wester identifies
African-American Gothic communicating the horror of racial oppression and
the traumatic legacies of slavery, Marie Mulvey-Roberts explores intersections
between Gothic fiction and anti-Semitism, slavery, and gendered surgical violence, Linnie Blake examines horror film engagements with national trauma,
and I examine how the Gothic of the Second World War British home front
expressed the suffering of many marginalised in that arena.[42] Yet notably, none
of us sees Gothic solely as a privileged mode for challenging social cruelties.
Each of us also identifies it as complicit in reinforcing toxic ideologies, othering
the marginalised as monstrous. Gothic is a genre and mode, not a politics, and
it can be bent to ends both reactionary and progressive.

This book seeks to advance historicist Gothic criticism in two ways. It
offers yet another 'unofficial history', in Punter's phrase, by examining ways
in which Gothic representations both mediate and destabilise discourses
around tissue transfer and its emergence.[43] In addition, it reflects on the critical conundrum that attends this historicist reading of Gothic as hallucinatory
mimesis, of reality become fantastic in its horrors. As Howard Malchow says
of his own writing, this kind of historicist criticism 'searches an area that
lies somewhere in the borderlands between literature and history, between
"representation" and reality',[44] and as his cautious quotation marks indicate
the distinction between reality and representation is hardly stable; reality is
discursively constituted. To describe the logics of such ambiguous discursive
positions, critics often combine social constructionist studies of the social
workings of power with theories about subjectivity, such as phenomenology or
Lacanian psychoanalysis.[45] In this book I navigate the intersection of the social
and the subjective by drawing on affect theory, post-structuralist theorisations
of embodiment, and contemporary biopolitics. As well as informing literary

and cinematic analysis with awareness of social and historical context, I offer an analytic framework which may also be of use to fellow critics working the terrain between imaginative representation and the suffering that it indirectly refracts. To that end, I offer the formulation of *bodies dis(re)membered* to describe four ways that Gothic can conduct ambiguous cultural work within these discursive borderlands.

Firstly, in their preoccupations with dismemberment – with dissection and vivisection – these works may mark efforts to subversively remember bodies and emotions that tend to be elided in the exultant register of dominant trans-plantation discourses. Secondly, any such work is always a *dis*remembering in the sense that it is a failed effort to represent, since it can always only ever be incomplete, necessarily impossible. The tortured negatives of the coinage reflect the impossibility of such a project, in that it reaches to hold images of suffering without co-opting the radical difference of an other, or accepting closure – instead, to remain aware of the suffering of others in ways that 'unset-tle and wound', as Jacques Derrida's work urges, actively embracing a state of uneasy haunting, refusing to lay ghosts to rest.[46] Thirdly, Gothic representa-tions can mediate a more conservative re-membering, more obedient to dom-inant trends, normalising particular forms of harvest or biomedical practice. This book is not only a reflection on the dangers of biomedicine when warped by economic pressures, but also about the dangers of representations that let us distance atrocities as performed by monsters. Gothic can dismember to forget, normalising certain suffering.

Fourthly, the prefixes *dis-* and *re-* speak of collapse and assembly and capture something of the way that tissue transfer is always already a process involving human and nonhuman entities, material and discursive: 'assemblages', in the sense used by Gilles Deleuze and Félix Guattari, combining 'states of things, bodies, various combinations of bodies, hodgepodges ... utterances, modes of expression, and whole regimes of signs'.[47] Margrit Shildrick and Deborah Steinberg suggest that the concept 'does the work of unravelling the conven-tional notion of the body as a stable, unified and bounded entity, and empha-sises the multiple connections that bodies form with other bodies, whether human, animal or machine'.[48] Transfer is assemblage in that it emerges not only from the intertwining of bodies and biotech or pharmacology but also elements like legislation, health insurance documentation, and waiting lists. Assemblage is a valuable term not only for describing any form of embod-iment but also for describing the systems of human and nonhuman agents in the acquisition of that tissue, from the life-support apparatus involved in cadaveric procurement (Chapter 1), recipients' ongoing pharmacological and medical surveillance (Chapter 4), and networks of surgical extraction and distribution (Chapters 2, 3, and 5). A Gothic mode, preoccupied with trans-formation and strangeness, may convey hybrid embodiment and biomedical processes. The coinage *dis(re)membering* thus captures four dimensions of transfer Gothic: the way these representations may represent suffering which is elided in transplant arenas; may mediate public and clinical discourses of transplantation or reinforce marginalisation; may describe assemblages of entities and materials involved in transfer; and will always necessarily fail and must remain respectfully cognisant of that failure.

I will briefly comment on ways that Gothic and medicine have been entangled since the former's inception, then review three different interpretative lenses which can be used for stories of transfer: the concept of the biomedical imaginary, the narrative of scientific progress, and theories of biopolitics, describing how certain lives are fostered while others are not. Transfer Gothic does contradictory work of dis(re)membering, simultaneously working to recall and to forget how particular bodies flourish and suffer within specific transfer economies.

Gothic medicine, medical Gothic

Gothic emerged as a literary category alongside the scientific and medical advances of the Enlightenment and Romantic periods, and was a corollary of new corpuses of knowledge.[49] Death, decay, and grief were part of the world of disorder that Enlightenment rationality sought to contain and explain, but Gothic fantasies were inextricably embroiled with these discourses of modernity because sites of 'darkness' were necessary fields of operation for rational illumination. Michel Foucault points out:

> A fear haunted the latter part of the eighteenth century: the fear of darkened spaces, of the pall of gloom which prevents the full visibility of things, men and truths ... The new political and moral order could not be established until these places were eradicated ... Gothic novels develop a whole fantasy world of stone walls, darkness, hideouts and dungeons ... [T]hese imaginary spaces are like the negative of the transparency and visibility which it is aimed to establish.[50]

These fictions dramatise efforts at illumination and control, as well as showing the frailties of such efforts.[51] Anachronism is central to this tension. Robert Mighall observes that 'the major organising figure in the Gothic throughout its development is the imputation of anachronism as a source of disorder or fear'.[52] Protagonists are menaced by ancient forces persisting into the modern present or by reversals of modern progress, and the contrast affirms modern values and institutions.[53] Concern with anachronism became especially interesting when science itself became the source of menace, because new technologies not only solved certain corporeal mysteries but also made bodies and minds strange in new ways. Terry Castle notes that 'the very psychic and cultural transformations that led to the subsequent glorification of the period as an age of reason or enlightenment ... also produced ... a new human experience of strangeness, anxiety, bafflement, and intellectual impasse'.[54] In this telling, science and technology are estranging forces rather than engines for reducing mystery, and indeed nineteenth-century fiction repeatedly positions medicine not as modern triumph but as Gothic threat. When Victor Frankenstein gathers flesh for his Creature or Dr Jekyll blends a pharmacological compound to bring forth a shadow self, archaic trappings of Gothic are not arrayed in opposition to modern medicine but identified with it. This trend continues in the twentieth- and twenty-first-century representations that predominate in this book.

Intersections between medical or scientific writing and Gothic fiction are not limited to medicine furnishing fiction with themes, for Gothic's intertextualities, narrative strategies, and tropes also informed nineteenth-century medical case histories and continue to operate in medical writing (see Chapter 1).[55] Fiction and scientific writing have different claims to truth-value, but both emerge from a shared cultural field; while scientific practice idealises objectivity, it is inevitably also informed by emotion, imagination, and sociocultural context.[56] Catherine Waldby notes, 'Despite, or perhaps because of, biomedicine's assertion of its own innocence of historical and political meaning, it constantly absorbs, translates and recirculates "non-scientific" ideas ... about social order, about culture in its technical discourses'.[57] Waldby uses the term the 'biomedical imaginary' to denote the fantasies and affects which underpin biomedical endeavours and public understanding of those endeavours. The 'imaginary' is the first of three stages of psychological development theorised by Jacques Lacan, and Waldby adapts the term to describe the subjective milieu within which biomedicine occurs. Both ideational and affective, this is the 'dream work' of science, 'the speculative, propositional fabric of medical thought, the generally disavowed dream work performed by biomedical theory and innovation', which supplements systematic scientific discourse.[58] Scientific endeavours and cultural representations inhabit a shared productive zone, not only reflective of, but in key ways constitutive of, discourses of medicine. Istvan Csicsery-Ronay Jr notes that science fiction, for example, can provide a 'thesaurus of images' to inform 'our metaphors and models for understanding our technologised world'.[59]

In the light of this speculative work done by the fantastic, it is important to challenge the assumption in the social-science commentary that opened this introduction – namely, the assumption that Gothic is solely an anxious form, mere expression of collective dreads. There are challenges with this model, not least that, as Mighall and Chris Baldick observe, Gothic is generically designed to evoke fear, though it is fair to say that there are historical trends in dread.[60] The anxiety model continues to be pertinent to transfer Gothic, but these representations can be understood also as speculative theorisations, as attempts to *think* about biotechnologically mediated states of extreme precarity.

In this vein, Kelly Hurley observes that *fin-de-siècle* Britain saw a profusion of texts concerned with human bodies transformed by forces evolutionary, pharmaceutical, or demonic. Hurley argues that in such moments Gothic can be a 'speculative art form' seeking 'new representational strategies by which to imagine human (or not-so-human) realities'.[61] Today, non-fiction writing uses Gothic tropes to describe patient experience in clinical descriptions of intensive care units, transplant receipt, cadaveric donor bodies' equivocal life or death status, and bodies shaped by genomic interventions.[62] The US government's Centers for Disease Control and Prevention even created a graphic novella *Zombie Pandemic*, a public-health publication encouraging disaster preparedness.[63] Gothic may be not only about expressing anxiety but also about exploring accelerated biotechnological transformations of the human. Such a mode may also help describe and think through the many dimensions of transfer for recipients, donors, kin, and practitioners.

Gothic historiography of transplantation science

To appreciate the biopolitical context for transfer, a review of transplantation history, biology, and pharmacology is required. Yet both history and biology are themselves highly contestable discourses, and transplantation historiography itself exemplifies Gothic's longstanding concern with conflict between progress and a dangerously unenlightened past.[64] Hamilton, as a transplant surgeon and historian, observes that progress in transplantation science was far from straightforward: 'Because progress in transplantation was not continuous, a "Whig" history, as some historians term the "onward and upward" traditional narrative, does not account for some remarkable gaps in the advance of tissue replacement. Progress not only halted at times but almost went into reverse, with insights already gained being lost.'[65] Histories of transplantation by Hamilton and fellow surgeon Thomas Starzl present transplantation progress as continually vulnerable to reversals. Research is mismanaged, international wars hinder co-operation, national legislation and economic interests are barriers, and the recipient's immune system continues to try to reinstate defences.

Histories of transplantation often begin by noting that fantasies of blended bodies date from ancient times. Myths from many cultures imagine human/ non-human hybridities, and the word 'chimera' originally described a creature of Greek mythology that blended lion, snake, goat, and dragon.[66] Religious narratives also used transfer tropes, and in Chapter 3 I discuss the Christian legend of Saints Cosmas and Damian attaching a dead Ethiopian man's leg to a white Christian man in the sixth century CE. Beyond fantasy, both ancient and medieval times saw attempts at transfer, autograft (transferring a person's tissues to another part of their body), allograft (between humans), and xenograft (between human and non-human).[67] Armenian archaeological research shows animal bone used to repair cranial injuries 2000 BCE, and manuscripts from the Indian subcontinent describe skin autografts 2500 BCE.[68] The Renaissance Italian surgeon Gaspare Tagliacozzi laid foundations for modern plastic surgery with his book on skin grafting in 1597.[69] The eighteenth-century Scottish scientist John Hunter experimented with avian tissue transfer and human tooth transfer, inspiring a brief fashion of living 'donor' tooth transplantation often coercive to donors or suppliers, and this phenomenon foreshadowed several aspects of contemporary tissue commodification. Blood transfusion was also an important precursor to transplantation science. First achieved in France in 1666, success was hard to replicate – blood typing was not known until 1900 – and until the invention of plastics it required surgically joining the blood vessels between two parties.[70] Skin transfer became increasingly attempted after French strides in technique in 1869, and by the end of the nineteenth century – at the time of Wells's *Moreau* – transfer attempts included bone, nerves, and muscles.[71] Furthermore, the first recorded internal grafts into a human were xenografts, not allografts: in two French experiments in 1906, kidney vessels from a sheep and a pig were connected to human kidneys, failing with hyperacute rejection.[72] Transfer was imagined and attempted for centuries before it became survivable in the late twentieth century.

Transplantation of internal organs became surgically feasible after Alexis Carrel developed a pioneering technique for microsuturing blood vessels in 1902, and this inspired an explosion of experimentation. People wrote begging for surgery and suggesting bodies that could yield tissue for themselves, including prisoners, the dead, and the poor.[73] Journalists celebrated skin grafts and blood transfusion so fervently that by 1920 the surgeon Hugh Baldwin lamented the 'theatrical and sensational' media portrayals, yet organ allografts continued to fail.[74] The first recorded attempt at human kidney transfer occurred in 1911 in Philadelphia, recorded in the *New York Times* but not in medical literature, and the first attempt recorded in the medical literature was a 1936 operation in Russia; both failed.[75] Kidney transfer did not succeed until that between identical twins in Boston in 1954, but this success was largely illusory since it required identical twins to prevent immune rejection. It was not until the 1960s that successful transplantation could be achieved between non-genetically identical parties.[76] Carrell himself warned in 1914 that, although advances had been achieved in surgical technique, the remaining challenge was preventing the recipient body from destroying transferred tissue.[77]

Indeed, the immunological hurdles are enormous. In summarising the conventional portrayal of these challenges, I will initially use the martial vocabulary that typically characterises description of immune function, but I will shortly problematise these metaphors. The immune system destroys (and partly incorporates) tissue coded with macromolecules that it does not recognise as 'self'; a recipient then dies due to organ failure and necrosis. (Avascular tissues such as corneas and aortic valves are exceptions, since they are not directly in contact with circulating blood and the lymphocytes it bears.) In Graft-versus-Host disease (GvH), rare except in bone marrow transfer, 'attack' may also occur when lymphocytes from the transferred tissue attack the recipient's tissue. In response to such immunological risks, one strategy is to make the transferred material as similar to the recipient's as possible. This goal was helped by the emerging sciences of heredity, later known as genetics, and by Karl Landsteiner's discovery of blood typing in 1900, but it was not until the mid-1960s that blood and genetic analysis could identify compatibility without surgical grafts.[78] Today 'histocompatibility' denotes compatible alleles on gene loci governing human leukocyte antigens, but histocompatibility alone does not prevent tissue rejection. The mechanisms of immunity were only dimly under-stood for much of the twentieth century, and indeed remain elusive. It took decades for surgeons and researchers to accept that allograft would fail unless between identical twins. Even when scientific consensus on this was reached early in the twentieth century, the 1920s saw experimental work resume until 1940s research reaffirmed the inevitability of allograft failure and formulated theories of immune defence.[79] Even in the 1950s, some scientists argued that endocrine gland tissues, foetal tissue, or tissue from children may be exceptions to the rule of graft failure.[80] The inevitability of rejection proved exceptionally hard to accept.

Experiments in the 1940s and 1950s indicated that graft failure could be delayed by certain agents such as the newly synthesised steroid cortisone, nitrogen-mustard derivatives, or sub-lethal doses of radiation. Immunosuppression was still seen as time-limited, but eventually evidence emerged that continuous immunosuppression accompanied modest increases in graft survival in non-human animals.[81] Some in the transplantation community reluctantly began to consider continuous immunosuppression. There was sub-stantial resistance to this move. The transplant scientist William Dempster warned that 'any measure which can suppress the homograft rejection process must also render the host an immunological cripple'.[82] None the less, long-term chemical immunosuppressants gradually became more acceptable. In 1960, 6-MP was used successfully in France to briefly reverse a late case of kidney rejection, and a breakthrough came in 1963 when Starzl showed a combination of steroids and azathioprine to be effective in reversing tissue rejection and increasing survival rates.[83] Survival was still far from a given, however, with mortality around 40 per cent within a year of transplant, and Starzl himself criticised exaggerations of the regimen's efficacy.[84] Not only was tissue rejection lethal without immunosuppression, but immunosuppression could be lethal itself.

In this milieu, December 1967 saw the South African surgeon Christiaan Barnard perform the first successful human heart transplant. The recipient survived only eighteen days, due to immunosuppression-related pneumonia, but Barnard's second heart transplant recipient survived nearly two years. Heart transplants were rapidly attempted around the world, most recipients dying within days, and these high-profile failures led to reduced research funding and legislation to circumscribe experimental transplantation.[85] As a result, the 1970s were a more cautious period in which kidney transplantation became established but other transfer more rare.

Much changed with the emergence of the immunosuppressant cyclosporine, approved for clinical use in the UK and US in 1983. The *New England Journal of Medicine* suggested that the drug might realise the legend of Cosmas and Damian.[86] Whilst cyclosporine never emulated that miracle, it extended recipient survival, eased some rejection crises, and overcame some tissue incompatibilities. As a result, it massively broadened viable donor pools with significant implications for global tissue economies (see Chapter 3). Yet rejection continues to be a challenge, be it acute rejection crisis or chronic rejection causing blood vessels to narrow. Recipient bodies remain antagonists.

This summary has drawn on histories of science and clinical writing in which the dominant metaphor for immunological function is military onslaught against alien invasion, an 'allophobic vocabulary', in Roberto Esposito's terms.[87] Yet martial metaphors obscure the strangeness of the process, which 'reproduces in a controlled form exactly what it is meant to protect us from … The body defeats a poison … by making it somehow part of the body.'[88] The immune system is about not only annihilation but also recognition, and this recognition is weirder than mere attack of material coded alien. Any body is always a composite of organic tissues, viruses, bacteria, inorganic nutrients, water, and toxins, meshed in dynamic relationships symbiotic, harmful, or neutral. Donna Haraway suggests that, instead of thinking of immune function in terms of a military arena, we can consider it in terms of 'a semi-permeable self able to engage with others (human and non-human, inner and outer)'.[89] The human body is far from a discrete, clearly demarcated entity, as research into the microbiome and microchimerism shows. The term 'holobiont' has been offered rather than 'individual', to convey entangled organisms, related in ways symbiotic, parasitic, or more ambiguous than either.[90] Scott Gilbert notes that the earlier idea of the immune system as 'defense network' with 'amazing … weaponry' 'constitute[s] a relatively minor part of the work that an immune system does. The immune system, rather than being imagined as a force of protective soldiers made by the host, can be thought of as a group of passport control agents. … They know who to let in and who to keep out. … [E]ven the immune system itself is built by microbes.'[91] Genetic material from other humans, too, circulates within bodies in a phenomenon known as microchimerism, in which parallel sets of DNA (and antigens) circulate within a body unassimilated, without evoking an immune defence response. Natural microchimeric states include pregnancy, in which foetal cells cross into the mother's bloodstream and may remain for years and be passed down to other children.[92] Twenty-first-century immunology continues to examine the subtle forms of recognition and tolerance mediated by the immune system, and other avenues of research include growing organs from adult stem cells. At the time of writing, however, long-term immunosuppression almost always remains necessary.

Even with advances in surgery, tissue-matching, and immunological pharmacology, transplantation could not have become the large-scale endeavour it is now without two discursive developments that transformed transfer biopolitics: new definitions of death and national apparatuses to regulate surgical procurement and allocation. These innovations were necessitated by a second somatic hurdle to transplantation: warm ischemia time causing tissue to degrade rapidly once removed from a functional circulatory system. With the emergence of life-support systems including artificial ventilation, certain bodies could be held in an unprecedented, ambiguous state with circulation intact, more favourable for transfer success. Life-support technology alone was not sufficient to facilitate surgical extraction of tissue from such bodies, however: discursive moves, too, were required, including legal recognition of new categories of neurological death and, later, 'nonheartbeating donation' (NHBD) or 'donation after circulatory death' (DCD). I discuss these death classifications and their Gothic intertexts in Chapter 1.

Transfer survival rates (for both recipients and living donors) depend on their context, but there is no doubt that the practice is now far more successful. As Peter Morris says of the US context, 'Loss of organs due to acute, irreversible rejection is now uncommon, and one-year graft-survival rates of 80 to 90% are the norm for all types of organ transplantation'.[93] That progress narrative included significant failure and death. For the majority of the twentieth century, transplantation of internal organs failed painfully. Historiographers of transplantation handle those decades of suffering in a variety of ways, choosing variously to emphasise the determination of surgeons and researchers,[94] the bravery of patients willing to accept experimental practices,[95] or the agony of participants, both human and non-human, that attended the decades of unsuccessful experiments.[96] Extreme striving and suffering are interwoven in the history of tissue transfer, and even now, Morris says, 'many problems remain to be solved ... the insidious loss of grafts from chronic allograft failure; the various complications associated with immunosuppressant drugs ... [and] an increased incidence of cancer'.[97] Tissue economies may also raise ethical concerns around predatorial harvest. The history of tissue transfer is not only about medical advances but also about sociopolitical milieux which foster certain bodies while diminishing protections for others.

Transfer biopolitics

Michel Foucault argues that the late seventeenth and eighteenth centuries saw a new kind of power emerge. In this view, prior to that, rulers forced compliance by threat of harm, power stemming from a sovereign's ability to kill: to '*take* life or *let* live' ('*de* faire *mourir ou de* laisser *vivre*').[98] The new form of power does not supplant sovereign violence but works alongside it, and hinges on 'the power of "make" live and "let" die'.[99] As such this is a 'biopower', fostering and regulating life, 'bent on generating forces, making them grow, and ordering them'.[100] Foucault identifies two interconnected forms such biopower could take: disciplinary power concerned with the body's 'optimization of capacities' and 'docility … its integration into systems of efficient and economic controls', and regulatory control of populations, efforts to 'calculate, interpret, and predict the overall health of the society writ large', such as statistical data-gathering and public health administration.[101] Biopolitics functions on both a micro and macro level: individual bodies are disciplined and regulated but 'precisely to the end of situating the particular body within a hierarchy that precedes it'; 'it was taking charge of life [*la prise en charge de la vie*] more than the threat of death, that gave power its access even to the body'.[102] Rather than bodies being mere fields on which external power works, they become part of the operation of power itself.

Foucault's early thoughts on biopolitics have been challenged since, including by Foucault himself. Among other things, critics challenge the notion of a clear break between epistemes,[103] or emphasise the processes of making live and letting die as 'a mutually reinforcing relation … wherein each presupposes the other',[104] or examine the ways that sovereignty and biopower have increasingly combined in appalling ways.[105] Giorgio Agamben offers a particularly influential critique, identifying a continuity of practice from ancient times to the present. Drawing on the Roman legal figure of the *homo sacer*, a person marked out as sacred who can be killed with impunity, Agamben differentiates between *zoe* or 'bare life', the basic biological state of being alive, and *bios*, political life, life with social meaning. Through 'states of exception' – which are anything but rare – certain people are reduced to 'bare life'. I will draw on Agamben's work at several points, but his theorisations, too, have been critiqued, notably for overemphasising the role of the state and failing to adequately differentiate between forms of dehumanisation. In Chapter 2 I discuss the critique that Agamben pays insufficient attention to the way that privatised biomedicine, rather than state sovereignty, implements exclusions that mark some lives off as less human; and in Chapter 3 I consider work that calls for a move away from Agamben's language of 'bare life' and towards a language which recognises a particular kind of sacrifice for subjects exploited within such encounter. The processes of dehumanisation must be made visible in their terrible heterogeneity, both the specific mechanisms of exclusion and the diverse subjective experiences of those excluded.

Judith Butler speaks of 'ungrievable lives', those of people whom society does not deem as meriting the same kind of mourning in the public sphere as others; such lives are already marked as less human before that death. Butler differentiates between 'precarity' and 'precariousness', the latter referring to the way all humans are interdependent, reliant on 'the hand of the other' to survive. Precarity, by contrast, describes life made even more uncertain, with differential distribution of basic social, economic, and political securities.[106] As Sherryl Vint says, we can identify a 'shifting of the right to "make life" or "let die" into engineering of life, the living kept in a state of vulnerability as vitality is unevenly distributed'.[107] To describe the plight of the precariat within this operational field, theorists have developed a vivid Gothic phraseology of torment: 'machines of social death' and 'zones of abandonment' (João Biehl), 'economies of abandonment' (Elizabeth Povinelli), 'death-worlds' and 'necropower' (Achille Mbembe), and 'anachronistic populations' (Priscilla Wald).[108] Here, the language of haunting, dismemberment, and undeath is used to bring exclusionary processes into the field of vision. Similarly, the vulnerable bodies, strange time, and confining spaces of a Gothic mode help to express biopolitical dimensions of particular transfer milieux.

Transplantation is advanced biotechnology used to extend and reshape life, and, even beyond surgery, there are other ways in which recipient life is 'made to live', is fostered and regulated.[109] To survive, recipients must comply with daily pharmaceutical regimens, self-monitoring, and ongoing medical surveillance for tissue rejection, immunosuppressant-associated infection, and side effects like nephrotoxicity or cancer. This individual compliance occurs within broader regulatory frames of the administrative bodies and legislation that govern tissue procurement, allocation, and distribution, such as tissue match algorithms, waiting lists, and national oversight bodies. Transfer recipients may also be subject to the affective disciplines central to neoliberal patienthood, the 'positivity imperative – to be hopeful, a warrior, a survivor, a meaning-finder', as I say elsewhere – but may experience a wide range of less triumphant emotions.[110] For some participants, haunting, confinement, and disjointed temporality can be apt figures for some of the affective and epistemological work attendant on transfer.

Rather than fostering life, this dimension of biopolitical process involves a *loosening* of that fostering, as in neglect or removing protections. Some critics, for example, see donation after brain death in this light (see Chapter 1), but even if one does not take issue with neurological death there are many ways in which particular economies of organ transplantation may be supported by loosened biopolitical protections. In transfer, the repair of certain bodies relies on injury to certain others. This is not to imply a conspiracy to engineer deaths, but rather to note that certain bodies are more likely to enter that encounter as donor or supplier than recipient, due to transnational mobilities of capital, economic precarity, cultural assumptions around gender roles or economic productivity, or a state choosing to prioritise the prevention of certain kinds of death while neglecting the prevention of other causes of mortality. Furthermore, '*making die*' also continues to be operational within some tissue economies, such as in the execution of Chinese political prisoners for transnational and national organ markets.[111]

Sacrificial asymmetry can be particularly overt in organ sales within illegal tissue markets and healthcare inequality, in which suppliers may suffer significantly as a result of tissue sale.[112] While such transfers are technically consensual, financial pressures drive consent to the extent that the United Nations' Bellagio Task Force has warned that 'inequities in political power and social well-being remain so profound that the voluntary character of the sale of an organ remains in doubt'.[113] Cyclosporine transformed the global biopolitics of organ transfer, for, as Lawrence Cohen says, 'Cyclosporine *globalizes*, creating myriad biopolitical fields where donor populations are differentially and flexibly materialized'.[114] The flow of tissue can be characterised by disturbing traces of older legacies of colonial force, tissue often flowing 'from South to North, from poor to rich, from black and brown to white, and from female to male bodies', as Nancy Scheper-Hughes observes, in a form of 'late modern cannibalism'.[115] Altruistic living donation, too, correlates with striking economic and gender divisions, including in the West.[116] However, transfer does not follow a universal blueprint, nor does it operate solely as a top-down exertion of force.[117] As Ciara Kierans says of people in Mexico involved with altruistic donation with whom she did ethnographic work, 'the practices, or "body-work", of these citizens are co-constitutive of medicine and the markets upon which it increasingly relies. This is about bodies which are at once medicalising as well as medicalised.'[118] Organ sales, too, can be 'intricate crimes', in which victimhood is not cancelled out by the 'agency' of the decision to sell.[119] Ethnographic research attends to particularities of transfer and warns against generalising: Crowley-Matoka warns, transplantation always 'reveals and enacts situated notions of who can and should risk their bodies through organ donation, as well as who can and should benefit from that risk ... neither the clinical practices nor the biopolitics are everywhere the same'.[120]

When I have mentioned working on a book on transplantation Gothic, the most common response was the expectation that it would focus on tissue moving along neocolonial trajectories, surgical extractions occurring outside North America and Europe and then flowing to benefit people in the latter. This assumption is echoed in media tendency to distance dysfunctional, unequal transfer as something exotic that happens 'elsewhere'. When Raj Chengappa wrote his exposé of exploitation of kidney suppliers in the *Villavakkam* ('kidney village') slums of Chennai in 1990, he was 'deluged with calls from American and European based media. *Villavakkam gothic became routinized*.'[121] Here,

Lawrence Cohen describes a Western appetite for stories of distant suffering. Gothic can be deployed to communicate harrowing corporeal violation, yet the sensationality and exoticism of some representations may simultaneously objectify organ suppliers, evacuate their interiority, and oversimplify the networks of encounter within which organ sales occur and the aftermath plays out. In this book, I wish to complicate such problematic exoticisation of representations of exploitative tissue sale misunderstood as uniquely a function of non-Western sites, and in that spirit I particularly consider inequalities and exploitations *within* the UK and the US, both imagined and real, resisting the trend to present dysfunctions of tissue economies as wholly distant from these sites in time or place. I explore texts which occupy complex transnational positions, including, for example, Trinidadian-American Gothic science fiction making use of non-Eurocentric spiritual traditions, and a play by an Indian author written in English for a European competition. Glennis Byron has coined the neologism 'globalgothic', to indicate how Eurocentric Gothic and horror vernaculars are transformed in dialogue with other cultural traditions of fantasy and haunting.[122] Primarily, however, this book examines British and American Gothic alongside scientific and legislative developments within these countries that paralleled these creative works. An even broader international scope would risk irresponsibly simplifying subtleties of legislation, economics, tissue procurement practice, and healthcare economies, and reinforce the misleading view that disordered transfer is exclusively an issue in non-Western contexts.

Cross-border transfer is far from the only aspect of tissue transfer characterised by biopolitical asymmetries. Hierarchies of life-value can also be discerned in postindustrial nations' healthcare inequalities and variable access to transplantation. Phillip Barrish argues that medical humanities should do more to consider the economics of medical care: 'who gets quality medical care, and who doesn't? ... How and by whom is it paid for? ... [W]e who study intersections of literature and medicine should devote more sustained attention to literary engagements with health care as a system: a complex, often fragmented set of financial models, institutions, government policies, and personnel.'[123] Gothic representations of abject embodiment can comment on the place of the human within contexts of economic precarity. Beyond the costs of surgery, recipients must also grapple with the costs of lifelong immunosuppression and medical surveillance. In countries without universal health care, a '"green screen" of ability to pay' is a disqualifying hurdle for many prospective recipients, and socialised medicine is not immune from inequalities either, in so far as privatised medical industries may exist in parallel or 'postcode lotteries' may apply.[124] Furthermore, in both privatised and socialised contexts, people may come to need an organ partly *as a result of* health inequalities.

Enhancing one life from the diminishing of another may sound vampiric, and, while vampires were fictional, power imbalance in blood transfusion was not. (When the Royal Society of London attempted to perform the first English blood transfusion in 1668, for example, they asked Bedlam Hospital for living subjects; Bedlam declined.)[125] Yet while Stoker's and Braddon's vampires are single, feudal figures, and while Frankenstein and Moreau are indicted in their texts for overweening individual scientific ambition, the locus of threat in the texts in this book tends to be multiple and distributed rather than a single villain. Social systems of ruination render certain bodies at risk from profit-driven corporations (Chapter 2), systems of 'slow violence' operate on extended timescales (Chapter 3), and governments implement a hierarchy of life (Chapter 5). In other words, a community, organisation, or society becomes the source of danger, and in this regard Gothic has long been interested in failed communities. Early fiction explored dysfunctional families or religious communities and, in the nineteenth century, alienating urban environments.[126] The economic and social ramifications of capitalism, too, have garnered Gothic tropes from the start. Karl Marx uses imagery of vampirism, spectrality, and werewolf hunger to critique the violence wrought by capital, and he describes commodities as fantastical things animated by the spectral traces of the disavowed labour that made them.[127] A Gothic lexicon continues to be invoked in attempts to describe hyper-networked neoliberal late capitalisms. Originally coined to describe a particular strand of economic philosophy including the work of the Chicago School, since the 1980s the term 'neoliberalism' has come to denote a combination of market deregulation, rise in privatisation, and reduction of the welfare state. Such systems work to 'produce desire and expectation on a global scale ... yet to decrease the certainty of work or the security of persons ... to offer up vast, almost instantaneous riches to those who master its spectral technologies – and, simultaneously, to threaten the very existence of those who do not', to quote Jean Comaroff and John Comaroff.[128]

Gothic's lurid images may seem to oversimplify the workings of neoliberalism, and caution must be taken not to generalise the term to 'a simple depiction of the "undermining" of the state and the "freeing" of markets'.[129] None the less, the sense in which neoliberal forms of late capitalism coincide with an expanding precariat is striking, and Gothic continues to be invoked to describe the attendant economic fragilities.[130] This book connects with – and seeks to respectfully complicate – scholarship on 'neoliberal Gothic'. The term 'neoliberal' has been criticised for oversimplifying top-down Big Capital and obscuring the differences between particular milieux, for, as Kaushik Sunder Rajan points out, 'capitalism is mutable and multiple – it is always *capitalisms*'; resistance requires scrutinising specific operations.[131] I specify privatised healthcare and biomedicalised imperatives for self-management (Chapter 4), and corporatisation of healthcare and profit imperatives (Chapters 2, 3, and 5). Language of haunting, dismemberment, and undeath can be apt for corporeal vulnerability

within marketisation of healthcare, globalised clinical labour, transfer economies, and health inequality.

Transplantation requires a shift in the cultural imaginary that makes it easier
to think of human bodies in terms of disaggregated parts. Organs explicitly
become 'commodities' only in illegal markets and in the few nations with legal
organ sales, or in controversies like the UK's Alder Hey scandal (1988–95)
where organs were removed from dead children without parental consent.[132]
Yet even in less explicit markets, the process of marking tissue off as transferrable echoes many of the detachment processes that accompany commodification. Mechanistic views of the human body existed in premodern contexts,
but the metaphor has become more prevalent in recent centuries and is central
to transfer discourse.[133] Starzl speaks of transplant recipients as 'puzzle people',
Waldby describes how organs and tissues have become 'detachable things',
and Silke Schicktanz and M. Schweda describe 'spare parts persons'.[134] In the
fictions I explore in this book, corporeal partitioning becomes gritty rather than
mechanically frictionless.

History abounds in examples of commodifications of body parts or body
capacities, the most appalling example being chattel slavery. I discuss some
of the legacies of that atrocity in Chapter 3, in the context of medicine and
care access. Other examples of bodily commodificaiton include the eighteenth-
century 'Resurrection Men', body snatchers, who exhumed graves or killed to
provide corpses for dissection in medical training and research; one London
gang sold corpses for 'two guineas and a crown' and charged for dismembered children's feet, prices correlating length of limbs.[135] Another example
of bodily commodification is living tooth transplantation, which briefly flourished in eighteenth-century England. Some wealthy recipients required serv-
ants to donate teeth or prevailed upon impoverished people to sell theirs. The
teeth were extracted without anaesthetic, since that was not developed until
much later. The dentist Charles Allen wrote, 'neither could this be called the
Restauration of Teeth, since the reparation of one is the ruine of another'.[136]
Tissue sale is not new: there have long been markets for skin, teeth, testes,
and hair.

Discussions of the ethics of such sale have long been dominated by an opposition between gift models and models of property rights and sale. The most
famous exposition of the gift/commodity dichotomy in transfer is Richard
Titmuss's *The Gift Relationship* (1971) which excoriated the US for legal blood
sales, arguing that the practice diminished the quality of stored blood and weakened community.[137] I discuss the gift/commodity dichotomy in Chapter 4 with
particular attention to gifts' coercive dimensions. Increasingly, however, the
gift/commodity dichotomy is inadequate, since neither excels at communicating the way that transfer is not a single momentary event between two
parties but involves multiple parties over an extended duration. Some critics

have sought to find an alternative language altogether. Kristin Zeiler and Eric Malmqvist, for example, have argued for 'sharing' to be a useful alternative framework.[138]

This book considers dark fantasias informed by all three framings for transfer: gift, commodity, and sharing. The conception of 'gift' that circulates in patient-facing discourse emphasises donation as a 'no strings attached' event, but studies have consistently indicated that many recipients feel the 'gift' of tissue requires reciprocation.[139] Chapters 2 and 3 consider commodification in a range of contexts, in each case showing how the texts engage in often surprisingly rich ways with both the changing forms of late capitalisms and the subtle processes attending economic 'disentanglement' of alienable goods. Chapter 4 looks at the impact of tissue transfer on the recipient, particularly conceptions of gift as oppressive, and Chapter 5 examines dystopian texts which blend all three frameworks – gift, commodity, and sharing – and extrapolate potential consequences of scarcity rhetoric and the moral imperative to share bodies as common resource. These works suggest that none of these models is immune from exacerbating participant distress or sanitising ethically problematic transfer.

At its heart, this book is about considering creative representations of affective enduring – grief work, pain work – within tissue transfer. Whilst Arlie Hochschild uses the term 'emotional work' to describe the ways workers are required to experience or perform emotions in remunerated labour,[140] I am using the term to describe emotional and physical effort that unfolds in time. This is labour and work in the sense of the labour of childbirth, or the *Trauerarbeit*, 'grief work', of Freud.[141] Living donors endure surgical aftermath, especially where lack of adequate healthcare makes that a grim deterioration; recipients may (gratefully) endure waiting lists, the aftermath of surgeries, the daily circuit of pharmacological compliance and medical surveillance; some healthcare practitioners endure emotionally challenging procurement contexts within institutions traversed by economic and social pressures; some donor kin endure irresolvable mourning. Gothic may be effective for representing such *durée*.

On the other hand, Gothic can also be complicit in hierarchilisations of life that reinforce biopolitical exclusions, deployed to racist, anti-Semitic, homophobic, and ableist ends.[142] Gothic can also weaken political critiques of care, by offering fantasy exaggerations that make it easier to distance oneself from the social context for suffering. There are two further ways in which Gothic may have a paradoxically deadening effect on ability to imagine suffering. On the one hand, Gothic's capacity to make the familiar strange can be useful in challenging taken-for-granted medical routines – the physician Steve Shlozman, for example, argues that graphic novels in a horror mode can help counter clinician detachment, 'allow[ing] us to resist the systemic pandemic of zombified medicine'.[143] Literary and cinematic Gothic may usefully render these practices strange. On the other hand, these representations can also help to normalise biotechnology, even if the texts are disturbing.[144] Gothic can also entrench assumptions of an inevitably dystopian futurity: Gerry Canavan has coined the term 'necrofuturist' to describe the way some fictions blend despair, political inertia and a kind of nihilistic celebration.[145] In all these senses, Gothic may dis(re)member to *forget*, to reinforce erasure or normalise suffering. Chapter 1, for example, examines how Gothic narrative frames, tropes, and intertextualities may bolster new thanatological classifications in the face of controversy and reduce affective complexities emerging from these new categories of death. Chapters 2, 3, and 5 examine donor/supplier vulnerability, but it can be argued that these fantastical, exaggerated renditions may make it easier to distance the ongoing reality of people rendered vulnerable to predatorial harvest. Chapter 4 acknowledges texts which dehumanise the donor as defence against recipients' compromised sense of self.

'Critical interloping': Gothic studies and critical medical humanities

One way to define a project's interdisciplinarity is to list the critical axioms it transgresses. This book performs a 'critical interloping', in Stella Bolaki's term, seeking to enrich medical humanities by broadening the range of illness representation explored and the range of critical practices invoked.[146] The metaphor implies 'unwelcome … intrusion', and indeed Gothic studies and medical humanities may both find this book to be a grim, unsolicited guest.

Representations of intense distress are often seen as unhelpful by healthcare practitioners, medical humanities scholars, and disability studies scholars. Each of these three constituencies has good reasons for historically discouraging attending closely to – or 'dwelling on' – expressions of individual anguish in physical or emotional extremity.[147] Yet prioritising narratives with a positive slant can mean that some people's experience may be implicitly denigrated.[148] Matti Hyvärinen *et al* warn, 'the imperative of coherence' – and, I would add, positivity – 'works to legitimise certain narratives while excluding or marginalising others from the narrative canon'.[149] Echoing scholars of trauma theory, gender studies, and postcolonial studies, this book seeks to trouble hierarchies of illness narration.[150] As such, it is connected with other research arguing for the validity of distress within medical contexts, the political importance of heeding grief, and the need to broaden medical humanities' capacity to engage with agony within a range of frameworks and registers.[151] In exploring the negative, however, I am not refuting work that is emerging on positive forms of relationality between recipient and donor or kin: this book is intended as a complement to more hopeful studies, and does not undermine creative visions for new forms of embodiment and less asymmetrical transfer relationships.[152]

This book also argues that Gothic representations can be particularly responsive to emerging questions of the 'critical' medical humanities. Critics have called for broadening attention to encounters beyond the patient–clinician dyad, to consider wider healthcare, economic, and cultural milieux and consider more than individual experience.[153] Viney, Callard and Woods call us to examine 'other kinds of relations, networks, nodes and entities through which health and medicine are made, and unmade'.[154] These fictions explore the distributed nature of health-related practice in a nexus of economics, altruism, and ideology, both global and local. This book also responds to the call to broaden discussion beyond the genres typically studied in medical humanities. Alan Bleakley has called for scholars to consider 'what kinds of arts and humanities are employed in medical humanities', warning that 'medical humanities culture can be seen as conservative', and Bolaki warns that seminal texts of medical humanities often privilege 'a specific canon and approach to texts', primarily 'realist fiction and autobiography'.[155] That canon is increasingly under challenge, with exciting work emerging in graphic novels, fine art, and science fiction.[156] Gothic and horror can be part of this broadening. Using Gothic as an organising principle enables a focus on distress, abjection, and the vulnerable subject, a focus highly responsive to the preoccupations of critical medical humanities.

Admittedly, since the Gothic mode does not yield 'realistic' representations, it may seem to be an odd resource for considering either illness experience or transfer biopolitics. Realist autobiography has often been privileged in discussions of illness representation.[157] As far back as 1978, however, Joanne Trautmann Banks questioned the divide between 'real' and 'fictional' in medical humanities contexts, recognising that even autobiography is always already constructed and partial.[158] Yet the argument for the value of fiction to medical humanities does not rest on evacuating the real from autobiography, for an argument can also be made in the opposite direction. Several critics have argued that non-realist representation may be *necessary* for representing extreme experience. In other words, distortion may be required in order to convey the epistemological challenge or the affective intensity of an experience. Several scholars of trauma have argued that representing the unrepresentable requires fantastical registers and textual artifice.[159] Susanna Egan, for example, suggests that 'genres that eschew traditional realism and challenge secure knowledge become the means for moments of reality and knowing'.[160] Vivid and hallucinatory, these texts can communicate fractured, distraught subjectivities within transfer milieux.

Gothic studies, too, can be enriched by scholarship from medical humanities and disability studies, not least in the way that these approaches encourage analysis aware of particular medical practice. This latter impetus chimes with the trend in Gothic studies towards historicised analysis. Roger Luckhurst, for example, calls for Gothic criticism to pay less attention to the 'generalised structure of haunting' and more to the specific 'generative loci' that give rise to the ghost.[161] In other respects, however, this book may thwart expectations of a Gothic studies monograph on transplantation. A more traditional approach would have been to structure my chapter progression as a chronological review of the development of transplantation science alongside scrutiny of fiction, but such a chapter progression would privilege science and the surgical moment, risking marginalising – again – the surrounding stages of recipients waiting, donation decisions, and aftermath for donor, recipient, and kin – experiences that occur outside 'the white space' of anaesthetised surgery, in the phrase of the poet Karen Fiser.[162] As such, rather than structure this book's chapters around the chronology of surgical advances, I have chosen to emphasise different figures throughout: practitioners (Chapter 1), donors, or suppliers, and the context of surgical procurement (Chapters 2, 3, and 5), and transfer recipients (Chapter 4). Whilst each chapter addresses a full gamut of participant roles, this chapter arrangement allows a range of readings to emerge beyond the story of scientific progress.

Chapter 1, 'Clinical necropoetics: medical and ethics writing of death and transplantation', explores how Gothic is used in representations of cadaveric harvest in work from within the disciplines of medical science and ethics: to excoriate contemporary processes of death management and surgical procurement, and, on the other hand, to advocate for such practice and to normalise a liminal position. Three chapters explore donor/supplier vulnerability. Chapter 2, 'The bioemporium: corporate medical horror in late twentieth-century American transfer fiction', explores 1970s American literary and cinematic fantasies of institutionally mediated organ theft, corporate Gothic changing medical institutions. These works dwell on the horror of forcible tissue extraction and the influence of finance's secondary forms including mortgages, repossession, and inherited debt. Chapter 3, 'Clinical labour and slow violence: transnational harvest horror and racial vulnerability at the turn of the millennium', considers turn-of-the-millennium transnational and intra-national tissue sale, in work from India, the US, and the UK, in contexts of economic marginalisation and slow violence. Chapter 4, 'Possession? Uncanny assemblage and embodied scripts in tissue recipient horror', makes a case for the value of a Gothic mode within tissue recipient narrative, exploring epistemological and affective challenges in post-transplant experience. Finally, Chapter 5, 'Scalpel and metaphor: "machines of social death" and state-sanctioned harvest in dystopian fiction', considers dystopian fictions of state-sanctioned harvest in which certain bodies are marked as less worthy of life. In the process this chapter shows how metaphors which dominate transfer representation today work to make predatorial practice acceptable in these fictional societies – with lessons for our own.

Spatial constraints necessitated three significant omissions: intrafamilial donation, artificial organs, and xenotransplantation. Whilst I explore financial coercion, emotional coercion can also be a concern, as in intrafamilial pressure to 'donate' as with 'saviour' siblings and spousal transfer. Given the Gothic's longstanding interest in dysfunctional families this would be a fruitful arena for future scholarship. With regard to artificial organs, my primary focus is human allograft, though I acknowledge that ventilators and dialysis units are already extracorporeal artificial organs. Xenotransplantation has been part of the history of transplantation experiment from the start, and a monograph exclusively exploring literary and cinematic study of xenotransplantation Gothic would draw on emerging scholarship on the treatment of non-human animal bodies within the contemporary 'Anthropocene', 'capitolocene', 'necrocene', or 'chthulucene' – just a few of the terms coined to convey different aspects of the ways human action has affected other beings and the ecologies we co-inhabit, and the urgent activist and imaginative work that must be undertaken as a result.[163] Human animals are far from the only animals whose bodies are dis(re) membered, in the multiple senses of that term.

The artist Andrew Carnie's digital drawing *Commonality in Liquidity* (2007) (Figure 1) shows two bodies layered inexactly, their differences remaining despite being linked by transfer. The image demands we think of both bodies simultaneously, as well as notice the shape around them – the systems and processes that make such corporeal entanglement feasible and survivable. Transplantation is a thing of networks corporeal, discursive, institutional, and international, and this insight also informs Carnie's *Gold Elysium* (2017), on the cover of this book. This work is made of gold metal and watercolour on stitched canvas. This work emphasises combinations, 'junctures of a haphazard kind', as the exhibition in which it appeared was titled. The paint, metal, threads, and canvas combine to make something new, but that new thing involves intricate layers, broken, with delicate cracks in their surfaces. The work speaks of assemblage, of networks, shadows, and forces intersecting within the body, and it also speaks of a range of emotional registers. Gold suggests transfiguration and healing but there is ambiguity in the grey heart's confinement, its separation from the rest of the body perhaps suggesting that the recipient has not yet come to terms imaginatively with the transplant, or that their body is rejecting it as immunologically other. The greyness and the box confinement may also be a marker of mourning for the loss of life that made transfiguration possible or, in the case of living transfer, the necessary wounding of the donor or supplier body, be that altruistic or incentivised. Transplantation saves lives but saying that does not obviate the way that like any human activity it may *also* involve grief, inequality, fear, or pain. Haunted and haunting representations may create spaces for thinking the unbearable. This book is about listening to the dark.

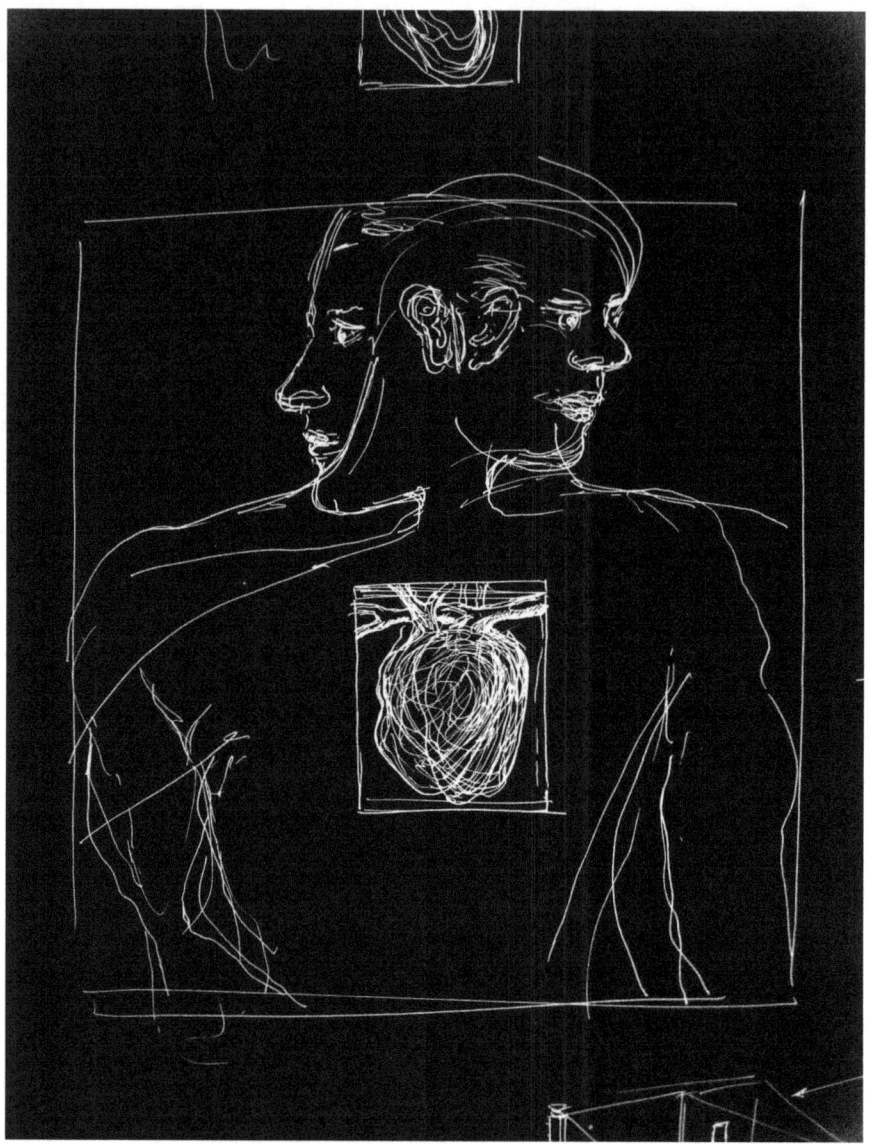

Figure 1   Andrew Carnie, *Commonality in Liquidity*. Digital drawing (2007).
© Image courtesy of Andrew Carnie.

Notes

1 J.D. Reed, 'Organ transplant', *The New Yorker* (26 September 1970), 126.
2 M. Gunnarson and S. Lundin, 'The complexities of victimhood', *Somatechnics*, 5:1 (2015), 32–51 (p. 47n1).
3 L. Sharp, *Strange Harvest* (Berkeley: University of California Press, 2006), pp. 3–4.
4 Ibid, pp. 3–4.
5 Gothic and horror are not synonymous in terms of either genre conventions or reader/viewer affect, but there is overlap and at times a work may merit both labels. Throughout this book I use 'horror' to describe intradiegetic protagonist emotion, rather than referring to genre. For audience affective responses to these genres, see X. Aldana Reyes, *Horror Film and Affect* (London: Routledge, 2016); A. Powell, *Deleuze and Horror Film* (Edinburgh: Edinburgh University Press, 2005).
6 S. Morgan, T. Harrison, S. Long, *et al.*, 'Family discussions about organ donation', *Clinical Transplantation*, 19:5 (2005), 674–82; C. Belling, 'The living dead', *Perspectives in Biology and Medicine*, 53:3 (2010), 439–51.
7 D. Hamilton, *A History of Organ Transplantation* (Pittsburgh, PA: University of Pittsburgh Press, 2012), p. xiv, emphasis added.
8 M. Crowley-Matoka and M. Lock, 'Organ transplantation in a globalized world', *Mortality*, 11:2 (2006), 166–81 (p. 167).
9 Sharp, *Harvest*, p. 9.
10 P. Simpson, 'What are the issues in organ donation in 2012?', *British Journal of Anaesthesia*, 108 (2012), Supplement 1: i3–i6 (p. 3).
11 T. Starzl, *The Puzzle People* (Pittsburgh, PA: University of Pittsburgh Press, [1993] 2003), p. 3; A. Tzakis, 'The miracle of liver transplantation', *British Journal of Surgery*, 100:12 (2013), 1547–8; P. Morris, 'Transplantation: a medical miracle of the twentieth century', *The New England Journal of Medicine*, 351:26 (2004), 2678–80; M. Siemionow, 'The miracle of face transplantation after 10 years', *British Medical Bulletin*, 120:1 (2016), 5–14; P. Terasaki (ed.), *History of Transplantation* (Los Angeles: UCLA, 1971), p. 7.
12 L. Cohen, 'Where it hurts', *Daedalus*, 128:4 (1999), 135–65; M. Moniruzzaman, '"Living cadavers" in Bangladesh', *Medical Anthropology Quarterly*, 26:1 (2012), 69–91 (p. 83); M. Goyal, R. Mehta, L. Schneiderman, and A. Sehgal, 'Economic and health consequences of selling a kidney in India', *Journal of the American Medical Association*, 288:13 (2002), 1589–93.
13 Sharp, *Harvest*; K. Overby, M. Weinstein, and A. Fiester, 'Response to open peer commentaries', *American Journal of Bioethics*, 15:9 (2015), W3–W5; I. Fukunishi, Y. Kita, W. Paris, S. Mitchell, and B. Nour, 'Relationship between posttraumatic stress disorder and emotional conditions in families of the cadaveric donor population', *Transplantation Proceedings*, 35:1 (2014), 295; S. Hurst and B. Ricou, 'Death at the door of the operating room', *American Journal of Bioethics*, 15:8 (2015), 31–3.
14 L. Sharp, *The Transplant Imaginary* (Berkeley: University of California Press, 2013), p. 38.

15 Sharp, *Harvest*; R. Fox and J. Swazey, *The Courage to Fail* (Chicago: University of Chicago Press, 1978); R. Fox and J. Swazey, *Spare Parts* (Oxford: Oxford University Press, 1992); M. Lock, *Twice Dead* (Berkeley: University of California Press, 2002); A. Sanal, *New Organs within Us* (Durham, NC: Duke University Press, 2011); S. Hamdy, *Our Bodies Belong to God* (Berkeley: University of California Press, 2012); M. Crowley-Matoka, *Domesticating Organ Transplant* (Durham, NC: Duke University Press, 2016).

16 L. Fiedler, 'Why organ transplant programs do not succeed', in S. Youngner, R. Fox, and L. O'Connell (eds), *Organ Transplantation* (Madison: University of Wisconsin Press, 1996), pp. 56–65 (p. 58); M. Shelley, *Frankenstein* (New York: Norton, [1818, 1823] 2012); H.G. Wells, *The Island of Dr Moreau* (London: Penguin, [1896] 2005); B. Stoker, *Dracula*, ed. by M. Hindle (London: Penguin, [1897] 1993); R.L. Stevenson, *Strange Case of Dr Jekyll and Mr Hyde* (London: Penguin, [1886] 2002).

17 S. Lederer, *Flesh and Blood* (Oxford: Oxford University Press, 2008), p. xvi.

18 J. Clute, 'Fantastika in the world storm' (2007), Lecture at the American Center, Prague, www.johnclute.co.uk/word/?p=15? [accessed 23 January 2016]. For more on the intersection of Gothic and science fiction, see S. Wasson and E. Alder (eds), *Gothic Science Fiction* (Liverpool: Liverpool University Press, 2011).

19 C. Spooner, *Contemporary Gothic* (London: Bloomsbury, 2017), p. 8.

20 R. Miles, *Gothic Writing*, 2nd edn (London: Routledge, 1993), pp. 1, viii.

21 E. Burke, *A Philosophical Inquiry into the Origin of Our Ideas of the Sublime and Beautiful* (Oxford: Oxford University Press, [1757] 1990), Kindle edn, p. 36.

22 D. Punter, *Gothic Pathologies* (Basingstoke: Palgrave Macmillan, 1998), p. 14.

23 F. Botting, *Gothic* (London: Routledge, 1996), p. 14.

24 Ibid., p. 3; Critics increasingly draw a firm distinction between affect and emotion (affect as visceral, pre-verbal, non-personal intensity; emotion as personal and particular). I do at times draw the same distinction, but I also recognise Sara Ahmed's warning about the dangers of differentiating these categories too rigidly. '[T]his model creates a distinction between conscious recognition and "direct" feeling, which itself negates how that which is not consciously experienced may itself be mediated by past experiences … Further, emotions clearly involve sensations … analytic distinction between sensation or affect and emotion risks cutting emotions off from the lived experience of being.' My own focus will primarily be on emotionality, but I also explore affects and particularly the way violence takes form in the grinding *durée* of everyday life. A. Smith, 'Rethinking the Gothic', *Gothic Studies*, 4:1 (2002), 79–85 (p. 84); B. Massumi, 'The autonomy of affect', *Cultural Critique*, 31 (1995), 83–109; S. Ahmed, *Cultural Politics of Emotion*, 2nd edn (Edinburgh: Edinburgh University Press, 2004), p. 40n4.

25 C. Spooner, *Postmillennial Gothic* (London: Bloomsbury, 2017); T. Jones, *The Gothic and the Carnivalesque in American Culture* (Cardiff: University of Wales Press, 2015).

26 A. Smith and J. Wallace, 'Introduction', in A. Smith and J. Wallace (eds), *Gothic Modernisms* (Basingstoke: Palgrave, 2001), pp. 1–10 (p. 4); Miles, p. 3.

27 G. Haggerty, *Gothic Fiction / Gothic Form* (University Park: Pennsylvania State University Press, 1989), p. 20; E.K. Sedgwick, *The Coherence of Gothic Conventions* (New York: Methuen, [1980] 1986), p. 38.

28 C. Baldick (ed.), 'Introduction', *The Oxford Book of Gothic Tales* (Oxford: Oxford University Press, 1992), pp. xi–xxiii (p. xv); D. Punter, *Literature of Terror*, vol. 2 (Edinburgh: Pearson Education, 1996), p. 137.

29 S. Zlosnik, 'Globalgothic at the top of the world', in G. Byron (ed.), *Globalgothic* (Manchester: Manchester University Press, 2013), pp. 65–76 (p. 65).

30 A. Carter, 'Afterword', in *Fireworks* (Cambridge, MA: Harper and Row, 1974), pp. 132–3.

31 Shelley, pp. 31, 35.

32 Wells, pp. 72, 50.

33 C. Knellwolff and J. Goodall, 'Introduction', in C. Knellwolff and J. Goodall (eds), *Frankenstein's Science* (London: Routledge, 2016). Kindle.

34 E. Poe, 'The premature burial' (1844), *Poestories.com*, poestories.com/text.php?file=premature [accessed 7 April 2018]; Stoker; M.E. Braddon, 'Good Lady Ducayne', in A. Ryan (ed.), *The Penguin Book of Vampire Stories* (London: Penguin, [1896] 1987), pp. 138–62.

35 M. Willis, K. Waddington, and R. Marsden, 'Imaginary investments', *Journal of Literature and Science*, 6:1 (2013), 55–73 (p. 65).

36 Lederer, p. 5.

37 M. Giacomini, 'A change of heart', *Social Science of Medicine*, 44:10 (1997), 1465–82 (p. 1465).

38 B. Rollin, *The Frankenstein Syndrome* (Cambridge: Cambridge University Press, 1995); Sharp, *Harvest*, pp. 23–4; D. Beidel, 'Psychological factors in organ transplantation', *Clinical Psychology Review*, 7:6 (2987), 677–94; M. Shildrick, *Embodying the Monster* (London: Sage, 2002).

39 D. Townshend, 'Gothic panoptics and the persistence of torturous enjoyment, 1764–1820', *Genre*, 37:3–4 (2004), 395–432; Spooner, *Postmillennial Gothic*; Jones, *Carnivalesque;* Aldana Reyes, *Horror Film*.

40 S. Bruhm, 'Butoh', in G. Byron (ed.), *Globalgothic* (Manchester: Manchester University Press (2013), pp. 25–35 (p. 31).

41 X. Aldana Reyes, 'What, why and when is horror fiction?', in X. Aldana Reyes (ed.), *Horror* (London: British Library, 2016), pp. 7–18 (p. 11).

42 M. Wester, *African-American Gothic* (Basingstoke: Palgrave, 2012); M. Mulvey-Roberts, *Dangerous Bodies* (Manchester: Manchester University Press, 2016); L. Blake, *The Wounds of Nations* (Manchester: Manchester University Press, 2008); S. Wasson, *Urban Gothic of the Second World War* (Basingstoke: Palgrave, 2010).

43 Punter, *Terror*, p. 187.

44 H. Malchow, *Gothic Images of Race in Nineteenth-Century Britain* (Stanford: Stanford University Press, 1996).

45 L. Diedrich, *Treatments* (Minneapolis: University of Minnesota Press, 2007); M. Bryson and J. Stacey, 'Cancer knowledge in the plural', *Journal of Medical Humanities*, 34:2 (2013), 197–212; M. Shildrick and D. Steinberg, 'Estranged

bodies', *Body and Society*, 21:3 (2015), 3–19; D. Townshend, *The Orders of Gothic* (New York: AMS Press, 2007).

46 J. Derrida, *Specters of Marx*, trans. P. Kamuf (New York: Routledge, [1993] 2006), p. xix. For a review of theories of politicised resistant mourning, see Wasson, *Urban Gothic*, pp. 162ff.

47 G. Deleuze, *Two Regimes of Madness*, ed. by D. Lapoujade, trans. A. Hodges and M. Taormina (New York: Semiotext(e), 2007), p. 177.

48 Shildrick and Steinberg, p. 16n4.

49 J. Monleón, *A Specter Is Haunting Europe* (Princeton, NJ: Princeton University Press 1990); Punter, *Terror*, vol. 1. For further discussion of medical Gothic, see Kennedy; A. Smith, *Victorian Demons* (Manchester: Manchester University Press, 2004); L. Talairach-Vielmas, *Wilkie Collins, Medicine and the Gothic* (Cardiff: University of Wales Press, 2009); W. Hughes, 'Gothic medicine', in M. Mulvey-Roberts (ed.), *The Handbook of the Gothic*, 2nd edn (Basingstoke: Palgrave Macmillan, 2009), pp. 144–5 (p. 144); A. Smith, *Gothic Death* (Manchester: Manchester University Press, 2016); Punter, *Pathologies*; T. Sparks, *The Doctor in the Victorian Novel* (Farnham: Ashgate, 2009); A. Stephanou, *Reading Vampire Gothic through Blood* (Basingstoke: Palgrave Macmillan, 2014); Willis, Waddington, and Marsden; L. Servitje and S. Vint (eds), *The Walking Med* (University Park: Penn State University Press, 2016), C. Davison (ed.), special issue on 'Addiction', *Gothic Studies*, 11.2 (2009); S. Wasson (ed.), special issue on 'Medical Gothic', *Gothic Studies*, 17.1 (2015).

50 M. Foucault, J. -P. Barou, and M. Perrot, 'Excerpt from *The Eye of Power*', in C. Gordon (ed.), *Power/Knowledge*, trans. C. Gordon, L. Marshall, J. Mepham, and K. Soper (New York: Pantheon, [1977] 1980), pp. 146–65 (pp. 153–4).

51 Townshend, *Orders*, p. 15.

52 R. Mighall, *A Geography of Victorian Gothic Fiction* (Oxford: Oxford University Press, 1999), p. 249.

53 C. Baldick and R. Mighall, 'Gothic criticism', in D. Punter (ed.), *A Companion to the Gothic* (Oxford: Blackwells, 2001), pp. 209–28 (p. 224).

54 T. Castle, *The Female Thermometer* (Oxford: Oxford University Press, 1995), pp. 8–9.

55 Talairach-Vielmas, pp. 1–3; M. Kennedy, 'The ghost in the clinic', *Victorian Literature and Culture*, 32:2 (2004), 327–51; Mighall; A. Smith, *Victorian Demons*.

56 Mighall, p. 168; Smith, *Victorian Demons*, p. 6; C. Waldby, *AIDS and the Body Politic* (New York: Routledge, 1996); Shildrick, *Monster*, p. 79; D. Haraway, *Simians, Cyborgs, and Women* (London: Free Association Books, 1991).

57 Waldby, *AIDS*, p. 5.

58 C. Waldby, *The Visible Human Project* (London: Routledge, 2000), p. 136.

59 I. Csicsery-Ronay Jr, *The Seven Beauties of Science Fiction* (Middletown: Wesleyan University Press, 2008), pp. 2–3.

60 Baldick and Mighall, p. 222.

61 K. Hurley, *The Gothic Body* (Cambridge: Cambridge University Press, 1996), p. 6.

62 S. Younger, 'The definition of death', in B. Steinbock (ed.), *Oxford Handbook of Bioethics* (Oxford: Oxford University Press, 2007), pp. 285–303; Lock, *Twice*

Dead; Sharp, *Harvest*; R. Luckhurst, 'Biomedical horror', in J. Edwards (ed.), *Technologies of the Gothic in Literature and Culture* (London: Routledge, 2015), pp. 84–98; R. Graulund, 'Nanodead', in Edwards (ed.), pp. 127–39; S. Wasson, 'Recalcitrant tissue', in Edwards (ed.), pp. 99–112.

63 M. Silver, *Preparedness 101*, US Centers for Disease Control and Prevention, www.cdc.gov/phpr/documents/zombie_gn_final.pdf [accessed 11 July 2016].

64 D. Haraway, 'The biopolitics of postmodern bodies', in T. Campbell and A. Sitze (eds), *Biopolitics* (Durham, NC: Duke University Press, [1989] 2013), pp. 274–309; R. Esposito, *Immunitas*, trans. Z. Hanafi (Cambridge: Polity, [2002] 2011).

65 Hamilton, p. 423.

66 P. Hernigou, 'Bone transplantation and tissue engineering, part I', *International Orthopaedics*, 38:12 (2014). 2631–8 (p. 2631).

67 For much of the twentieth century the terminology was 'homograft' (to describe human-to-human transfer) and 'heterograft' (for grafts between different species), but since the late twentieth century the terms have become 'allograft' and 'xenograft' respectively. In describing xenotransplantation, I avoid the false human/ animal dichotomy.

68 Hernigou, p. 2637.

69 G. Tagliacozzi, *De Curtorum Chirurgia per Insiotonem* (Venice: Berolini, 1597).

70 Hamilton, pp. 29; 47–8, Lederer, p. 33.

71 Lederer, pp. 4–6; A. Ehrenfried, 'Reverdin and other methods of skin-grafting', *Boston Medical and Surgical Journal*, 161 (1909), 911–27.

72 Morris, p. 2678.

73 Lederer, pp. 22–5.

74 H. Baldwin, 'Skin grafting', *Medical Record*, 97 (1920), 686–8; Hamilton, pp. 195–9.

75 Lederer, pp. 23, 30n105.

76 Hamilton, p. 259.

77 Morris, p. 2678.

78 Hamilton, p. 316.

79 T. Gibson and P. Medawar, 'The fate of skin homografts in man', *Journal of Anatomy*, 77:4 (1943), 299–310.

80 Hamilton, pp. 130, 190–1.

81 Ibid, pp. 272–5.

82 W. Dempster, 'Rejection of renal homografts', *The Lancet*, 275:7123 (1960), 551.

83 Hamilton, pp. 275–9.

84 Starzl, pp. 112, 134.

85 Hamilton, pp. 340–58.

86 Fox and Swazey, *Spare Parts*, p. 3.

87 Esposito, pp. 154–8, 195n20.

88 Ibid, p. 8

89 Haraway, 'Biopolitics', p. 299.

90 S. Gilbert, 'Holobiont by birth', in A. Tsing, H. Swanson, E. Gan, and N. Bubandt (eds), *Arts of Living on a Damaged Planet* (Minneapolis: University of Minnesota Press, 2017), pp. M73–M90.

91 Ibid, pp. M81–M82.
92 M. Shildrick, 'The biopolitics of heart transplant and microchimerism', *Medical Humanities Futures*, 2nd Congress, Leeds University, October 2018.
93 Morris, p. 2679.
94 Hamilton; Starzl.
95 T. Starzl and C. Barker, 'Foreword' to Hamilton, pp. vii–ix (p. viii).
96 Fox and Swazey, *Courage*; *Spare Parts*; L. Sharp, 'Monkey business', *Social Text*, 29:1 (2011), 43–69; *Harvest*; *Transplant Imaginary*.
97 Morris, p. 2679.
98 M. Foucault, *History of Sexuality*, vol. 1 (London: Penguin, [1976] 1987), p. 138, italics in original.
99 M. Foucault, 'Society must be defended', in T. Campbell and A. Sitze (eds), *Biopolitics* (Durham, NC: Duke University Press, [1976] 2013), pp. 61–81 (p. 62).
100 Foucault, *Sexuality*, p. 136.
101 Foucault, 'Society', p. 67.
102 V. Cisney and N. Morar, 'Why biopower?' in V. Cisney and N. Morar (eds), *Biopower* (Chicago: Chicago University Press, 2016), pp. 1–25 (p. 9); Foucault, *Sexuality*, p. 143.
103 G. Agamben, *Homo Sacer*, trans. D. Heller-Roazen (Stanford: Stanford University Press, [1995] 1998); Townshend, *Orders*; G. Canavan, 'Fighting a war you've already lost', *Science Fiction Film and Television*, 4:2 (2011), 173–203.
104 C. Mills, 'Biopolitics and the concept of life', in V. Cisney and N. Morar (eds), *Biopower* (Chicago: Chicago University Press, 2016), pp. 82–101 (p. 98).
105 J. Butler, *Precarious Life* (London: Verso, 2004); A. de Boeve, *Narrative Care* (London: Bloomsbury, 2013), p. 37.
106 J. Butler, *Frames of War*, 2nd edn (New York: Verso, 2016).
107 S. Vint, 'Suspending death, reinventing life', *Embodying Fantastika* Conference, 8–10 August 2019, Lancaster University.
108 J. Biehl, *Vita*, 2nd edn (Berkeley: University of California Press, 2013), p. 366; E. Povinelli, *Economies of Abandonment* (Durham, NC: Duke University Press, 2011), pp. 4, 29; A. Mbembe, 'Necropolitics', trans. L. Mentjes, *Public Culture*, 15:1 (2003), 11–49; P. Wald, *Contagious* (Durham: Duke University Press, 2008).
109 A. Clarke, L. Mamo, J. Fishman, J. Shim, and J. Fosket, 'Biomedicalisation', *American Sociological Review*, 68 (2003), 161–94 (p. 162); P. Conrad, 'Medicalisation and social control', *Annual Review of Sociology*, 18 (1992), 209–32; R. Harris, N. Wathen, and S. Wyatt (eds), *Configuring Health Consumers* (Basingstoke: Palgrave Macmillan, 2010).
110 S. Wasson, 'Creative manifesto', *Translating Chronic Pain*, AHRC-funded Research Network (2017), wp.lancs.ac.uk/translatingpain/creative-manifesto/ [accessed 28 March 2018].
111 D. Kilgour and D. Matas, *Bloody Harvest* (Niagara Falls: Seraphim, 2009); E. Gutmann, *The Slaughter* (Amherst, NY: Prometheus, 2014).
112 L. Cohen, 'The other kidney', *Body and Society*, 7:2 (2001), 9–29; Moniruzzaman; Cohen, 'Where it hurts'; Goyal *et al.*

113 D. Rothman, E. Rose, T. Awaya, *et al.*, 'The Bellagio Task Force report', *Transplantation Proceedings*, 29:6 (1997), 2739–45 (p. 2742).

114 Cohen, 'Other kidney', pp. 11–12, emphasis in original.

115 N. Scheper-Hughes, 'Bodies for sale', in N. Scheper-Hughes and L. Wacquant (eds), *Commodifying Bodies* (London: Sage, 2002), pp. 1–8 (p. 1).

116 A. Ojo and F. Port, 'Influence of race and gender on related donor renal transplantation rates', *American Journal of Kidney Disorders*, 22:6 (1993), 835–41; L. Kayler, C. Rasmussen, D. Dykstra, A. Ojo, F. Port, R. Wolfe, and R. Merion, 'Gender imbalance and outcomes in living donor renal transplantation in the United States', *American Journal of Transplantation*, 3:4 (2003), 452; N. Biller-Andorno, 'Gender imbalance in living organ donation', *Medicine, Health Care and Philosophy*, 5:2 (2005), 199–204; P. Khajehdehi, 'Living non-related versus related renal transplantation', *Nephrology Dialysis Transplantation*, 14:11 (1999), 2621–4; N. Scheper-Hughes, 'Commodity fetishism in organs trafficking', in N. Scheper-Hughes and L. Wacquant (eds), *Commodifying Bodies* (London: Sage, 2002), pp. 31–62 (pp. 45, 54).

117 C. Kierans, 'Biopolitics and capital', *Body and Society*, 21:3 (2015), 42–65; Crowley-Matoka; K. Sunder Rajan, *Biocapital* (Durham, NC: Duke University Press, 2006).

118 Kierans, pp. 46–7.

119 Gunnarson and Lundin, p. 44.

120 Crowley-Matoka, pp. 2–3.

121 R. Chengappa, 'The great organs bazaar', *India Today* (31 July 1990), 60–7; Cohen, 'Where it hurts', p. 137, emphasis added.

122 G. Byron, 'Introduction', in G. Byron (ed.), *Globalgothic* (Manchester: Manchester University Press, 2013), pp. 1–10 (p. 4).

123 P. Barrish, 'Health policy in dystopia', *Literature and Medicine*, 34:1 (2016), 106–31 (paras 1–2).

124 Fox and Swazey, *Spare Parts*, p. 75; J. Aleccia, 'Wallet biopsy', *CNN.com* (24 December 2018), t.co/WXXjGkaiC3 [accessed 19 May 2019].

125 Hamilton, p. 30.

126 S. Wasson, 'Gothic and the built environment', in D. Punter (ed.), *Gothic and the Arts* (Edinburgh: Edinburgh University Press, in press); S. Wasson, 'Gothic cities and suburbs, 1880–present', in G. Byron and D. Townshend (eds), *The Gothic World* (London: Routledge, 2014), pp. 132–42.

127 S. Shapiro, 'Transvaal, Transylvania', *Gothic Studies*, 10:1 (2008), 29–47 (pp. 30, 44n2); S. Shapiro, 'Material Gothic', *Gothic Studies*, 10:1 (2008), 1–3; K. Marx, *Capital*, vol. 1 (London: Penguin [1976] 1990), pp. 163–77.

128 J. Comaroff and J. Comaroff, 'Millennial capitalism', *Public Culture*, 12:2 (2000), 291–343.

129 J. Guyer, 'Prophecy and the near future', *American Ethnologist*, 34:2 (2007), 409–21 (p. 412); cf. E. Povinelli, *Economies of Abandonment*, p. 19.

130 L. Blake, 'Neoliberal adventures in neo-Victorian biopolitics', in J. Edwards (ed.), *Technologies of the Gothic in Literature and Culture* (London: Routledge, 2015), pp. 166–78 (p. 167). Cf. also B. Murnane, '*In the Flesh* and the Gothic pharmacology of everyday life', *Text Matters*, 6:6 (2016), 227–44; H. Giroux, *Zombie*

Politics and Culture in the Age of Casino Capitalism (New York: Peter Lang, 2011); D. McNally, *Monsters of the Market* (Brill: Leiden, 2011); S. Shaviro, 'Capitalist monsters', *Historical Materialism*, 10:4 (2002), 281–90; G. Byron (ed.), *Globalgothic* (Manchester: Manchester University Press, 2013).

131 Sunder Rajan, p. 7; A. Ong, *Neoliberalism as Exception* (Durham, NC: Duke University Press, 2006), p. 3; R. Venugopal, 'Neoliberalism as concept', *Economy and Society*, 44:2 (2015), 165–87 (pp. 171–81).

132 S. Squier, *Liminal Lives* (Durham, NC: Duke University Press, 2004), pp. 175–8.

133 H. Zwart, 'Transplantation medicine', *Subjectivity*, 9:2 (2016), 151–80 (p. 157); J. Riskin, *The Restless Clock* (Chicago: University of Chicago Press, 2016).

134 Starzl, *Puzzle People*; C. Waldby, 'Biomedicine, tissue transfer and intercorporeality', *Feminist Theory*, 3 (2002), 235–50 (p. 239); S. Schicktanz and M. Schweda, '"One man's trash is another man's treasure"', *Journal of Medical Ethics*, 35:8 (2009), 473–6.

135 R. Richardson, *Death, Dissection and the Destitute* (London: Penguin, 1989), p. 57.

136 Hamilton, pp. 47–8.

137 R. Titmuss, *The Gift Relationship* (New York: Vintage, [1971] 1972).

138 K. Zeiler and E. Malmqvist, 'Bodily exchanges, bioethics, and border crossing', in E. Malmqvist and K. Zeiler (eds), *Bodily Exchanges* (London: Routledge, 2016), pp. 1–18 (p. 9).

139 E. Malmqvist and K. Zeiler, 'Concluding reflections', in Malmqvist and Zeiler, pp. 197–207 (p. 205n2); Fox and Swazey, *Spare Parts*; R. Shaw, 'Perceptions of the gift relationship in organ and tissue donation', *Social Science and Medicine*, 70:4 (2010), 609–15; N. Scheper-Hughes, 'The tyranny of the gift', *American Journal of Transplantation*, 7:3 (2007), 507–11. For Gothic aspects of the coercive dimension of the gift, see S. Wasson, 'The "coven of the articulate"', *The Journal of Popular Culture*, 45:1 (2012), 197–213.

140 A. Hochschild, *The Managed Heart*, 3rd edn (Berkeley: University of California Press, 2012).

141 S. Freud, 'Mourning and melancholia', *Penguin Freud Library*, vol. 11, trans. J. Strachey, ed. by A. Richards (London: Penguin, [1917] 1984), pp. 245–68.

142 Wester; Malchow; Mulvey-Roberts, *Dangerous*, p. 2; S. Wasson, 'Spectrality, strangeness and stigmaphilia: Gothic and disability studies', in A. Hall (ed.), *Routledge Companion to Literature and Disability* (London: Routledge, in press).

143 S. Schlozman, 'Preface', in L. Servitje and S. Vint (eds), *The Walking Med* (University Park: Pennsylvania State University Press, 2016), pp. vii–x (p. ix–x).

144 Squier, pp. 212–13.

145 G. Canavan, '"If the engine ever stops, we'd all die"', *Paradoxa*, 26 (2014), 41–66.

146 S. Bolaki, *Illness as Many Narratives* (Edinburgh University Press, 2016), p. 13.

147 S. Wasson, 'Before narrative', *Medical Humanities*, 44:2 (2018), 106–12; Wasson, 'Stigmaphilia'.

148 S. Wendell, 'Unhealthy disabled', *Hypatia*, 16:4 (2001), 17–33; L. Crow, 'Including all of our lives', in J. Morris (ed.), *Encounters with Strangers* (London:

The Women's Press, 1996); D. Price-Herndl, 'Disease versus disability', *PMLA*, 120:2 (2005), 593–8.

149 M. Hyvärinen, L.-C. Hydén, M. Saarenheimo, and M. Tamboukou (eds), 'Introduction', *Beyond Narrative Coherence* (Philadelphia: John Benjamins, 2010), pp. 1–15 (p. 7).

150 See for example the discussion of 'narrative fetish' in E. Santner, 'History beyond the pleasure principle', in S. Friedlander (ed.), *Probing the Limits of Representation* (Cambridge, MA: Harvard University Press, 1992), pp. 143–54.

151 Wasson, 'Before narrative'; Wasson, 'Stigmaphilia'; S. Wasson, 'Creative manifesto', *Translating Chronic Pain*, AHRC-funded Research Network (2017), wp.lancs.ac.uk/translatingpain/creative-manifesto/ [accessed 28 March 2018]; S. Wasson, 'Useful darkness', *Gothic Studies* 17:1 (2015), 1–12.

152 Sharp, *Harvest*; D. McCormack, 'Living with others inside the self', *Medical Humanities*, 42:4 (2016), 252–8.

153 T. Jones, D. Wear, and L. Friedman (eds), 'Introduction', *Health Humanities Reader* (New Brunswick: Rutgers University Press, 2014), pp. 1–9 (p. 7); A. Whitehead, 'A literary perspective', in V. Bates, A. Bleakley, and S. Goodman (eds), *Medicine, Health and the Arts* (Abingdon: Routledge, 2014), pp. 107–27 (p. 118).

154 W. Viney, F. Callard, and A. Woods, 'Critical medical humanities', *Medical Humanities*, 41 (2015), 2–7 (p. 5).

155 A. Bleakley, 'Towards a critical medical humanities', in V. Bates, A. Bleakley, and S. Goodman (eds), *Medicine, Health and the Arts* (Abingdon: Routledge, 2014), pp. 17–26 (p. 23); Bolaki, p. 9; cf. K. Waddington and M. Willis, 'Rethinking illness narratives', *Journal of Literature and Science*, 6:1 (2013), iv–v (p. iv).

156 M.K. Czerwiec, I. Williams, S. Squier, M. Green, K. Myers, and S. Smith, *Graphic Medicine Manifesto* (University Park: Penn State University Press, 2015); *Configurations*, 22:2 (2014), special issue edited by S. Squier and J. Marks; and the GraphicMedicine.com blog and annual conference. Fine art and visual arts are explored by, among others, Bolaki, and A. Radley, *Works of Illness* (Harrow: InkerMan, 2009), and conjunctions between science fiction and medical humanities have been examined by, among others, Glasgow University's Wellcome Trust project on Science Fiction and the Medical Humanities.

157 P. Crawford and C. Baker, 'Literature and madness', *Journal of Medical Humanities*, 30 (2009), 237–51 (p. 247).

158 J. Trautmann, 'The wonders of literature in medical education', in D. Self (ed.), *The Role of the Humanities in Medical Education* (Norfolk, VA: Eastern Virginia Medical, 1978), pp. 32–44; cf. K.M. Hunter, 'Toward the cultural interpretation of medicine', *Literature and Medicine*, 10 (1991), 1–17 (p. 2).

159 J. Semprun, *Literature or Life*, trans. L. Coverdale (New York: Viking, [1994] 1997), pp. 13–14, 123–5; U. Teucher, 'The incomprehensible density of being', in V. Raoul, C. Canam, A. Henderson, and C. Paterson (eds), *Unfitting Stories* (Waterloo, Ontario: Wilfrid Laurier University Press, 2007), pp. 71–8; M. Rothberg, *Traumatic Realism* (Minneapolis: University of Minnesota Press, 2000).

160 S. Egan, *Mirror Talk* (Chapel Hill: University of North Carolina Press, 1999), p. 28.

161 R. Luckhurst, 'The contemporary London Gothic', *Textual Practice*, 16:3 (2002), 527–46 (pp. 528, 542).

162 K. Fiser, 'Why not be wholly changed into fire?', *Losing and Finding* (Denton: University of North Texas Press, 2003), p. 11.

163 D. Haraway, *Staying with the Trouble* (Durham, NC: Duke University Press, 2016); J. Moore (ed.), *Anthropocene or Capitalocene?* (Oakland: PM Press, 2016); Sharp, *Transplant Imaginary*; 'Monkey business'.

1

Clinical necropoetics: medical and ethics writing of death and transplantation

In 1875, Francis Gerry Fairfield invoked period understandings of neurology to offer a striking view of the human nervous system. Experiments at the time indicated that white and grey nervous tissue have different functions, the former governing movement and sensation, and the latter involving higher thought. '[T]he physiologist thus finally encounters a gray nervous spectre that thinks and feels and longs, wills and determines and controls … a thin and filmy ghost … matter's final *Doppelgänger*'.[1] While the science of that passage is flawed, it foreshadows more recent medical thought in differentiating neurological functions and seeing consciousness wholly as a function of the body rather than the function of a separate spirit. Yet the language of this materialist vision is spectral: the subject is haunted by the *material* body, the 'thin and filmy ghost' of nerves themselves, 'matter's final *Doppelgänger*'.

A kind of materialist haunting can also be discerned within the medico-legal redefinitions of death that have accompanied the progress of the transplantation project. While haunting usually connotes disembodied spirits, here the term implies that bodies themselves can be recalcitrant and mysterious, not quite explained by a diagnostic label. This chapter explores affective and epistemological challenges posed by the novel diagnostic entities of 'whole-brain death', 'brain-stem death', and 'controlled circulatory death' as they developed in transfer milieus in the US and UK. As life-support technologies progressed, cardiopulmonary functions could be maintained despite catastrophic neurological damage. New states of being emerged, cyborg hybridities of machine and flesh dependent on machines for oxygen but still breathing, sweating, growing, sighing, and – sometimes – even weeping.[2] My goal is not necessarily to challenge the validity of these criteria, or to question that these states indicate irreversible decline. Rather, I want to address how Gothic imagery, intertextualities, and narrative strategies are marshalled to variously express uncertainty or unease or, by contrast, to manage doubt and normalise. As described in my Introduction, Gothic can facilitate contradictory meanings, dis(re)membering to communicate troubling affects or to elide that very strangeness.

Reading the dead

Of necessity, a significant proportion of this interdisciplinary chapter will review the new deaths and their controversies, conventions of scientific communication, and theories of diagnosis. Diagnosis is historically and culturally specific, in that social factors shape how symptoms are understood; it is also always an enacted practice, an assemblage, as discussed in my Introduction, a network of human and nonhuman entities and forces tangible and intangible.[3] Death diagnoses are enacted by assemblages of diverse elements – a body, cotton ear-buds, cardiac defibrillators, EEG machines, nurses, neurologists, anaesthesiologists, ventilators, thermometers, legal criteria for death, death certificate documentation, ice water poured into an ear. Each era has its own methods for enacting such diagnosis.

Thanatological uncertainty is hardly new, and has been especially prevalent at periods when new resuscitation technologies increased uncertainty about boundaries between life and death, notably 1740–1850 and the 1960s onwards. I will briefly review the eighteenth- and nineteenth-century context since it influenced the way these questions played out in the late twentieth century. In 1740, Leander Paget and Jacques-Bénigne Winslow wrote a short book in Latin, *The Uncertainty of the Signs of Death*. Expanded by others and translated into many languages, this text spawned a vast literature of thanatological doubt.[4] By 1850 books and articles on the difficulty of diagnosing death 'could be counted in the hundreds'.[5] Societies were founded dedicated to resuscitation, especially of the drowned, such as England's Humane Society founded in 1773. Considered as assemblage, early resuscitations drew on human and nonhuman actants including blankets, massage, and sal volatile. Electricity joined the paraphernalia of resurrection in 1774, and in 1803 Aldini used electricity to make a hanged man twitch, later to influence Mary Shelley's *Frankenstein* (1818). By 1796 the London Society claimed over two thousand successful resuscitations.[6] The Society's work increased uncertainty over death's finality, one of its Society's founders arguing in 1780 that only bodily decay was a reliable indicator and some physicians contending that even that could be confused with gangrene.[7] When the physician Charles Kite listed signs of death in 1788, he added that 'these signs will not afford certain and unexceptionable criteria, by which we may distinguish between life and death'; likewise, Mathieu Orfila's influential work on poison lists many signs of death but concludes that 'no one of the signs, taken singly (except decided putrefaction) is sufficient to ascertain, positively, that an individual is dead'.[8] By the end of the nineteenth century, physicians used a list of up to twenty possible signs of death.[9] Checklists remain applicable in clinical diagnoses of death today, with some of the same challenges.

Fear of premature burial inspired creative measures such as escapable coffins and waiting mortuaries – 'shelters of doubtful life' – and as medical research and training make increasing use of dissection, fear also rose around unwitting vivisection.[10] Uncertainties around death were exacerbated by popular awareness of other deathlike states, including those induced by trance, poison, or chloroform anaesthesia.[11] Scientific innovations like the stethoscope and thermometer seemed to offer the possibility of simplifying death diagnosis, but instead added even further confusion by indicating that organs cease functioning at different times.[12]

At the same time as the corpse was brought under such scrutiny, death also became more hidden. Public-health reforms shifted to the margins of towns, and mourning conventions changed. There are risks in generalising about cultural attitudes towards death in particular eras, yet multiple commentators have identified a range in attitudes to death emerging at various moments from the late eighteenth century to the present, ranging from sentimentalising death in a cult of family through to seeing death in terms of prurience and taboo.[13] Some critics have suggested that Gothic fiction offered ways to contemplate forms of mourning not socially acceptable at the time, as well as opportunities to muse over the corporeal mysteries of decay. With regard to the former, Dale Townshend speaks of early Gothic offering a socially acceptable expression of 'negated grief', mediated by descriptions of 'macabre realities of corporeal decomposition and religious insecurity', and Elisabeth Bronfen describes how, at times, art and literature could facilitate a kind of 'death by proxy', an imaginative engagement with this visceral and final experience.[14] Carol Davison argues that Gothic writing offers a 'necropoetics', using 'death-focused symbols and tropes such as spectrality and the concept of *memento mori*' to express the complex relationship between the living and the dead, as well as the work of mourning.[15] As the nineteenth century progressed, Gothic writing also increasingly imaginatively enacted the inquiry of professional medical discourse in deciphering death processes.[16] By contrast with late eighteenth-century Gothic, nineteenth-century protagonists typically respond to the sight of a corpse less with horror than with either grief or quasi-scientific detachment: as Andrew Smith notes, in the late nineteenth century in particular, the dead body 'either elicits empathy or invites forms of scientific understanding', rather than terror or dread.[17] In a range of ways, then, these fictions pose invitations to contemplate the affective and epistemological challenges posed by the dead.

Gothic fiction and scientific writing differ not only in formal characteristics but also in intended relationship to truth. Scientific writing is an 'epistemic genre', in Gianna Pomata's phrase, driven by the goal of 'knowledge-making' (with the caveat that what counts as knowledge is historically variable).[18] The nineteenth century saw professional pressure to move away from eighteenth-century sentimentality and Romantic language of emotional response, which had sometimes characterised elements of scientific writing previously.[19] This distancing was informed not only by a need to meet the emerging epistemic virtue of objectivity but also by medicine's claims on modernity, as Meegan Kennedy says, 'defin[ing] itself in opposition not only to disciplinary others but to its own disciplinary ancestry'.[20] However, traces of the sentimental or Romantic remained, particularly in contexts where physicians were emotionally moved.[21] Nineteenth-century medical writing could invoke tenderness or fascinated horror, or emulate Gothic's 'interest in the supernatural and the unexplainable and its narrative aim of arousing suspense, horror, and astonishment'.[22] Clinicians' writing could also slide into emotional prose characteristic of Gothic fiction, such as James Bower Harrison's description of fatal haemorrhage in his book *The Medical Aspects of Death* (1852): 'The sufferer becomes pale and faint, his lips white and trembling … [E]xhaustion and prostration are more and more alarming. Soon a curious restlessness arises, and he tosses himself from side to side … In vain the pulse is sought at the wrist – in vain efforts are made to re-excite warmth – the body is like a living corpse … [C]onvulsive gaspings arise, and the countenance sets in the stiff image of death.'[23] Elsewhere, Harrison interrupts a detached and clinical exposition of signs of death to exclaim, 'Shall we "look upon those lips that we have kissed we know not how oft", pale, cold, and repulsive, and not experience the immensity of this change!'[24] Medical texts could even be illustrated with pictures that would not be out of place in Gothic fiction, such as multiple plates in Winslow's text depicting people rising from graves after premature burial, and onlookers fleeing in fear. As late as 1947, a medical textbook uses dramatic prose to describe the mystery of death. Stefan Jellinek, Professor of Electro-Pathology at the University of Vienna, warns that 'Not only has life pulsing freshly in each one of us its own peculiar motif, its own rhythm; but the sonorous finale, death, has in each one of us its individual cadence', and he asks 'is there certainty that the dark door is passed for ever?'[25]

Even today, despite new conventions of scientific prose, clinical case reports remain narrative and at times echo literary genres, notably the detective story and the Gothic tale: 'the urge to conjure up the enigmatic', says Brian Hurwitz, 'to entertain and shock with spectacle … is still at work in case reporting today', and Rick Rylance describes how case reporting, in particular, may still shift 'between gothic make-believe and the modernised medical mode'.[26] As I will show, contemporary journal correspondence pages, too, can serve as a site where emotion and thanatological uncertainty may be voiced, and scientific journal articles may also invoke Gothic intertextuality, tropes, or narrative structures.

This chapter identifies a clinical necropoetics in writing exploring transfer from within the disciplines of medical science and ethics. Gothic representations can 'give a voice to the silenced dead', in the words of Sarah Webster Goodwin and Elisabeth Bronfen, imbuing a dead body with social meaning.[27]

At the same time, Gothic can be part of a process of *silencing* the dead, reducing the dangerous superfluity of meanings that such bodies may bear.

The new deaths: determination of death by neurological criteria and donation after circulatory death

'Organ donors must be dead before procurement of organs begins, [and] organ procurement itself must not cause the death of the donor'.[28] This 'dead donor rule' has been called 'a centerpiece of the social order's commitment to respect for persons and human life', and has led to stringent efforts to clearly identify the exact moment of death.[29] Different parts of the body cease functioning at different times, and cultures privilege particular organs as the seat of life; even the term 'brain death' elides whether it describes brainstem or whole-brain death, since countries differ in their definition.[30] Death determined by neurological criteria differs from conventional cardiac death, after which the entire body rapidly begins degeneration. In donation after diagnosis of brain death, it is cross-clamping the heart artery which directly causes cardiac death. For this reason, some practitioners have spoken informally of cardiac death as 'real' death.[31]

The nineteenth century saw attempts to define a form of neurological death, but such efforts became more urgent in the twentieth century after increasingly reliable ventilator life support began extending lives despite severe neurological damage.[32] One of the biggest influences on definition was the concept of *coma dépassé* by the French physicians Mollaret and Goulon in 1959, 'a state surpassing/exceeding coma'.[33] They did not see this as death and their criteria would today be closer to those for chronic disorders of consciousness (CDoCs), but the concept influenced the Belgian surgeon Guy Alexandre's criteria for brain death criteria in 1963 and was used in Belgium's first cadaveric transplant.[34] The most influential event in the formulation of criteria for brain death was the 1968 'Report of the Ad Hoc Committee of the Harvard Medical School to Examine the Definition of Brain Death'. The Report argued that a definition was needed for two reasons: the emotional and financial burdens of extended life support in futile cases, and the fact that '[o]bsolete criteria for the definition of death can lead to controversy in obtaining organs for transplantation'.[35] The Report admits, 'The question before the committee could not simply be to define brain-death. *This would not advance the cause of organ transplantation* since it would not cope with the essential issue of when the surgical team is authorised ... in removing a vital organ.'[36] Committee records indicate that transplantation concerns influenced the recommendations.[37] Mita Giacomini observes that the archives indicate that the Committee 'suppressed professional uncertainty from public view', and that 'transplantation interests ... played a particularly influential role in tailoring the final criteria'.[38] The Harvard Report's definition of 'irreversible coma' fed into the President's Commission on Defining Death, which in turn underpinned the Uniform Determination of Death Act (UDDA) in 1980.[39] The latter gave a rubric for the US states to pass individual laws recognising 'irreversible cessation of all functions of the entire brain' as a form of death, although US states still vary in their legal definitions.[40] Nations, too, continue to use different criteria for neurological death. From the start, the UK differed from the US by defining neurological death in terms of brainstem rather than whole-brain death and emphasising clinical examination over scans.[41] Transatlantic differences flared into public view in 1980 and 1981 when the BBC ran two episodes of *Panorama* featuring American neurologists suggesting that British methods of brain-death diagnosis might lead to extracting organs from people 'not really dead'.[42] In turn, some UK neurologists argued that the American criticism indicated inadequate history-taking and clinical observation, which could also lead to misdiagnosis.[43]

Just as deathlike states confused popular understanding of death in the nineteenth century, so too did the early years of the brain-death definition see cases that complicated popular grasp of the concept. Most notable among these was the case of Karen Quinlan – ironic, since Quinlan was never diagnosed as brain-dead.[44] In April 1975, Quinlan inexplicably stopped breathing and was admitted to hospital where she did not respond to painful stimuli. She was diagnosed as in a persistent vegetative state, placed on a ventilator, and never regained consciousness. Her parents wished to withdraw life support, but the hospital refused because that would technically have been homicide. The New Jersey Supreme Court ruled for the parents in March 1976, but after Karen was removed from ventilator support she continued to breathe independently and lived, unconscious, for another nine years. Her permanent unconsciousness and the fact that she was dependent on medical equipment for oxygen and nourishment made the case overlap (inaccurately) with popular conceptions of neurologically determined death.

Today there is overwhelming consensus in both the UK and US medical communities that, despite differing national criteria for brain death, the state is irreversible and organ extraction is justifiable. None the less, two kinds of uncertainty can still gather around the life status of the patient or body within these new frameworks. Firstly, there is the possibility, as with all human activity, of error; secondly, neurologists identify real obstacles to complying with current legal language of 'irreversibility' and 'whole-brain' death.

Any diagnostic practice has the chance of fallibility due to practitioner error, flaws in the diagnostic model itself, or 'necessary fallibility' due to the unknowable idiosyncrasies of any particular case.[45] Discussions of the new death categories use qualifying phrases like 'virtually' certain and acknowledge there may be at times an 'element of uncertainty' that requires confirmatory tests.[46]

Yet as Paul Byrne and Richard Nilges note, it is hard to countenance fallibility in death diagnosis that leads to surgical procurement: 'In brain death there can be no "necessary fallibility" of diagnosis'.[47] There are several reasons why neurological death might be inaccurately diagnosed. Neurological death cannot be solely ascertained through EEG or fMRI – indeed, these may not be used at all, and they cannot indicate whether the brain-stem is still alive – but also requires history-taking and clinical examination. Confounders include certain narcotics, a body temperature below 95°F/35°C, and undiagnosed conditions like brain-stem encephalitis or locked-in syndrome.[48] Infants and neonates have neurophysiologies that may falsely indicate irreversible brain death, including electrocerebral silence.[49] There can also be failures to follow diagnostic protocol. Even an enthusiastic supporter of neurological criteria for determining death admits that it is of 'significant concern' that 'deviation from practice guidelines is relatively widespread'.[50] In 2016, David Greer *et al.* studied how brain death was diagnosed in multiple US hospitals and found extensive failures to meet the American Academy of Neurology guidelines, and in 2013 C. Shappell *et al.* found that in chart reviews of 226 patients in 68 hospitals, 'only 44.7% of the brain death determinations met AAN practice parameters'.[51] Amid the complexities of varying clinical practice and disagreements within the profession, Margaret Lock notes that 'the possibility of actual mistakes ... cannot be ruled out'.[52]

Challenges are also sometimes posed to the diagnostic categories themselves. Michael Nair-Collins, Sydney Green, and Angelina Sutin argue that 'There is legitimate scientific dispute among experts as to whether "brain dead" donors are truly dead, and this information is not routinely disclosed'.[53] At the time of writing there continues to be no international consensus on the specific protocols or legal terminology for determination of neurological death, and as Basil Matta notes, 'A brain might be defined as dead in the United Kingdom, yet the same brain would not be dead in Europe and vice-versa'.[54] None the less, regardless of nuances in national criteria, several decades of evidence reliably indicate that patients diagnosed as neurologically dead do not recover, provided the diagnosis has omitted confounders.[55] Yet legal terminology has become increasingly vexed. Neurological research indicates that 'Irreversible cessation of all functions of the entire brain', as the US UDDA requires, is virtually impossible to demonstrate, and even in the more specific UK definition of brain-*stem* death, several basic neurological functions may persist.[56] Halevy and Brody observe that 'any sharp dichotomy [of alive/dead] based on brain functioning ... is biologically artificial', and the 2008 US President's Council on Bioethics acknowledged that legal definitions should be amended in the light of current knowledge.[57]

The need to increase organ supply led to a second expansion of death criteria to include 'donation after determination of circulatory death' (DDCD), previously known as Non-Heartbeating Donation (NHBD). I will use the more widespread acronym DCD. DCD has two forms: 'uncontrolled' DCD, rapid procurement after an unexpected heart attack, and 'controlled' DCD, where a patient already on life support has it withdrawn in a manner to optimise transplant success.[58] My discussion will focus on the latter, which is more common in the UK and US. Patients may be conscious or unconscious before the death process is initiated and are not neurologically dead. The procedure deviates from normal terminal wean. The patient is taken into theatre where a procurement team are ready to operate. Life support is withdrawn and staff wait to see if the heart will stop beating; if it does, a set time is allowed to elapse, death is declared and a surgical team extracts the organs.

While it may sound straightforward to say the moment of death occurs at the moment the heartbeat ceases, several controversies have gathered around DCD, especially in its early forms. Spontaneous resumption of cardiac function can occur, notably in cases where CPR was previously applied.[59] As with neurological death, national guidelines vary widely. Some waits have been as brief as 75 seconds, and as first developed in the 1990s at Pittsburgh University Hospital required a lack of pulse or breathing for only two minutes, despite recorded cases of spontaneous cardiac recovery even after five minutes asystole.[60] By contrast, Switzerland's Maastricht protocol mandates a ten-minute wait.[61] In addition to disagreement over a safe time span to elapse, there are also complications around legal definition of death. As various supporters of DCD admit, controlled DCD is technically incompatible with mandating 'irreversible' cessation of cardiac function, since resuscitation is not only not attempted but has to be actively *prevented* during surgery, as I discuss shortly.[62] There is also a paradox when a patient is declared dead on the grounds of irreversible cardiac failure yet that same heart is retrieved and successfully transplanted.[63] Several strong supporters of DCD state that we should use 'not a literal definition of irreversible'.[64]

Some physicians have raised concerns about pain due to uncertainties about neurological status at point of procurement. DCD donors are not neurologically dead before life support is withdrawn, and evidence has shown brain-stem function persisting as long as ten minutes after cardiopulmonary cessation.[65] Rady and Verhejde note, 'surgical procurement is performed on donors without general anaesthesia', and 'it is clinically challenging to confirm irreversible cessation of brainstem reflexes on ECMO [extracorporeal membrane oxygenation] support'.[66] Frank Chaten observes, 'Even advocates of DCD ... recommend that additional research is needed in "the chronology of brain destruction after complete cessation of circulation"'.[67] In this regard, a surgeon supportive of DCD has expressed concern over a case where a cardiomyopathy developed during DCD surgery, a response that typically indicates 'extreme emotional stress'.[68] Furthermore, advocates of DCD acknowledge that the process of procurement surgery itself may inadvertently reawaken elements of pain-related neurological function, raising concerns over 'lingering responses of the nervous tissue to restoration of cerebral blood flow', unless countermeasures are taken, since '[r]estoring brain circulation also raises the possibility of ... consequent potential for suffering'.[69]

Donation after controlled circulatory death may also impact end-of-life care. The 1990s Pittsburgh practice could include painful lymph node removal and drugs to optimise tissue for transfer but which could mask a pulse or hasten death.[70] Deviation from end-of-life care targets has been documented in several other DCD contexts.[71] Patients and families choosing DCD may be motivated by a desire to avoid artificially prolonging life, but DCD itself involves a more technologically mediated death. Bion *et al*, note that 'the processes we have developed for permitting a peaceful death in the ICU must now take place in an environment which allows rapid intervention to optimise organ retrieval, for example, the operating theatre'.[72] The President's Council for Bioethics warned that DCD means a more technologically mediated death than would occur otherwise.[73] Despite a lack of public awareness about the procedure, controlled DCD is an increasing part of national procurement strategies.[74]

Death diagnosis in the context of organ procurement, then, can still pose some conceptual and affective challenges. Two solutions have been proposed for the current impossibilities of the legal wording. Death could be redefined in terms of 'loss of personhood', in which 'the loss of certain key human functions (such as the ability to be conscious or apply reason) is sufficient for the philosophical and ethical justification of a diagnosis of death' (which risks being interpreted broadly to include CDOCs, dementia, or psychosis).[75] Another option is to discard the dead donor rule altogether and reframe surgical organ extraction as semi-euthanasia in the service of a social good.[76] Robert Truog, for example, says that 'the so-called dead donor rule ... seeks to establish a bright line, or ethical firewall, between the dying process and organ procurement. But this bright line has always been an illusion', and recommends 'creation of legal exception to ... homicide laws'.[77] Physicians have also argued that this candour would benefit DCD donors, by enabling anaesthesia in the light of the possibility that donors may feel pain.[78] Vernez and Magnus, supporters of DCD, warn that the possibility of donor pain 'should be taken seriously and ... care should be taken not to allow semantics and the definition we have of death to stop us from providing adequate pain relief'.[79] So vigorous are challenges to the rule that it is itself figured as hovering on a life/death boundary, as in articles entitled 'Life or death for the dead donor rule?', 'Burying the dead donor rule', and 'Can the dead donor rule be resuscitated?'[80]

Cadaveric procurement may also be emotionally challenging for practitioners at times, even when they are highly committed to the endeavour.

It could be especially taxing in the early years. The surgeon René Küss recalls extracting kidneys from executed prisoners minutes after decapitation in a Paris prison in 1951, operating in 'extremely precarious conditions … which strongly offended the sensitivity of some of us', 'performed on the ground by torchlight' in an *'atmosphere extrêmement pénible'* (extremely harrowing atmosphere), and, a few years later, his team were extracting kidneys from cadavers in morgues in 'a Dantesque adventure … dissecting cadavers secretly at night by candlelight'.[81] Even within hospital settings, surgeons recall that the extraction surgery could be 'rushed, undignified, and often unpleasant', with 'suboptimal anaesthetic preparation' for recipients.[82] The surgeon Roy Calne recalls an incident where a nurse superintendent barred cadavers from the operating theatre, 'So we had to remove the kidneys in the open ward. Looking back on the procedure it must have resembled a horror film.'[83] The surgeon Thomas Starzl describes many emotionally challenging scenarios, including harvesting blood vessels in the hospital morgue and seeing 'a parade of sorrow' of violent death: 'I dreaded the summons to the morgue, not wanting to know what had happened to the blood vessel donor, but realising that this knowledge would be the price for providing the vessel graft to someone who needed it'.[84] Here, Starzl strikingly identifies transplant surgeons' labour as being affective as well as surgical, a willingness to bear knowledge. Lock describes a surgeon vomiting with distress after he had to assist with surgical procurement of a child he had treated while alive, in which he felt the team 'swarmed in' and 'cannibalised' the boy (today, protocols assign such work to different teams, in recognition of the emotional challenge).[85] Even now, some medical staff may occasionally find elements of the process disturbing.[86] Barbara-Anne Wren describes an experienced transplant surgeon overcome with emotion when he realised that under the body of the child donor from whom he had extracted organs, there were pages of hand prints from family members so that the child could 'die in their arms'.[87] Surgeons are not the only medical practitioners who may at times find it hard; Lock quotes several anaesthesiologists in this regard, one of whom I quote from here:

> Procurements are not a pretty sight. I always get the hell out of the operating room as soon as I possibly can. As soon as they've got the heart out. Everyone starts to scrabble at that point. It's ghastly, absolutely ghastly. I sort of have to sit down by the machines and just keep checking the dials every couple of minutes so I don't have to watch what's going on. It's ghoulish.[88]

Some practitioners also describe uneasy experiences. One surgeon recalls that in the middle of procurement surgery on a man, 'suddenly I felt the guy's arm rise behind me, and this was obviously some sort of neurological reflex, but it is – I mean, deep down, it's pretty spooky … Yes, I did just call it a patient – because they're still breathing. It's definitely a sort of in-between state.'[89]

The slide between pronouns mirrors the ambiguity of the body: '*it*' is a patient because '*they're* still breathing'. Surgical procurement may evoke a range of feelings, even if practitioners are dedicated to the process.

Yet despite such reasonable potential distress, there may be pressure to suppress such responses. Lesley Sharp observes, 'Involved professionals – be they surgeons, transplant nurses or social workers, or organ procurement specialists – invest significant effort in denying the strange, uncanny, and troubling aspects of organ transfer ... [through] elaborate forms of rhetorical policing, word play, and metaphorical representations that both objectify fleshy parts and obscure their troubled human origins'.[90] Sharp reports encountering 'the uncanny assertion that human suffering does not exist, as long as clinical staff respond immediately to patients' reports of physical pain'.[91] Lock warns, 'It is inappropriate, even if it were possible, to suppress emotional responses to organ procurement in the interest of finding rational answers. We are scrutinizing extraordinary activities: death-defying technologies in which the creation of meaning out of sudden destruction produces new forms of human affiliation. These are profoundly emotional matters.'[92] A Gothic discursivity is part of clinical rhetorics in response to such uncertainties, distress, and unease.

'Closure rhetoric' and clinical necropoetics

To present a diagnosis as a stable truth inherent within a body, the practices that enact the diagnosis must be 'bracketed', in Mol's terms, eliding the processes, people, and paraphernalia that comprise the diagnostic assemblage. Through such bracketing, the diagnosed state becomes naturalised, 'a virtual common object ... projected into the body, an object that is hidden under the skin', and this bracketing also occurs in writing.[93] Mol identifies a 'closure rhetoric' in research publications, in which 'once outcomes are accepted as facts that the methods by which they are reached are, at least for the time being, abbreviated, allowed to fade out, forgotten. The two movements seem to go together: the consolidation of a fact and the bracketing of the means of its production.'[94] Late twentieth- and twenty-first-century scientific writing is characterised by stylistic markers that downplay both affective response and individual action, using 'suppressed-person passive verb and verbs that relate to the activities of things rather than people', and condensed syntax with complex noun phrases in the subject position but few clauses per sentence.[95] 'Epistemic hedging' is abundant, cautiously marking limitations to current knowledge, but expressions of uncertainty are rare, particularly around the implications of diagnostic fallibility: while diagnostic fallibility is admitted, it is regularly followed by a renewed statement reiterating the need to avoid fruitlessly prolonging life.[96] Articles in scientific journals do address elements of diagnostic assemblage, as when reviewing diverse clinical protocols for declaring brain death or donation after circulatory death, but, at the same time, these texts are invested in the stability of the new death diagnoses and the need to bracket assemblage.

Gothic discursivity can work both sides of that process, to express doubt and to reinforce consensus. In the remainder of this chapter, I will identify three ways that a clinical necropoetics functions in writing emerging from both transplantations science and medical ethics. I will differentiate each across two dimensions: its representation of thanatological ambiguity (the extended temporality of the biological process of death and the parallel process of social death), and its representation of death's affective impact on the medical witness. I will briefly comment on these two dimensions.

Every culture has social processes that go alongside reclassification of a body from living to dead. The anthropologist Robert Hertz observes, 'Death does not confine itself to ending the physical bodily life of an individual; it also destroys the social being grafted upon the physical individual'.[97] Hertz's particular model has been critiqued, but the concept of social death is useful in examining constructions of death prior to surgical extraction. Giorgio Agamben is also interested in the way that bodies are stripped of social meaning, differentiating between *zoe* (bare life) and *bios* (political life, a life recognised as having social form), as discussed in my Introduction.[98] Bruno Latour's work is also helpful, identifying as he does the operation of two processes, which happen in tandem yet must remain distinct: 'translation', which combines living and inorganic elements into new hybridities, and 'purification', which 'render[s] mixtures unthinkable ... by leaving out what was in the middle. "It's nothing, nothing at all ... merely residue".'[99] Hybrids of body and technology, these bodies manifest qualities of living and dead. They are radically between, but they are relentlessly 'purified' in a range of medical discourses: these bodies must be constructed as 'just' dead – 'merely residue'. Clinical necropoetics can intensify or obscure these bodies' social and temporal complexity.

With regard to affect, it has been persuasively argued that the affective charge of Gothic has diminished since the late twentieth century. Fred Botting argues that Gothic has lost 'its specific intensity, shedding the allure of darkness, danger and mystery', and Sue Zlosnik notes, 'The familiarity and popularity of gothic monsters such as the zombie and vampire suggest that they have other cultural work to do'.[100] None the less, some of the texts I explore in this chapter continue to use Gothic in affectively charged ways to communicate apprehension around these practices, or, on the other hand, to communicate unease at delaying such diagnosis and condemning a patient to technologically mediated undeath. At still other times, Gothic elements can indeed be used to *leach* emotion from representations of cadaveric ambiguity, helping to normalise these processes.

'Ghouls', 'shudder' and 'twitch': Gothic in critiques of cadaveric transfer practice

Brain death emerged as a diagnostic category alongside a profusion of popular culture representations of neurological decay – notably George Romero's zombie film oeuvre – and fantasies of predatory medical institutions profiting from bodies in suspended states (see Chapter 2). Gothic tropes, intertextualities, and narrative strategies have also been used by some medical practitioners and ethicists to communicate unease at perceived risk of hasty surgical procurement, lingering signs of life, the ambiguities of EEG, and the technological context for death in controlled DCD.

Early in the emergence of the new death category, some clinical practitioners drew on Gothic tropes to express concerns about transfer protocols, invoking fantastical and supernatural figures. In a 1993 article, for example, the neurologists Byrne and Nilges warned that physicians in that era could experience time pressures distorting judgement. They describe 'the haunting question' of ambiguity of life/death, and argue:

> Too many third party interests potentially contaminate the brain death decision. There is the glorious vision of the recipient patient in a new life … There is the transplant surgeon always ready to add another successful transplantation to his and his hospital's record. There are third party payers not willing to pay for prolonged intensive care given to a 'dead brain in a live body' … [T]here is the patient's family … brainwashed by the transplanters' propaganda … entranced by the pied pipers of thanatology.[101]

While this sounds dramatic, such pressure was – and is – more likely in contexts without clear protocols, as in the early years of transplantation. In the extract above, Byrne and Nilges use dramatically binary language, 'glory' contrasted with horror, and families 'entranced', mesmerised by malevolent, folkloric figures leading people to doom. Other physicians and ethicists invoke cannibalism and necrophagia. A 1964 editorial in *Annals of Internal Medicine* expressed fears of 'cannibalizing' patients for organs, and a few years later a public health official in Washington, DC, drew on similar imagery, admitting, 'I have a horrible vision of ghouls hovering over an accident victim with long knives unsheathed, waiting to take out his organs as soon as he is pronounced dead'.[102] A creature both supernatural and subhuman, an eater of dead human flesh, *ghoul* here implies that donor bodies are vulnerable to violation and positions surgeons as other, inhuman. The ghoul analogy was echoed in a 1973 ethics article from the theologian William May, who suggests that there is 'a tinge of the inhuman', 'ghoulish in its consequences', in those who see the benefits of procurement easily override unease around the process.[103] As recently as 2015, the neurologist Joseph Fins mentions instances where kin of people in minimally conscious states have been urged to opt for organ donation, despite the patients not being brain-dead ('Too often, these patients are viewed as if they are destined to die, even when their prospects for recovery are not exhausted') and invokes vulture symbolism, describing staff who 'hover' for the dead, 'waiting to swoop'.[104] Predatorial imagery also appears in 1990s critiques of early DCD procurement protocols, particularly in the form first developed at Pittsburgh. Renée Fox averred that 'the Pittsburgh protocol is the most elaborately macabre scheme for obtaining organs that I have encountered. It borders on ghoulishness.'[105]

A second way Gothic imagery enters critique of procurement practice is in negative descriptions of technologically mediated death in controlled DCD. These critiques may evoke Gothic spectacles of ritualistic vivisection. Alan Weisbard, for example, writes:

> in its rawest form, the Pittsburgh protocol envisions wheeling a ... still living prospective donor into the O.R., prepping the individual's body for subsequent expeditious removal of organs, presiding over a series of events ... hopefully culminating in the individual's death ... and finally removing the individual's organs for transplant – all this unless something goes dreadfully wrong, and the patient survives.[106]

Fox describes the early Pittsburgh protocol as 'gruesome', 'fearful', and 'ghastly', and evokes a vivid scene: 'If asked to identify what is most dreadful about it, I would single out the desolate, profanely "high tech" death that the patient/donor dies, beneath operating room lights, amidst masked, gowned, and gloved strangers, who have prepared ... [their] body for the eviscerating surgery that will follow'.[107] Passages such as this present a single moment in dramatic terms, a vivid spectacle of profane ceremony. Fox speaks of a 'powerful sacrificial meaning' of controlled death and organ removal occurring on the same operating table, and the President's Council for Bioethics quotes her description of DCD as potentially a 'profane, high-tech death'.[108] Staging desolate spectacle is central to these authors' critiques of what they perceive as overly technological death.

In the foregoing examples, Gothic tropes and intertextualities are deployed not to emphasise ambiguity over the cadaveric body, but rather to underscore an impression of *certainty*. This version of the necropoetics of procurement responds to the challenge of thanatological uncertainty by situating the moment of death later in the dying process, and handles the challenge of affect by intensifying affect around the surgery itself. In these scenes, the locus of Gothic threat is the surgical and administrative procedures that go into marking off a living body for procurement. This form of necropoetics requires the cadaveric body to be defiantly imbued with human meaning, demanding it be re-recognised as *bios*, in Agamben's terms, and presenting the procurement as medicalised sacrifice – *homo sacer* on the operating table.

Gothic imagery, intertextualities, or narrative strategies can also feature in expressions of the difficulty of reading signs of death. Death diagnosis has long involved a checklist of signs, and deciphering signs has been a central trope of Gothic since the eighteenth century.[109] One of the uncanny aspects of some bodies diagnosed as dead by neurological criteria is the way they may still seem to react.[110] The physician Gregory Liptak describes how some bodies may respond when removed from ventilators: 'goose bumps, shivering, extensor movements of the arms, rapid flexion of the elbows, elevation of the arms above the bed, crossing of the hands reaching of the hands towards the neck, forced exhalation, and thoracic respiratory-like movements'.[111] The most dramatic reflexive response is the 'Lazarus sign', in which the person raises their arms, brings them together across the body over their chest or towards their neck, and may simultaneously seem to exhale. When their hand is taken, they may squeeze the hand in response.[112] These actions may happen spontaneously or in response to painful stimuli, pauses in ventilation support, or flexing the neck of the patient (for example, when a child is embraced by the parent). Such bodies also continue to present subtle legal complexities, since some such movements indicate a greater degree of neurological integrity than others.[113]

These phenomena may be experienced as disconcerting even by some medical practitioners. In the correspondence pages of the *Journal of the American Medical Association*, for example, the physician Thomas Poulton responds to Liptak's abovementioned description with alarm:

> patients who have been competently diagnosed to be brain dead *neither shudder, nor gasp, nor twitch* when ventilator support is disconnected. The absence of such response is, in fact, part of the process of certification of brain death ... If Dr. Liptak's 'brain-dead' patients are indeed responding to disconnection of the ventilator in the manner described, then it is *chillingly* clear that they are not, in fact, brain dead.[114]

Liptak replies that spinal reflexes are compatible with brain-death diagnosis.[115] What I draw attention to here, however, is that even if spectators accept new death criteria they may still have difficulty with accepting the counterintuitive idea that a moving, sighing body is not alive. A body's movements and behaviour may be experienced as uncanny while none the less still explicable within the new model of death, and a language of undeath and 'chill' may help to express that response.

In other cases, there has been concern among some procurement surgical staff and neurointensivists that some cadaveric donors may feel pain, in, for example, rare cases in which donor bodies react to unanaesthetised surgical incision with massive drop in blood pressure and increase in heart rate, suggesting an organism in distress.[116] Anaesthetising before procurement is controversial. On the one hand, it has been shown to help reduce cardiac shock and radical changes in blood pressure, which can harm organs. On the other hand, using anaesthetic can send mixed messages about whether the body is really dead, and thus negatively impact consent rates. In describing these concerns, a striking shift in register can at times be found in letters printed in medical journal correspondence pages. One anaesthesiologist, for example, speaks of the cadaveric donor body as in a 'warm, pink, pulsating, breathing (albeit by machine), reactive state'.[117] Unlike the usual register of the writing alongside them, such passages are not only adjectivally rich but specifically rich in adjectives formed from verbs in the present participle, attributing a strange degree of agency to these ambiguous bodies.

Finally, a language of mystery clusters around electroencephalography. As in the nineteenth century, technological advances may complicate rather than simplify death diagnosis. Invented in 1929, the electroencephalograph (EEG) made it possible to track some neural electrical signals.[118] 'Flat line' electro-cardiograms or electroencephalograms have acquired iconic status in popular film, imagined as stable mechanical records of the cessation of heartbeat or brain function respectively. In reality, EEG interpretation is more complex. Instrument-induced artefacts may mislead, and electrocortical silence may be caused by hypothermia, drug intoxication, or other confounders; further-more, EEG cannot indicate whether the brain-stem is still alive.[119] In looking at professional and popular representations of EEG, one can discern a tension between two different modes of scientific knowing: 'mechanical objectivity', in which instrumental records of the natural world were prized over scientists' subjective apprehension of the same phenomena, and 'trained judgement', in which accurate insight requires expert interpretation.[120] Describing EEG interpretation in 1941, the experts Frederick Gibbs and Erna Gibbs warned that subjective criteria and a 'seeing eye' were required.[121] Even as recently as 2015, a blind experiment gave experienced neurologists multiple EEGs repeatedly to assess for indications of neurological death, and found that they offered a different interpretation 25 per cent of the time on the unknowing second attempt.[122]

Unsurprisingly, then, a lexis of strangeness gathers around EEG in the context of the new deaths. The neurologists Pallis and Harvey describe 'bizarre and difficult' artefacts that can warp readings, and Fins warns, 'In this early stage of their development, neuroimaging methods do more to *deepen the mys-teries* of the mind than to resolve them'.[123] Even post-mortem some portions of the human brain 'have been shown to retain capacities for electrophysiological responsiveness'.[124] Most disconcerting of all, however, is EEG data that sug-gest pain during post-mortem surgery. There have been surges of EEG activity even when in cardiac flatline,[125] and on rare occasions EEG scans show linger-ing traces of cellular brain activity in some patients diagnosed as brain-stem dead. Matta, who is strongly supportive of transplant, none the less mentions cases in which EEG recordings after brain-stem death produce 'data suggesting organized brain activity and perfusion in a minority of brainstem dead [and] is unsettling'.[126] Phrasing such as this can convey both epistemological uncertainty and unease. In an echo of the example of materialist haunting that opened this chapter, here electricity is a flickering presence, an energy lingering in death.

Ancient threats and tortured twilight: the necropoetics of procurement advocacy

While Gothic tropes may seem best suited to critique, there is also a body of work that uses Gothic tropes to defend death diagnoses in the transplantation context. Such writing tends to focus on the risks of *not* diagnosing. Here, Gothic works to help manage thanatological uncertainty and distressing affect by reaffirming the new death categories, erasing uncertainties around diagnostic practice, and reinforcing medical jurisdiction around death declaration.

Language of Gothic horror can be invoked to present a fruitlessly extended existence on life support and the torment that loved ones may feel at witnessing it.[127] In the influential textbook *The ABC of Brainstem Death*, the UK neurologists Christopher Pallis and D. Harley declare that 'A dead brain in a body with a still beating heart is one of the more macabre products of modern technology', speak of the 'spectre of a patient on a ventilator', and describe the process of ventilating until heartbeat ceases as 'harrowing' and 'grotesque'.[128] Pallis and Harley use evocative imagery and adjectives to describe the prolonged ventilation of the dead as a threat to the human. As before, Gothic is being deployed in the service of certainty, but this time from the opposite side: here *bios* is seen as impossible, the body barely even *zoe*. Also like the first cluster of examples, these evoke intense horror, even if the locus of that horror is in the opposite place: the life-support machinery is no longer succour but torment. This strand of clinical necropoetics manages the temporal complexities of dying by compressing the moment of death, of losing humanness, to earlier in the dying process, and handles affect by intensifying affect around obstacles to procurement.[129]

A second way a Gothic discourse can be defensively marshalled around procurement is in depicting scientific progress as itself threatened, and here it is not only symbolism or lexis but also a Gothic *narrative structure* that is in play. Whilst scientific prose must be emotionally neutral, transplantation's scientific writing of the 1960s and 1970s often included highly affect-laden terms, mentioning 'dark days', 'black years', 'bizarre organisms', describing experimental conditions as 'grim', 'bleak', and 'dismal' and lamenting 'clinical heartbreaks', 'pathos', and 'miseries'.[130] Such terms were invoked to communicate the struggle for progress hindered by immune defences, administrative complexities, and obstacles to pharmaceutical manufacture. As awareness of transplantation spread with the international flurry of (mostly doomed) attempts at heart transplant from 1967 to 1969, the enterprise also met increasing resistance from legislation and moratoriums on experimentation.

Gothic can be recruited to narrative strategies presenting medicine as a vulnerable body of knowledge, itself under threat. Such a formulation echoes a defining structure of Gothic writing as Robert Mighall has defined it, as texts in which modernity is under threat from anachronism.[131] Scientific writing can draw on such tropes to bolster the modernity of the transplantation endeavour and to rebut challenges to it. In an influential 2012 article on neurological death, for example, Dale Gardiner and his co-writers open by invoking historical death practices to illustrate antiquated attitudes to death like 'security coffins with alarm mechanisms and permanent air supply'.[132] After establishing the contrast between past folly and present reason, they adopt an unexpected turn of phrase in defence of contemporary cadaveric procurement protocols. To appreciate the force of this excerpt one must read it within the context of the detached scientific prose that precedes and follows it, within the article itself and the journal as a whole. When addressing the problem that DCD violates irreversibility criteria for death, they abandon that measured register, responding that irreversibility can simply never be known for sure:

> if a literal definition of irreversible is used … then for the brain this would be 1 hour of cerebral circulatory arrest, whilst for the heart it would be many hours. *This would lead to a death watch in which there would be no place for a stethoscope and modern medicine would be turned back 150 years*, to a time when only the satisfaction of somatic criteria, such as rigor mortis, was widely accepted, yet still not publicly trusted.[133]

Here modern transplantation practice itself becomes a potential Gothic victim, at risk of being dragged into a dark past. As in Mighall's framing of Gothic anachronism, this structure presents medical discourse as itself a potential victim to be guarded against irrational attempts on modernity.

The approaches discussed so far recruit Gothic imagery, intertextualities, or narrative structures to arguments with certainties, albeit in contrasting ways. By contrast, in my final cluster of examples, a clinical necropoetics is used with a different emphasis, managing uncertainty by creating a liminal space using highly Gothicised tropes, yet *emptied* of horror. In this, these texts exemplify the cultural trend mentioned earlier, for Gothic to increasingly lack the affective charge of earlier uses. Numerous terms for the cadaveric donor were coined between 1966 and 1997, at conferences and in journal articles exploring the new deaths. At the CIBA Foundation Conference on Ethics in Medical Progress in London in 1966, Starzl speaks of a 'living cadaver', Alexandre speaks of a 'heart-lung preparation', and J. Revillard speaks of the 'potential cadaver'.[134] Lock observes that 'it is evident from the language used that participants were sensitive to the ambiguous state of the patient-cadaver. Scare quotes were placed around words such as *dead* and *irreversible* to qualify their meaning.'[135] In 1968, J. Hamburger and J. Crosier spoke of cadaveric donors as 'dead but in a state of artificial survival'.[136] At the 1977 New York Academy of Sciences conference on brain death the cadaveric donor was described several times as a 'respirator brain', Julius Korein defining this state as 'the presumed end point of brain destruction in a patient who is brain dead and maintained in a respirator'; Korein notes the 'difficulty in use of this term' in that the process of brain deterioration is gradual and little-understood.[137]

Death as a gradual process is central to all these terms, which acknowledge that the body is in transition between states, while also grouping certain bodies at different stages in that process together; in other words, these terms simultaneously emphasise bodies in process and create a clearly bounded entity. As before, this is language to manage the temporal complexity of the donor body – but with a difference. While the previous two approaches were about entrenching certainty and obscuring the extended duration of the death process, this cluster of texts simultaneously emphasises liminality and *reduces* its affective charge. In my prior examples, corporeal ambiguity is managed by clearly locating death to earlier or later in the dying process. By contrast, this strand of necropoetics creates a container *for* ambiguity, a noun or noun phrase to convey a span of time during which the body is in an ambiguous state. The grammatical process of nominalisation is central to the effect of these coinages, for the nouns are about a body enmeshed with the processes and technologies that sustain certain physical processes – a changing entity, a thing of verbs, an active assemblage – into a stable, single part of speech. As such, the noun simultaneously conveys and contains a span of time. Interestingly, many of these coinages explicitly unbracket machinic components. Hyphenations and noun phrases like 'respirator brain' emphasise the inorganic components of the assemblage, highlighting the conjunction of organic and inorganic and joining them into a single, time-limited entity. These blended noun constructions, then, emphasise assemblage; as Lisa Diedrich says, a hyphen can become 'the condition of possibility for the formation of other links across time and space ... a sign of the process of assemblage, the placing side by side of various discourses, practices, figures, and spaces'.[138]

DCD, too, generated a new nomenclature for the dead. Early DCD was dominated by the term 'non-heartbeating cadaver', a phrase coined to differentiate these donor bodies from brain-dead donors at the time called 'heartbeating cadavers'. The tautology of non-heartbeating cadaver implies that the two terms – non-heartbeating and cadaver – are not actually equivalent, and thus makes the death-status of *both* terms less secure.

Overall, to invoke Agamben's terms, in these coinages the cadaveric body is *zoe*, but the hybrid language dramatises the discursive work of *zoe*-ing, the machine of *zoe*. The Gothic language of undeath, living death, can simultaneously destabilise the legitimacy of the new death categories and enable exactly those concepts, in giving a language for expressing these ambiguous states.

A similar manoeuvre occurs in terminology for one of the most uncanny elements of donation after controlled circulatory death: the risk of the dead donor returning to life during procurement surgery, due to the way the body is handled. Mohamed Rady and others describe processes required during surgery to actively prevent the donor coming back to life or the brain becoming reperfused with blood, such as blocking the aortic arch with a balloon. These life-suppressing actions during procurement surgery are termed 'reanimation suppression'.[139] Notably, these practices are specifically not called 'resuscitation' suppression. 'Resuscitate' is derived from Latin *resuscitāt*, 'rouse again, reawaken' or 'to raise from the dead'.[140] 'Reanimate' derives from the Latin *redanimatio* (restoring to life, to blaze up anew, resurrection) or the French *reanimer* (restore to life), and like 'resuscitate' it can historically denote both reawaken and resurrect.[141] With 'resuscitation' becoming the dominant term for restoration of life, 'reanimate' has gained a more ambiguous valence, sometimes describing conventional emergency care medicine and sometimes describing clinically dead patients or bodies which have a degree of life temporarily restored, or particular organs targeted for resumed function. In popular contexts, the connotations of 'reanimate' have become distinctly menacing, not least for the way the term is now often chosen to describe inhuman reanimation, zombies, or other subhuman entities. What is fascinating about the clinical use of the term here is that it, too, describes nonhuman, partial resurrection, yet without the horror that this image carries in popular media. This is Gothic leached of dread, as Botting and Zlosnik describe it.

A language of ambiguous life can also be useful for legal categories. The new deaths are enabled by an understanding that dying is a process rather than a momentary event, yet the dead donor rule and current laws make it legally necessary to frame death as a clear and momentary event in time. As discussed earlier, some have called for moving away from the 'dead donor' rule that organs can be extracted only from patients irreversibly dead. Linda Emanuel suggests that people could pre-declare their own death definitions in a customised 'life cessation certificate' that states at what point in the dying process one would wish oneself to be considered dead.[142] She speaks of a 'bounded zone' between life and death within which neither category is fully adequate. Here, a state that matches neither life nor death is described not to evoke dread but to reassure by creating more stable legal frameworks for procurement. These twilight states are presented not to evoke horror but to personalise and normalise.

Describing intersections between Gothic fictions and late nineteenth-century science, Kelly Hurley says that these fictions not only express popular anxieties about evolution and degeneration but also function as 'fundamentally speculative, even theoretical'.[143] Gothic representations, in their focus on corporeal extension, ruination, and strangeness, may help to conceptualise inadmissible excess, including the diverse practices that have to be 'bracketed' to make death diagnosis uniform. Amidst all these labours of purification, however, cadaveric donor bodies may remain strange. Like Fairfield's quotation that opened this chapter, these bodies may offer a modern-day materialist haunting, both secular and spectral.

Notes

1 F. Fairfield, *Ten Years with Spiritual Mediums* (New York: D. Appleton, 1875), p. 173.

2 J. Christie, T. O'Lenic, and R. Cane, 'Head turning in brain death', *Journal of Clinical Anesthesia*, 8:2 (1996), 141–3; M. Lock, *Twice Dead* (Berkeley: University of California Press, 2002), p. 243; cf. M. Lock, 'On making up the good-as-dead in a utilitarian world', in S. Franklin and M. Lock (eds), *Remaking Life and Death* (Santa Fe, NM: School of American Research Press, 2001), pp. 165–93 (p. 172).

3 R. Aronowitz, *Making Sense of Illness* (Cambridge: Cambridge University Press, 1998); L. Gardner, K. Dew, M. Stubbe, T. Dowell, and L. Macdonald, 'Patchwork diagnoses', *Social Science and Medicine*, 73:6 (2011), 843–50; A. Jutel, *Putting a Name to It* (Baltimore, MD: Johns Hopkins University Press, 2011); A. Mol, *The Body Multiple* (Durham, NC: Duke University Press, 2002).

4 J.-B. Winslow [and Leander Paget], *An Mortis Incertae Signa Minus Incerta a Chirurgicis, Quam ab Aliis Experimentis?* (Paris: Quillau, 1740).

5 M. Pernick, 'Back from the grave', in R. Zaner (ed.), *Death* (Dordrecht: Kluwer, 1988), pp. 17–74 (p. 21); R. de Réaumur, 'Avis pour donner du secours à ceux que l'on croit noyés', in A. Louis, *Lettres Sur la Certitude des Signes de la Mort* (Paris: Michel Lambert, [1740] 1752), pp. 250–60; J. Fothergill, *Observations on the Recovery of a Man Dead in Appearance* (San Francisco: Garth Hudson, [1745] 1980).

6 Pernick, p. 22.

7 W. Hawes, *An Address to the Public on Premature Death and Premature Interment* (London: Royal Humane Society, 1780), p. 40; Pernick, p. 61n2.

8 C. Kite, *An Essay on the Recovery of the Apparently Dead* (London: Dilly, 1788), p. 125; M. Orfila, *Directions for the Treatment of Persons Who Have Taken Poison*, trans. R. Black (London: Longman, 1818), p. 189.

9 Pernick, p. 39.

10 P. Ariès, *The Hour of Our Death*, trans. H. Weaver (Harmondsworth: Penguin, [1977] 1983), p. 401; Pernick, pp. 31–7; Lock, *Twice Dead*, p. 66; R. Richardson, *Death, Dissection and the Destitute* (London: Penguin, 1989); W. Bynum, *History of Medicine* (Oxford: Oxford University Press, 2008).

11 Orfila; Pernick, p. 40; B. Richardson, 'Suspended animation', *Living Age*, 142 (1879), 99–103.

12 Kite, p. 95; Pernick, p. 38.

13 C. Howells, 'The Gothic way of death in English fiction, 1790–1820', *Journal for Eighteenth-Century Studies*, 5:2 (1982), 207–15; P. Ariès, *Western Attitudes Towards Death*, trans. P. Ranum (London: Marion Boyars, [1974] 1976); J. Whaley, 'Introduction', in J. Whaley (ed.), *Mirrors of Mortality* (London: Europa, 1981), pp. 1–14 (pp. 7–9); D. Cannadine, 'War and death, grief and mourning in modern Britain', in Whaley, pp. 187–242 (pp. 188–9).

14 D. Townshend, 'Gothic and the ghost of Hamlet', in D. Townshend and J. Drakakis (eds), *Gothic Shakespeares* (Abingdon: Routledge, 2008), pp. 60–97 (p. 89); E. Bronfen, *Over Her Dead Body* (Manchester: Manchester University Press, 1996), p. 10.

15 C. Davison, 'Introduction', in C. Davison (ed.), *The Gothic and Death* (Manchester: Manchester University Press, 2017), pp. 1–2.

16 A. Smith, *Gothic Death* (Manchester: Manchester University Press, 2016); Howells; Townshend; L. Talairach-Vielmas, *Wilkie Collins, Medicine and the Gothic* (Cardiff: University of Wales Press, 2009).

17 A. Smith, *Gothic Death*, pp. 5, 2.

18 G. Pomata, 'The medical case narrative', *Literature and Medicine*, 32:1 (2014), 1–23 (p. 2).

19 J. Riskin, *Science in the Age of Sensibility* (Chicago: University of Chicago Press, 2002); M. Kennedy, 'The ghost in the clinic', *Victorian Literature and Culture*, 32:2 (2004), 327–51.

20 Kennedy, 'Ghost', p. 332.

21 M. Kennedy, '"Let me die in your house"', *Literature and Medicine*, 32:1 (2014), 105–32 (p. 106); Talairach-Vielmas; J. Thrailkill, 'Killing them softly', *American Literature*, 71:4 (1999), 679–707; J. Matus, *Shock, Memory and the Unconscious in Victorian Fiction* (New York: Cambridge University Press, 2009); A. Smith, *Victorian Demons* (Manchester: Manchester University Press, 2004).

22 Kennedy, 'Ghost', p. 327.

23 J. Harrison, *Medical Aspects of Death* (London: Longman, 1852), pp. 42–3.

24 Ibid, p. 20.

25 S. Jellinek, *Dying, Apparent-Death, and Resuscitation* (London: Baillière, Tindall and Cox, 1947), pp. 39, 38.

26 B. Hurwitz, 'Narrative constructs in modern clinical case reporting', *Studies in History and Philosophy of Science*, 62 (2017), 65–73 (p. 68); R. Rylance, 'The theatre and the granary', *Literature and Medicine*, 25:2 (2006), 255–76 (p. 270).

27 S. Goodwin and E. Bronfen, 'Introduction', in S. Goodwin and E. Bronfen (eds), *Death and Representation* (Baltimore, MD: Johns Hopkins University Press, 1993), pp. 3–28 (p. 6).

28 J. DuBois cited in N. Nikas, D. Bordlee, and M. Moreira, 'Determination of death', *Journal of Medicine and Philosophy*, 41:3 (2016), 237–56 (p. 239).

29 J. Robertson, 'The dead donor rule', *Hastings Center Report*, 29 (1999), 6–14 (p. 6).

30 Lock, *Twice Dead*, pp. 78–129, 199.

31 L. Sharp, *Strange Harvest* (Berkeley: University of California Press, 2006), pp. 80, 84.

32 Pernick, p. 55; D. Duckworth, 'Some cases of cerebral disease', *Edinburgh Medical Journal*, 3 (1898), 145–52; H. Cushing, 'Some experimental and clinical observations concerning states of increased intracranial tension', *American Journal of the Medical Sciences*, 124 (1902), 377–91; C. Machado, 'The first organ transplant from a brain-dead donor', *Neurology*, 64:11 (2005), 1938–42.

33 P. Mollaret and G. Goulon, 'Coma dépassé et nécroses nerveuses centrales massives', *Revue Neurologique*, 35 (1959), 211–18.

34 C. Machado and G. Leisman, 'Towards an effective definition of death and disorders of consciousness', *Reviews in the Neurosciences*, 20:3 (2009), 147–150 (p. 148).

35 Ad Hoc Committee of the Harvard Medical School to Examine the Definition of Brain Death, 'A definition of irreversible coma', *Journal of the American Medical Association*, 205:6 (1968), 85–8.

36 Ibid, emphasis added.

37 M. Giacomini, 'A change of heart', *Social Science of Medicine*, 44:10 (1997), 1465–82.

38 Ibid, pp. 1465–6.

39 Lock, *Twice Dead*, pp. 74, 104.

40 Nikas *et al.*, p. 241.

41 C. Pallis, 'Diagnosis of brain death', *British Medical Journal*, 281:6253 (1980), 1491–2; C. Pallis and D. Harley, *ABC of Brainstem Death*, 2nd edn (London: BMJ, 1996).

42 'Transplants: are the donors really dead?', *Panorama*, BBC (13 October 1980); 'A question of life or death: the brain death debate', *Panorama*, BBC (19 February 1981).

43 By 1995, the American Academy of Neurology parameters brought US and UK practice closer, although differences continue to exist. For transatlantic differences in diagnosis of neurological death, see E. Wijdicks, 'The transatlantic divide over brain death determination', *Brain*, 135 (2012), 1321–31; P. Byrne and R. Nilges, 'The brain stem in brain death', *Issues in Law and Medicine*, 9 (1993), 3–21 (p. 9); M. Smith, 'Brain death', *British Journal of Anaesthesia*, 108 (2012), Supplement 1, i6–i9 (p. i9).

44 'The living dead', *The New York Times* (12 October 1975), www.nytimes.com/1975/10/12/archives/the-living-dead.html [accessed 20 January 2019]; C. Belling, 'The living dead', *Perspectives in Biology and Medicine*, 53:3 (2010), 439–51.

45 S. Gorovitz and A. MacIntyre, 'Toward a theory of medical fallibility', *Hastings Center Report*, 5:6 (1975), 13–23.

46 M. Smith, 'Brain death', p. 145.

47 Byrne and Nilges, p. 17.

48 K. Ragosta, 'Miller Fisher Syndrome', *Clinical Pediatrics*, 32:11 (1993), 685–7; R. Hughes and G. McGuire, 'Neurologic disease and the determination of brain death', *Critical Care Medicine*, 25 (1997), 1923–4.

49 Byrne and Nilges; Lock, *Twice Dead*, pp. 239–40; J. Pasternak and J. Volpe, 'Full recovery from prolonged brainstem failure following intraventricular hemorrhage', *Journal of Pediatrics*, 95:6 (1979), 1047–9; W. Szurhaj, M. Lamblin, A. Kaminska, and H. Sediri, 'EEG guidelines in the diagnosis of brain death', *Neurophysiologie Clinique*, 45:1 (2015), 97–110; Pallis and Harley, p. 23.

50 M. Smith, 'Brain death', p. i7.

51 D. Greer, P. Varelas, S. Haque, and E. Wijdicks, 'Variability of brain death determination guidelines in leading US neurologic institutions', *Neurology*, 70:4 (2008), 284–9; G. Yanke, M. Rady, and J. Verheijde, 'When brain death belies belief', *Journal of Religion and Health*, 455:6 (2016), 2199–213 (p. 2209); C. Shappell, J. Frank, K. Husari, M. Sanchez, F. Goldenberg, and A. Ardelt, 'Practice variability in brain death determination', *Neurology*, 81:23 (2013), 2009–14.

52 Lock, *Twice Dead*, p. 124.

53 M. Nair-Collins, S. Green, and A. Sutin, 'Abandoning the dead donor rule?' *Journal of Medical Ethics*, 41:4 (2015), 297–302 (p. 301).

54 B. Matta, 'The implications of anaesthetising the brainstem dead', *Anaesthesia*, 55:7 (2000), 695–6 (p. 696).

55 P. Young and B. Matta, 'Anesthesia for organ donation in the brainstem dead', *Anaesthesia*, 55:2 (2000), 105–6 (p. 106).

56 R. Truog, F. Miller, and S. Halpern, 'The dead-donor rule and the future of organ donation', *New England Journal of Medicine*, 369:14 (2013), 1287–89 (p. 1288); S. Shah and F. Miller, 'Can we handle the truth?', *American Journal of Law and Medicine*, 36:4 (2010), 540–85; A. Halevy and B. Brody, 'Brain death', *Annals of Internal Medicine*, 119 (1993), 519–25.

57 Halevy and Brody, p. 523.

58 N. Zamperetti, R. Bellomo, and C. Ronco, 'Defining death in non-heart beating organ donors', *Journal of Medical Ethics*, 29 (2003), 182–5 (p. 182).

59 It has been argued that autoresucitation is not relevant to DCD contexts, but a rebuttal is offered by A. Joffe, J. Carcillo, N. Anton, *et al.*, 'Donation after cardiocirculatory death', *Philosophy, Ethics, and Humanities in Medicine*, 6:1 (2011), 1–20.

60 Shah and Miller, p. 548; M. Rady, J. Verheijde, and J. McGregor, '"Non-heart-beating," or "cardiac death" organ donation', *Journal of Hospital Medicine*, 2:5 (2007), 324–34.

61 Rady *et al.*, '"Non-heart-beating"', pp. 325–7.

62 M. Nair-Collins and F. Miller, 'Is heart transplantation after circulatory death compatible with the dead donor rule?', *Journal of Medical Ethics*, 42:5 (2016), 319.

63 Zamperetti *et al.*, p. 183.

64 D. Gardiner, S. Shemie, A. Manara, and H. Opdam, 'International perspective on the diagnosis of death', *British Journal of Anaesthesia*, 108 (2012), Supplement 1, i14–i28 (p. 19).

65 Zamperetti *et al.*, p. 183; Rady *et al.*, '"Non-heart-beating"', pp. 325–7; G. Martin, E. Rivers, N. Paradis, M. Goetting, D. Morris, and R. Nowak, 'Emergency department cardiopulmonary bypass', *Chest*, 113:3 (1998), 743–51.

66 M. Rady and J. Verhejde, 'Lazarus phenomenon', *Resuscitation*, 85:4 (2014), 63.

67 F. Chaten, 'The dead donor rule', *Journal of Medical Ethics*, 40:7 (2014), 496–500 (p. 498).

68 M. Yacoub, 'Cardiac donation after circulatory death', *The Lancet*, 385:9987 (2015), 2554–6 (p. 2555).

69 A. Manara, P. Murphy, and G. O'Callaghan, 'Donation after circulatory death', *British Journal of Anaesthesia*, 108 (2012), Supplement 1, i108–i121 (p. i109); J. Bernat, 'The debate over death determination in DCD', *Hastings Center Report*, 40:3 (2010), 3.

70 R. Fox, 'An ignoble form of cannibalism', in R. Arnold, S. Youngner, R. Schapiro, and C. Spicer (eds), *Procuring Organs for Transplant* (Baltimore, MD: Johns Hopkins University Press, 1995), pp. 155–64; Sharp, *Harvest*, p. 71; Manara *et al.*, p. i114.

71 M. Rady, J. Verheijde, and J. McGregor. 'Organ donation after circulatory death', *Critical Care*, 10:5 (2006), ccforum.com/content/10/5/166, 2–3.

72 J. Bion, P. Nightingale, and B. Taylor, 'Will the UK ever reach international levels of organ donation?', *British Journal of Anaesthesia*, 108 (2012), Supplement 1, i10–i13 (p. i12); Manara *et al.*, p. i113. For more on DCD's impact on donor kin see K. Overby, M. Weinstein, and A. Fiester, 'Response to open peer commentaries', *American Journal of Bioethics*, 15:9 (2015), W3–W5 (p. W4); S. Hurst and B. Ricou, 'Death at the door of the operating room', *American Journal of Bioethics*, 15:8 (2015), 31–3.

73 A. Rubenstein, E. Cohen, and E. Jackson, 'The definition of death and the ethics of organ procurement from the deceased', *The President's Council on Bioethics* (2006), bioethicsarchive.georgetown.edu/pcbe/background/rubenstein.html [accessed 4 May 2017]; cf. M. Solomon, 'Maximizing benefits, minimizing harms', in Institute of Medicine (ed.), *Non-Heart-Beating Organ Transplantation* (Washington, DC: National Academy Press, 2000), pp. 67–86; Gardiner *et al.*, 'International perspective', p. 15; Overby *et al.*

74 In the UK, for example, in 2019 DCD donors comprised 39.8 per cent of total deceased donation, with DBD accounting for 60.2 per cent. NHS Blood & Transplant, 'Organ donation and transplantation: activity figures for the UK as at 8 April 2019', *NHS Blood & Transplant*, nhsbtdbe.blob.core.windows.net/umbraco-assets-corp/15720/annual_stats.pdf [accessed 8 June 2019].

75 M. Smith, 'Brain death', p. i7; D. Rodríguez-Arias, M. Smith, and N. Lazar, 'Donation after circulatory death', *American Journal of Bioethics*, 11:8 (2011), 36–43 (p. 42).

76 Sharp, *Harvest*; Lock, *Twice Dead*.

77 R. Truog, 'The price of our illusions and myths about the dead donor rule', *Journal of Medical Ethics*, 42:5 (2016), 318; Truog, Miller, and Halpern, p. 1288; cf. N. Fost, 'The unimportance of death', in S. Youngner, R. Arnold, and R. Schapiro (eds), *The Definition of Death* (Baltimore, MD: Johns Hopkins University Press, 1999), pp. 161–78 (p. 162); Lock, 'Making up', pp. 174–7.

78 Rodríguez-Arias *et al.*, pp. 37, 41; Chaten, p. 498.

79 S. Vernez and D. Magnus, 'Can the dead donor rule be resuscitated?', *American Journal of Bioethics*, 11:8 (2011), 1.

80 Rodríguez-Arias *et al.*, pp. 36–43; J. Bernat, 'Life or death for the dead donor rule?', *New England Journal of Medicine*, 369:14 (2013), 1289–91; Vernez and Magnus, p. 1.

81 R. Küss, 'Human renal transplantation memories, 1955 to 1981', in P. Terasaki (ed.), *History of Transplantation* (Los Angeles: UCLA, 1971), pp. 37–60 (pp. 39, 48).

82 D. Hamilton, *A History of Organ Transplantation* (Pittsburgh, PA: University of Pittsburgh Press, 2012), p. 283.

83 R. Calne, *Ultimate Gift* (London: Headline, 1998), p. 56.

84 T. Starzl, *The Puzzle People* (Pittsburgh, PA: University of Pittsburgh Press, [1993] 2003), pp. 48–9, emphasis added.

85 Lock, *Twice Dead*, p. 254.

86 S. Youngner, 'Organ retrieval', *Transplantation Proceedings*, 22:3 (1990), 1014–15. Without stereotyping, it is also the case that different medical roles may invite particular affective responses to tissue procurement process. In ethnographies of transplantation professionals, for example, Lock notes differences between intensive-care neurologists and transplant surgeons (*Twice Dead*, pp. 94, 106), but it is impossible to generalise about practitioners' affective response during procurement. Responses vary widely, influenced by diverse elements such as the practitioner's role during the procurement, clinical field, the age and appearance of the harvestee, and the practitioner's personal history.

87 A. Schuman, 'Review of Barbara-Anne Wren, *True Tales*', *BMJ Blogs* (6 February 2017) blogs.bmj.com/medical-humanities/2017/02/06/book-review-true-tales-of-organisational-life/ [accessed 10 January 2019].

88 Lock, *Twice Dead*, pp. 254–5.

89 Ibid, p. 261.

90 L. Sharp, *The Transplant Imaginary* (Berkeley: University of California Press, 2013), p. 12.

91 Ibid, p. 45; cf. R. Richardson, 'Fearful symmetry', in R. Fox, L. O'Connell, and S. Youngner (eds), *Organ Transplantation* (Madison: University of Wisconsin Press, 1996), pp. 66–100; Youngner, 'Organ retrieval'.

92 Lock, *Twice Dead*, p. 13.

93 Mol, p. 163.

94 Ibid, pp. 88, 161.

95 A. Gross, J. Harmon, and M. Reidy, *Communicating Science* (New York: Oxford University Press, 2002), p. 215.

96 Ibid, p. 215.

97 R. Hertz, *Death and the Right Hand*, trans. R. Needham and C. Needham (Oxford: Routledge, [1907] 2004), p. 77.

98 G. Agamben, *Homo Sacer*, trans. D. Heller-Roazen (Stanford: Stanford University Press, [1995] 1998).

99 B. Latour, *We Have Never Been Modern*, trans. C. Porter (Cambridge, MA: Harvard University Press, [1991] 1993), pp. 42, 47.

100 F. Botting, *Gothic Romanced* (London: Routledge, 2008), pp. 39–40; S. Zlosnik, 'Globalgothic at the top of the world', in G. Byron (ed.), *Globalgothic* (Manchester: Manchester University Press, 2013), pp. 65–76 (p. 68).

101 Byrne and Nilges, p. 18.

102 'Moral problems in the use of borrowed organs, artificial and transplanted', *Annals of Internal Medicine*, 60:2 (1964), 309–13; 'When are you really dead?', *Newsweek* (18 December 1967), 87. See Chapters 2 and 3 for similar symbolism.

103 W. May, 'Attitudes to the newly dead', *Hastings Center Report*, 1 (1973), 3–13 (p. 5).

104 J. Fins, *Rights Come to Mind* (Cambridge: Cambridge University Press, 2015), pp. 55–6; cf. 29–30.

105 Fox, 'Ignoble', p. 156.

106 A. Weisbard, 'A polemic on principles', in S. Youngner, R. Arnold, and R. Schapiro (eds), *The Definition of Death* (Baltimore, MD: Johns Hopkins University Press, 1999), pp. 141–54 (p. 147).

107 Fox, 'Ignoble', pp. 159–60.

108 Ibid, p. 160; Rubenstein *et al.*; cf. Solomon, pp 67–86.

109 V. Sage, *Horror Fiction in the Protestant Tradition* (New York: St Martin's, 1988), p. xvi.

110 S. Palacio, G. Zeppa, and C. Lucero, 'Spontaneous movements in brain dead patients', *Journal of the Neurological Sciences*, 150 (1997), S243; L. Döşemeci, M. Cengiz, M. Yılmaz, and A. Ramazanoğlu, 'Frequency of spinal reflex movements in brain-dead patients', *Transplantation Proceedings*, 36:1 (2004), 17–19.

111 G. Liptak, 'In reply', *Journal of the American Medical Association*, 255 (1986), 2028, emphasis in original.

112 Lock, *Twice Dead*, p. 247.

113 Christie *et al.*, p. 142.

114 T. Poulton, 'Spontaneous movements in brain-dead patients', *Journal of the American Medical Association*, 255 (1986), 695, emphasis added.

115 Liptak, p. 2028, emphasis in original.

116 L. Hogle, *Recovering the Nation's Body* (New Brunswick: Rutgers University Press, 1999), pp. 16ff; Young and Matta; Byrne and Nilges, p. 15. For counter-argument, see B. Poulton and M. Garfield, 'Implications of anaesthetising the brainstem dead', *Anaesthesia*, 55:7 (2000), 695; Matta, p. 696.

117 D. Hill, 'Issues in organ donation and transplantation', *Journal of the Royal Society of Medicine*, 92:9 (1999), 493–4 (p. 493).

118 Brainclinics Research Institute, 'History: from EEG to quantitative EEG (QEEG)', www.brainclinics.com/history-of-the-eeg-and-qeeg [accessed 27 May 2019].

119 Joffe *et al.*, p. 7; Szurhaj *et al.*; Byrne and Nilges, p. 6.

120 L. Daston and P. Galison, *Objectivity*, 2nd edn (New York: Zone, 2010).

121 Ibid, pp. 323–4.

122 Szurhaj *et al.*, p. 101.

123 Pallis and Harley, p. 36; Fins, p. 41, emphasis added.

124 M. Rady and J. Verheijde, 'Advancing neuroscience research in brain death', *Journal of Critical Care*, 39 (2017), 293–4 (p. 293).

125 Joffe *et al.*, p. 7.

126 Matta, p. 696.

127 H. Chimowitz and R. Sade, 'Benefits and harms to organ donors', *The American Journal of Bioethics*, 15:8 (2015), 19–20.
128 Pallis and Harley, pp. 1, 45, 28.
129 E. Santner, 'Terri Schiavo and the state of exception', *University of Chicago Press Blog* (29 March 2005), www.press.uchicago.edu/Misc/Chicago/05april_santner. html [accessed 27 May 2018].
130 R. Fox and J. Swazey, *The Courage to Fail* (Chicago: University of Chicago Press, 1978), p. 87; J. Dossetor, 'Transplantation', in P. Terasaki (ed,), *History of Transplantation* (Los Angeles: UCLA, 1971), pp. 295–306 (p. 297).
131 R. Mighall, *A Geography of Victorian Gothic Fiction* (Oxford: Oxford University Press, 1999).
132 Gardiner *et al.*, 'International perspective', p. 15.
133 Ibid, p. 15.
134 T. Starzl, G. Alexandre, and J. Revillard, 'Discussion', in G. Wolstenholme and M. O'Connor (eds), *Ethics in Medical Progress* (Boston, MA: Little, Brown, 1966), pp. 70, 156.
135 Lock, *Twice Dead*, p. 94.
136 J. Hamburger and J. Crosnier, 'Moral and ethical problems in transplantation', in F. Rapaport and J. Dausset (eds), *Human Transplantation* (New York: Grune and Stratton, 1968), pp. 37–44 (p. 42).
137 J. Korein, 'Terminology, definitions and usage', in J. Korein (ed.), *Brain Death* (New York: New York Academy of Science, 1978), pp. 6–10 (p. 9).
138 L. Diedrich, 'Illness as assemblage', *Body & Society*, 21:3 (2015), 66–90 (p. 72).
139 Rady *et al.*, '"Non-heart-beating"', pp. 327–8 (p. 327).
140 'Resuscitate, v.', *OED Online*, Oxford University Press (March 2019), www.oed. com/view/Entry/164120 [accessed 31 May 2019].
141 'Reanimate, v.', *OED Online*, Oxford University Press (March 2019), www.oed. com/view/Entry/158980 [accessed 31 May 2019].
142 L. Emanuel, 'Re-examining death', *Hastings Center Report*, 25:4 (1995), 27–35.
143 K. Hurley, *The Gothic Body* (Cambridge: Cambridge University Press, 1996), p. 6.

2

The bioemporium:
corporate medical horror in late
twentieth-century American transfer fiction

In his 1974 article 'Harvesting the dead', Willard Gaylin imagines a near-future in which brain-dead bodies are stored in warehouses for organ extraction and medical experimentation. He writes that these bodies may seem indistinguishable from patients in deep coma and that the sites may look identical to hospital wards. To mark the way these bodies and spaces will not be what they appear, he coins two terms: the brain-dead are 'neomorts', and the place that houses them is a 'bioemporium'.[1] The semantic field of transactionality informs the whole article, Gaylin lamenting the 'debit-credit ledger of limbs and lives'.[2]

This chapter explores such fantasies of commodification-inflected institutionalised living death as they emerged in 1970s American fiction and the ways these tropes have persisted and morphed in the decades since. Such fictions flourished with the emergence of transplantation as a feasible large-scale project due to immunosuppressant pharmacology, medical advances in life support, and the new legal categories of death discussed in my previous chapter. Rather than a threat from a single ambitious scientist in the vein of Moreau or Victor Frankenstein, here menace inheres in a system of state and corporate forces shaping medical sites. In these fictions, the gravest threats are institutions. Simultaneously symbolic and partially mimetic, the works comment on period concerns around organ procurement practice and critique a political economy that erodes compassion in healthcare, particularly when healthcare depends on private funding. The terror in these fictions is not only located at the moment of sale or theft. These fictions can also extrapolate how, when transfer is commodified, it may morph into finance's intricate secondary forms, body parts being repossessed or mortgaged. These works explore bodies at risk within certain forms of political economy.

To communicate these perils, these fictions use spatial conventions characteristic of Gothic. They stage their action in disorienting sites in which protagonists' physical and emotional vulnerability makes the space seem claustrophobic and hallucinatory.[3] Such framings of the built environment are particularly pertinent to a social history of hospital spaces. Whilst places of healing have been common to cultures since ancient times, the eighteenth century saw particular changes in how those sites could be organised and understood. Michel Foucault observed that hospitals instantiated a new kind of corporeal discipline and medical surveillance, organising space to classify and control the bodies within it, and sites for mental health underwent a similar change, their architectural and infrastructural forms becoming framed less as carceral and more as rehabilitative.[4] Foucault's model has been criticised on several grounds, not least for understating the complex local subtleties of hospital process and the persistence of clinicians' imaginative practice.[5] Without denying those flaws, what I seek to do here is note the logic underpinning representations of medical institutions as threat – namely a sense of being controlled and contained within an efficient system that may well feel far from tender.

Arthur Frank warns that clinical spaces can be experienced as hostile: 'Professionals forget what they are often demanding of patients and families, including the self-mastery required to enter environments that are confusing, stressful, uncomfortable, and often unfriendly. In hospitals, the maze of corridors mirrors the bureaucratic maze … It takes work to recognise – to pause and to *see* – what daily routine can render transparent.'[6] Rendering the familiar unfamiliar may usefully estrange that which has been normalised by routine, and Gothic representations of medical space make that carcerality explicit. The texts of this chapter not only set their horrors in institutional environments but make those institutional edifices the very engines of the horror. These edifices – and particularly their infrastructural, peripheral interior spaces – become metonymic of the management and administrative processes that underpin the corporeal violations. Representations of American medical process during the transplantation era cannot be understood without reference to the corporatisation of healthcare under late twentieth- and twenty-first-century biomedicalisation, the 'medical-industrial complex', a term coined by HealthPAC in 1971, or the 'U.S. Biomedical Technoservice Complex, Inc.', as Clarke *et al.* observe:

> Trends in corporatization and commodification are embodied in the moves by private corporate entities to appropriate increasing areas of the health-care sector under private management and/or ownership. In biomedicalization, not only are the jurisdictional boundaries of medicine and medical work expanding and being reconfigured, but so too are the frontiers of what is legitimately defined as private versus public medicine, and corporatized versus non-profit medicine.[7]

This chapter explores corporate and institutional transfer Gothic in American fiction, particularly from the 1970s and 1980s. These works respond to the emergence of neurological death as a legal category and increasing corporatisation of care.

A significant component of the horrors in these texts stems from the factory imagery, conveying the scale, mechanical automation, and impersonal efficiency of the organ theft. The political economy of capitalism requires a constant supply of raw material on which to work its production. The fantasies in this chapter show human bodies that become that raw material for the voracious machine of capital, that systemic hunger. Transplantation technologies 'add value' to severed organs and tissues by virtue of the chemical, surgical, and mechanical processes required to effect the transfer.

'Banking' bodies

Advances in extracorporeal preservation were central to the large-scale viability of transfer. The late nineteenth century saw attempts at creating mechanical devices to enable biological material to last longer outside the body, but it was only in 1935 that Alexis Carrell and Charles Lindbergh invented an organ perfusion device that could keep internal organs viable outside the body.[8] Certain biomaterial could be stored earlier, notably red blood cells, which – lacking a nucleus – can be frozen and thawed more readily, and in the 1920s Soviet scientists developed collections of stored blood, notably from cadavers.[9] In 1937, a Chicago hospital emulated some elements of the Soviet endeavour, with the emphatic exception of cadaveric blood. Bernard Fantus, the doctor who devised the project, condemned transfusions from the dead as 'revolting to Anglo-Saxon susceptibilities'.[10]

Fantus coined the term 'blood bank' to describe the 1937 Cook County Hospital blood storage facility. In using the banking metaphor, Fantus did not intend to put blood within an exclusively commercial framework (although blood sale was well established at the time and more common than altruistic donation). Rather, Fantus intended the 'bank' metaphor to emphasise the finitude of the resource: 'Just as one cannot draw money from a bank unless one has deposited some, so the blood preservation department cannot supply blood unless as much comes in as goes out'. He envisioned individual records of saving and loan. Both the terminology and the concept were popular, other 'blood banks' opening along Fantus's lines. Surgeons spoke of refrigerators storing blood as 'vaults', maintained 'reserves', nurtured 'capital', recorded 'bank assets', kept 'blood ledgers', and recorded debits in red ink, and 'eye banks', 'skin banks', and 'gene banks' (for sperm) and 'human milk banks' followed.[11] So central was the language of finance that there was even debate over whether blood donation should be tax-deductible or subject to state sales taxes, and so professional did some of the 'donor' base become that in the 1930s a blood sellers' union was recognised by the American Federation of Labor.[12] In 1971, American blood markets incurred trenchant criticism from the British sociologist Richard Titmuss, who argued that, in contrast to the UK system of voluntary donation, the American system weakened social connections and impaired the quality of the blood supply, and his critiques led to reforms.

None the less, the American blood donation system continues to feature paid components, particularly with regard to blood plasma. As Susan Lederer says, 'More than a metaphor, banking captured the transactional nature of commerce in the body'.[13]

Blood and tissue banks could be directly profitable. After tissue banks began to be established in the UK and US in the late 1940s and 1950s, for example, there were instances where some surgeons agreed to sell banked tissue for profit to buyers in other countries: David Hamilton says, 'These profitable opportunities were not always turned down by the surgeons involved'.[14] In 1968, Henry Davidson speculated that the need for organs might spawn new professions, sardonically invoking the spirit of free enterprise. 'Maybe a new profession is being born: that of organ snatcher, or, perhaps, a "transplant supply engineer"... American ingenuity is limitless ... Who says the old spirit of innovation and know-how is dead?'[15] When US national procurement mechanisms emerged in the late twentieth century, there was vociferous enthusiasm for optimising the systems through corporate 'efficiency' and enterprise. The US National Organ Transplant Act (1984) not only criminalised organ sale but also established a centralised national network to monitor and foster donation, procurement, and transplantation, the United Network for Organ Sharing (UNOS), and *Fortune* magazine voiced a common criticism when it asked, 'Will this emerging high-tech industry be run efficiently by dynamic entrepreneurs of the capitalist persuasion, or will it be semi-socialised and smothered by regulators?'[16] In multiple ways, then, trends in economic management and political economy influenced expectations of transfer administration.

The financial benefits that accrue from disaggregating bodies are manifold and exceed mere 'organ sale'. Most countries have made it illegal to sell most human material; there are exceptions, such as Iran where living kidney sale is legal, and the market in blood in the US. Yet even in countries where organs cannot be legally sold, transfer is a nexus for significant cash and capital flow. Economically speaking, transfer is exceptionally generative in the labour that maintains procurement allocation and distribution networks, the cost of the surgery, the cost of ongoing medical surveillance, ongoing pharmaceutical profit from lifelong immunosuppression, and the cost of treating rejection or side effects, without even including the appreciable economic benefits accruing to particular hospitals as a result of the 'reputational benefit' of having a transplant centre. Although biomaterial is not usually sold per se, profits are engendered by the engineering of biomaterial to make it transferable, and effecting the transfer itself. It is transferable only through surgeries and technological processing.[17] Transfer is not a simple movement from x to y, but involves, as Catherine Waldby and Robert Mitchell say, 'a ... network of donor-recipient relations ... mediated by biotechnical processes and an institutional complex of tissue banks, pharmaceutical and research companies, and clinics'.[18] Each stage may see direct or indirect financial benefits accrue to certain participants, and Lesley Sharp observes:

> Without question, much money is exchanged, but payments made by insurance companies, individual patients, transplant hospitals, and procurement agencies are typically described as covering technical, transportation, and other support services, rather than being directly linked to the cost of the organ itself ... [T]he miracle of transplantation may quickly dissolve into a dollar-driven medical nightmare.[19]

Scott Carney notes that US hospitals 'increasingly turn profits on organ transplants; some even return revenues to shareholders'.[20] Money is also involved in more subtle ways. In the US, organ procurement is managed by government-contracted non-profit Organ Procurement Organisations (OPOs), which have responsibility for evaluating and procuring organs in cadaveric donation. These organisations are non-profit, but retaining contracts can hinge on meeting certain targets, and these targets can affect staff career security. This funding structure can become a potential ethical problem if, for example, end-of-life care of potential donors is put into the hands of OPO professionals, without family necessarily being aware that the new nurses and doctors with whom they are working are employed by an OPO and that their personal success in their role is linked to meeting targets; Sharp observes that, at times, some staff have been given 'monthly and annual quotas, and their inability to meet these puts their own jobs at risk'.[21] In addition to institutional benefits, financial burdens are also in play, notably with regard to the costs of extended life support for patients with no prospect of recovery but not yet meeting any new death classification. Such patients may inhabit a 'billable' grey zone, in Sharon Kauffman's terms.[22] The costs of such life extension were foregrounded in the Harvard Ad Hoc Committee's Report and were especially publicised during Karen Quinlan's extended coma (see Chapter 1).

With such institutional benefits and burdens in play, the international 1979 Declaration of Sydney states that the practitioners who diagnose death before donation must be separate from those would be professionally involved with either surgical procurement or transplant.[23] In some cases, however, a complete distinction between teams and concerns may be hard to achieve, and healthcare practitioners must balance care for a patient while working towards optimising donation consent even before death occurs. The US-government-funded Organ Donation Breakthrough Collaborative project, for example, identifies ways to increase donation consent rates, and recommends multiple incentives to encourage staff to strive to acquire consent to cadaveric organ donation. Recommendations include linking 'hiring, supervision and recognition ... to performance [rates of consent to organ donation] and financial incentives for meeting targets', requiring 'Nurses [to] automatically look at white boards to see if any patients look like potential donors', 'assign[ing] only those nurses [named champions of donation] to potential donor cases', and '"setting the stage" for consent well ahead of the declaration'.[24] These endeavours are of course motivated not by profit but by a desire to maximise organ donation with a view to saving lives, as well as arguably to benefit donors posthumously in agreeing to their wishes and offering comfort to donor kin through good emerging from tragedy.[25] None the less, even a strong supporter of maximising donation concedes that integrating donor optimisation into critical care 'can make those involved ... feel that they are required to commoditise the patient as a community resource'.[26] The processes may evoke a sense of individuals vulnerable to opaque institutional processes.

The threat to the human in these texts requires a different approach to the analysis of dehumanisation from that of Giorgio Agamben's thanatopolitical model of the *homo sacer*, discussed in my Introduction and previous chapter.[27] While Agamben's model of sacrificial biopolitics is valuable in cultural studies of transfer, its emphasis on state power makes it less helpful in exploring the combinations of private and public finance that inform the process. Thomas Lemke argues that Agamben puts too much weight on the state as salient agent:

> biopolitics is not only the purview of government regulation ... The principal danger today is not that the body or its organs will succumb to state control ... On the contrary, the danger is that the state will, in the name of 'deregulation', retreat from the domains it once occupied in society and hand over decisions pertaining to the value of life and determinations of when it begins and ends to the realm of science and commercial interests.[28]

The medical institutions imagined in these fictions are funded with blends of state and private funding, and each presents corporate and financial imperatives as central drivers for predation.

'The hospital itself harboured considerable violence': fantasies of medical predation and profit

The US saw rapid public acceptance of the concept of brain death (though acceptance is still not universal), but none the less the late 1960s and 1970s saw anxieties about the new death manifest in a range of media.[29] The *New York Times*, for example, warned in 1967 that 'One need not be a science fiction writer to envision the possibility of future murder rings supplying healthy organs for black-market surgeons whose patients are unwilling to wait until natural sources have supplied the heart or liver or pancreas they need'.[30] Preoccupations with neurological death also found expression in other ways, including George Romero's horror film *Night of the Living*

Dead.[31] Released contemporaneously with the 1968 Harvard Report naming 'irreversible coma', this film engages contemporary preoccupations with the brain; Roger Luckhurst notes that in these films 'it is the brain that remains stubbornly "minimally conscious" whilst the cardiopulmonary system has died off'.[32] Luckhurst admits that such comparisons do not imply that Romero's team were filming while poised waiting for the latest issue of the *Journal of the American Medical Association*, yet elements of such popular work can be read as hallucinatory refractions of debates circulating at the time. Within a decade of the Harvard Report, the most famous tale of predatorial harvest is Robin Cook's novel *Coma* (1977).[33]

The protagonist Susan Wheeler is a medical student at a prestigious hospital, Boston Memorial. When an unexpected number of patients fall into coma under anaesthetic, Wheeler discovers that the oxygen line to operating room 8 has been poisoned. People who subsequently enter stable coma are transferred to the mysterious 'Jefferson Institute'. Not all the bodies stored there are classified as dead; some suffer what are now called chronic disorders of consciousness (CDoCs), including conditions once labelled 'persistent vegetative states'. Ostensibly a benevolent site to support long-term coma patients, it is actually 'a clearinghouse for black-market human organs', bodies tissue-matched with recipient requests and harvested on demand for tremendous fees (p. 276). Susan is threatened, including with sexual assault. The hospital director drugs her to induce false symptoms of appendicitis, and takes her to OR8 for surgery, intending to induce brain damage and consign her to the Institute. Her lover tries to rescue her but her fate is ambiguous. Michael Crichton's film adaptation was released a year later with a similar plot, except that she is successfully rescued. The adaptation from novel to film was also influenced by the Quinlan controversy. As Catherine Belling observes, 'The novel could assume it was routine to keep coma patients indefinitely on life support; by 1978 Crichton cannot trust his film audience to agree'.[34] I will discuss the film and novel in tandem.

Cook's novel became a bestseller, was adapted to film in 1978, became a TV mini-series in 2012, and influenced subsequent medical thrillers.[35] Cook, himself a doctor, maintains that he wrote *Coma* to try to encourage popular debates around medical ethics with a view to encouraging organ donation. In fact, evidence suggests the novel caused consent rates to drop.[36] The novel's medical minutiae and the fact it was written by a doctor made some readers regard it as a semi-disguised exposé – not of actual practices, but at least of callous and deceptive hospitals within which people were vulnerable. Belling says, 'To understand its overt agenda, one must read *Coma* as a kind of hypothetical bioethics case; to understand its actual impact, we must also read it as a horror story'.[37] Featuring a young woman rushing around subterranean tunnels of a menacing edifice, threatened with corporeal violation only to be rescued by a male beloved – described thus, both novel and film evoke tropes of early Gothic fiction. The terror and horror of the narration, however, accrue around a very particular component of the story: specifically, less the surgery than the *site*.

Whilst the surgical action and thriller events are described in detached and matter-of-fact prose, the hospital buildings and interior spaces accrue febrile and vivid descriptions, imbued with Gothic intertextualities and the triad of qualities discussed in my Introduction: claustrophobic space, disoriented affect, and disrupted temporality. The intensive care unit is presented as especially disorienting and strange to both patients and students, Susan as baffled by the space and its signs as any early Gothic heroine struggling to decipher manuscripts. Within this isolated space: 'the outside world faded and disappeared', 'a surrealist alien environment emerged out of the gloom', patients are 'lost in layer upon layer of mummylike bandages', and Susan struggles to decipher oscilloscope screens and medicine labels, feeling 'sickening' bewilderment (pp. 40–1). Outside fiction, the sensory distress of ICUs is well-established and contributes to the recognised phenomenon of ICU psychosis.[38] Despite the disturbing qualities of the ICU, however, the most dramatic Gothic descriptions in the novel are reserved for internal peripheral spaces: stairwells and corridors. As Susan descends to the ICU she notices the squalor and dilapidation of the stairwell:

> By leaning out over the metal banister Susan could see down into the sub-basement and up to where the spiralling stairs became lost in collapsing perspective ... The decaying darkness of the walls seemed to move in on her, awakening some atavistic fear. Perhaps because it reminded her of a recurrent dream. ... [which] involved moving through a tunnel of twisted shapes which would ... impede her progress. She never made it to the end of the tunnel ... (pp. 59–60)

The space has a profound impact on Susan, the collapsing perspective rendering her dizzy and the confinement making her feel 'caught within a vertical prison' (p. 61). These interior spaces seem to take an unnaturally long time to traverse, and the decay is ominous. Things hardly improve when she reaches corridors, as the following example shows:

> The light from each bulb met the light from the next in an uneasy penumbra, causing a strange interplay of shadows from the tangle of pipes along the ceiling ... The atmosphere was oppressive ... She had seemingly been walking for a hundred yards as the corridor twisted first in one direction then in another ... With increased misgivings she continued. At several places, the light bulbs were not functioning and Susan's shadow would appear in front of her and lengthen. Then as she moved into the sphere of influence of the next functioning light her shadow would pale and disappear. (pp. 131–2)

The morphing shadows of the protagonist – extended into unnatural forms and then erased altogether – parallel the way that the human becomes oddly malleable and vulnerable within the processes of the hospital site. Similarly, Crichton's film adaptation features repeated, extended scenes of Susan in basements, corridors, and crawl-voids and these confined infrastructural spaces become sites of repeated physical threat and mystery. The film uses extradiegetic music and camerawork to imbue the medical edifices and their interiors with menace. The soundtrack, for example, is generally minimal and music-free, but an ominous musical score coincides with the approach to the Jefferson Institute, dramatic spikes in sound coinciding with the sight of its façade. From that point on, the film features repeated shots of Susan moving through disorienting and vertiginous spaces, through empty corridors, up vertical shafts, and along cramped overhead access passages, always accompanied with disruptive camerawork to destabilise the viewer's position. The building is a menacing antagonist. Furthermore, the camera frames and contains her within multiple barriers (Figure 2). Threatening musical cues continue to build over images of the internal peripheral spaces of both institutions, operating as affective triggers.

These passages may be approached by considering both the phenomenology of the spaces themselves and the historical legacies of buildings with such designs, which have long functioned to control and discipline bodies.[39] In terms of the phenomenology of the space, Luckhurst notes that a corridor's bounded architectural volume simultaneously confines the individual body and multiplies potential threats to that body, and film can intensify those,

Figure 2 Corridors. Film still from *Coma*, dir. by Michael Crichton
(US: Metro Goldwyn-Mayer, 1978).

'multipl[ying] the anticipatory fear from the off-screen spaces of the doorways and voids that it passes'.[40] The social meaning and form of the corridor has morphed since its earliest appearance as a passage to enable rapid communication within fortified towns and then within fifteenth-century palazzos. Since then, and notably since nineteenth- and twentieth-century transformations in hospital and asylum architecture, corridors have become associated less with enabling rapid connection than with effecting containment and separation. In other words, these texts are influenced by changing architectures and managements of medical sites, and affective legacies of such institutional spaces.

These spaces also take on symbolic functions, metonymically denoting the predatorial systems within which the sites are achieving profit and creating (and un-creating) social meaning for the bodies within them. Tellingly, in Crichton's film, when a senior doctor finally seeks to justify the conspiracy to Susan, he uses an architectural metaphor: 'These great hospital complexes are the cathedrals of our age … We must always take the long view. Not of the individual, but of society as a whole, because medicine is now a great social force. The individual is too small.' In this speech, the doctor supports his utilitarian rationale for selective execution through the symbolism of a magnificent edifice, its scale outstripping a mere human body. Individual human vulnerability within the medical site is rendered with similar effect, but with a different strategy, in the Jefferson Institute. Unlike the dilapidated Boston Memorial, the Institute is presented as hypermodern in architectural form, purpose, and funding structure. The economics of the project's construction and management are foregrounded throughout, with the reader being told no fewer than three times that the Institute's construction was state-funded, with subsequent administration under private finance. From inception it blends state and private forces in the ways Clarke and others describe as paradigmatic of biomedicalisation, and it has been so successful at cutting costs for care for those in coma that most US cities already have or are building their own version (p. 263). Amid this profit-inflected framing, economies of scale are foregrounded. Susan's lover Bellows explains, '"It's an intensive care facility built as part of the area's Health Maintenance Organisation design. Supposedly it's been designed to cut clinical costs by applying economics of scale in relation to intensive care … I saw it from the outside once. It's very modern … massive and rectilinear"' (p. 156). This segue from the institution's financing to its architecture is not a *non sequitur*. Throughout the novel, the Jefferson's architectural idiosyncrasies are presented as both symbolic of and materially mediating its inhuman detachment from conventional conceptions of care.

Our first glimpse of the structure is memorable. It is a 'strikingly modern structure', with slanting walls. The first 25 feet of the façade are sheer, with no windows or doors apart from the front entrance. 'The second story [*sic*] had windows but they were recessed and could not be seen from the street. Only the sharply geometric embrasures were visible and the glow of lights from within … It gave the impression of a two-storey ancient Egyptian mastaba, or the base of an Aztec pyramid' (p. 261). The description evokes a blend of massive, imposing architectural designs, ancient and modern. The 1978 film adaptation uses the former Xerox headquarters in Lexington, Massachusetts, a modern concrete structure with multiple blank exterior walls. When Susan enters, she finds herself in a 'stark white' interior, devoid of windows, any ornamentation, or visible lighting, dominated by mirrors. 'The sameness was … disorienting … She had to blink and make an effort to focus' (p. 262). This space is not for human comfort, but at best marginalises humans and at worst processes them into highly profitable products. When Susan sees the room where the patients are warehoused:

> she stopped in astonishment. There were more than a hundred patients in the room, and all of them were completely suspended in air about four feet from the floor. All of them were naked. Looking closely, Susan could see the wires piercing multiple points in the patients' long bones. The wires were connected to complicated metal frames and pulled taut. The patients' heads were supported by other wires from the ceiling which were attached to screw eyes in the patients' skulls. Susan had an impression of grotesque, horizontal, sleeping marionettes. (pp. 265–6)

Naked human bodies are suspended horizontally on wires piercing their bones, monitored, medicated, and moved by machinery on a 'bewildering' maze of tracks (p. 267). Care is neither delivered by humans nor readily comprehensible by them. This scene also furnished the cover illustration for the first edition as well as yielding the most widely reproduced stills from the 1978 film adaptation (Figure 3).

The site dehumanises the patients. Even though not all the people are brain-dead, the novel's Nurse Michelle says, 'They aren't people. They *were* people; now they're brain stem preparations' (p. 267). In addition to its visual connotations of marionettes and puppetry, the wire-hung semi-corpses also evoke associations with an abattoir's cold room for hanging slaughtered animals, and later fictions of institutional organ theft elaborate more overtly on this connotation, as I will shortly discuss.

Whilst the Institute is a factory for spare parts, the hospital, too, is described in factory terms. Describing the work of the operating room suite, we hear, 'Within a five minute interval, twenty-one scalpels sliced through unresisting human skin as the scheduled operations commenced' (p. 20), and the first character to moot the possibility of procuring organs from not-quite-dead patients is not a villain but a good doctor. The implied connections between the two sites culminate in Susan's hallucination as she

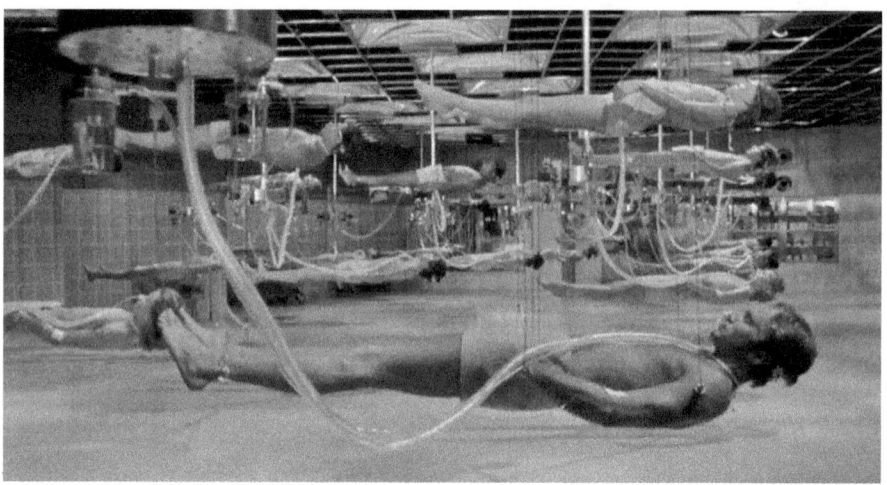

Figure 3 Bodies in storage. Film still from *Coma*, dir. by Michael Crichton
(US: Metro Goldwyn-Mayer, 1978).

partially wakes in OR8, dimly aware she is about to be rendered comatose and
sent to the Institute:

> A phantasmagoria of geometric images … [T]he image of a hand being stabbed
> by scissors preceded a sequence of chase. The autopsy room at the Memorial
> appeared with a realism that included auditory and olfactory aspects. A spiral
> staircase took dominance then a corridor … The corridor twisted and turned
> kaleidoscopically. (p. 300)

Her vision accurately conveys the blending of the site of healing and the site of
surgical violation. The locus of threat is a medical institution driven by profit
concerns. In the novel and its subsequent adaptations to screen, the buildings and their interiors become symbolic of the rapacious economic and social
machinery that drives the surgical extractions. The site is as scary as the scalpel.

A similar aesthetic and logic of institutional threat characterises Robert
Fiveson's film *Parts: The Clonus Horror* (1979).[41] Bearing the tag lines, 'The only
thing they don't use … is the scream', and 'Where science and nightmare merge',
this film imagines a government-run secret facility in rural Milwaukee, breeding
clones for elite scientists and politicians. Senators and the president-elect are
shown to be aware of the project and the latter has received a heart from a clone
two years before the film's action begins. By the end of the film, he has received
a second clone heart. Most clones are rendered brain-damaged through viral
warping of the embryo or lobotomy, but some are left intact and one uncovers
the truth and (briefly) escapes. As with *Coma*, a large part of the horror lies
in the storage of the bodies, in this case cryogenically frozen and hanging in

shrink-wrapped bags. Whilst the low-budget effects are unintentionally hilarious for contemporary viewers (and remind us how horror can often veer into comedy), the film does draw maximum effect from the way that the victims are conscious for the final stage of the freezing procedure, screaming as the plastic encases their faces and then remaining frozen in anguished postures. The film opens with shots of wrapped bodies, unnerving camerawork caressing them in close-ups, the partialising shots foreshadowing the partitioning that these stored bodies are destined to undergo. Whilst the nature of the 'clonus horror' is thus disclosed to the audience early in the film, the climactic reveal of the film is the sight of these bodies *en masse*, when the protagonist Richard finds the storage facility (Figure 4). The massed collection of bodies is central to the impact of this shot, underscoring the factory scale of production.

The compound that enables this processing of bodies is a vast modern concrete structure, again with an impassive façade, and, tellingly, the opening title shot makes that edifice the backdrop. As with *Coma*, much of the dramatic action revolves around flight through the institution's infrastructural interior spaces of deserted corridors, lift shafts, basements, ceiling access panels, and pipelines. The protagonist Richard runs frantically through these spaces amid intermittent illumination, repeatedly dramatising bewilderment at institutional

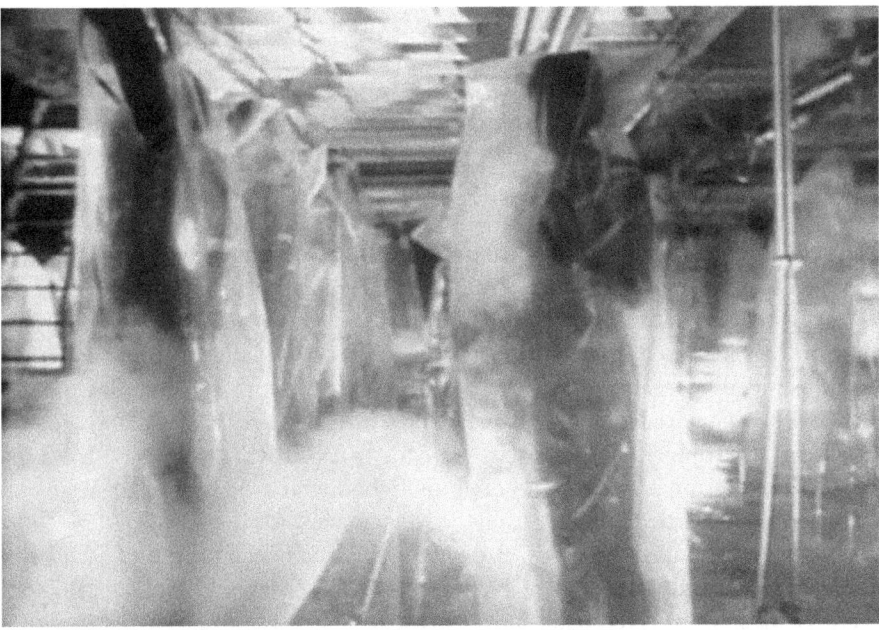

Figure 4 Still from *Parts: The Clonus Horror*, dir. by Robert Fiveson
(Group I Films, 1979).

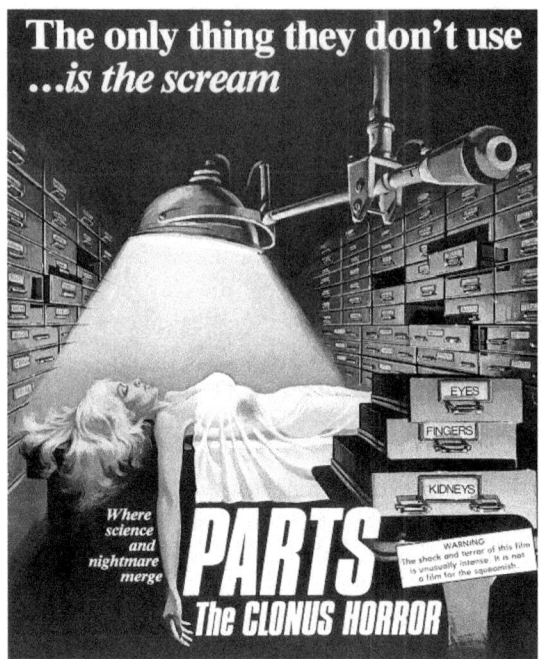

Figure 5 Theatrical release poster for *Parts: The Clonus Horror*, dir. by Robert
Fiveson (Group I Films, 1979).

sprawl as he looks for guidance and seeks maps. The film even adds a dose of
what might be called administrative dread, in which extensive screen time is
given over to rummaging in filing cabinets for secrets. Metal file storage even
acquires a (hilarious) charge of dread in one of the posters for the theatrical
release (Figure 5). The poster deploys the classic Gothic trope of a pros-
trate female figure, her body sensuously swathed in white fabric, violated and
bloody, but reframes it with a contemporary medical setting. The white fabric
is a surgical drape, and the body is illuminated by a surgical theatre spotlight.
The body is hemmed in, however, not by dungeon walls but by filing cabinets,
and this metallic organ bank seems to have more vitality than the supine human
body. The staggered metal drawers open and protrude towards the viewer,
claiming attention with the labels 'EYES', 'FINGERS', 'KIDNEYS'. This
medical institution is a factory where human bodies are the raw material, stored
en masse to satisfy demand.

Institutional transfer Gothic also characterises another strand of 1970s fiction, one exemplified by John Hejinian's novel *Extreme Remedies* (1974).[42]
Like Cook's *Coma*, Hejinian's novel presents itself as rooted in the author's
own experience as a hospital doctor, but unlike Cook's omniscient narrator
Hejinian offers a first-person narration from a doctor's perspective. Womack,

a weary neurologist, discovers that patients are being raided for organs or used in doomed medical experiments. The hospital stages scenes of compassionate care but in fact is rife with malpractice and callous ineptitude. Racism abounds among the staff, with the character Billy Liggons dismissed as a young African-American man with a drug problem and falling into coma as a result of clinical neglect. His brother recognises that Billy is being mistreated because of his race: 'Billy ain't no hunk of black meat for you to fuck around with', 'I'm onto all your crap. Operate on his brain. Stick needles in him. Tie him down on the bed. Don't let him eat or nothing' (pp. 14, 165). One staff member admits that among the African-American community the hospital's reputation is 'A place to die ... No return' (p. 194). Staff refer to Billy dismissively as 'that Negro', and repeatedly urge the protagonist Womack to mark him as brain-dead prematurely so his kidneys can be taken. Institutional racism is not confined to the hospital, with police asserting 'what's another nigger killing? It's us or them, right?' (p. 257). Whilst all the hospital's patients are neglected, the patients targeted for too-hasty organ extraction and experimentation are African-American, Mexican, and disabled. In this, the text is informed by long histories of African-American torment in medical contexts, and my next chapter will discuss narratives of African-American transfer horror in more detail.

Hejinian's novel represents the corporate nature of the hospital as the engine of its cruelties. Senior partners of the hospital complain, as shareholders, about coma patients taking too long to reach brain-death status, on the grounds that the life support is using taxpayers' money. One says, 'This is supposed to be a hospital, not a hotel, I'm going to be wiped out this year on capital gains alone. It's getting so bad I can't afford to take any profits' (p. 87).

Again, the building itself comes to symbolise the threats. Womack sees the hospital's peripheral and infrastructural spaces as somehow inviting brutality:

> the hospital itself harboured considerable violence: each year, two or three women usually were raped in the bathrooms and an occasional intern was stabbed, but these matters were hushed up by the city administration. The most recent rape had been committed by one of the hospital's own security policemen, who had dragged a lady visitor down to the asphalt between two parked cars.
>
> We chose the damp tunnel. Water dripped from the sagging ceiling, and our voices echoed as if we were entering a crypt. Many of the bare bulbs were broken, and we moved through shadows between yellow islands of light. (p. 44)
>
> The emergency ward was the usual evening chaos – babbling with pleas and curses and moans, slippery with urine and blood and splats of vomit ... At the nadir of urban decay, the emergency ward was a major drain. (pp. 4–5)

The hospital is a stage for neglect and misery. Working there, Womack feels despair and a sense of contamination and resentfulness. 'I wondered why I had to be awake and entangled with souls whose desperation and illness allowed none of us any rest' (p. 30); 'Wrestling with so many ill bodies, I felt polluted' (p. 53); 'My arms were tired from wrestling with so many stiff bodies. Past midnight, in the eerie, shadowed glow of the night lights, the different cases blurred together as if their similar blood and sweat and destroyed brains made them into a single human wreck, and I got the nightmare feeling that I was somehow grappling with the angel of death' (p. 309). At such moments Womack indulges grandiosity and self-pity, while problematically dehumanising the patients as a monstrous, contaminating mass of 'blood and sweat and destroyed brains'. Unlike *Coma*, the novel resists a heroic narrative of villain brought to justice, ending far more ambiguously. Disturbed at what he uncovers about the hospital's exploitative practices, Womack helps one patient escape medical experimentation but refuses to publicly expose the hospital's ongoing atrocities. A student accuses him of being just another 'fucking butcher' (p. 342) and Womack does not dispute it. Like *Coma*, this novel imagines a medical institution driven by economic rapacity and an indifference to individual patients. The profit-driven nature of these hospitals is central to their becoming sites of horror rather than healing.

Perhaps the most disturbing 1970s American transplant horror fictions, however, are those in Dennis Etchison's 'transplant trilogy', as Ramsay Campbell calls a sequence of three short stories: 'The machine demands a sacrifice' (1972, rev. 1982), 'Calling all monsters' (1972, rev. 1982), and 'The dead line' (1979, rev. 1982).[43] The first two will be discussed in subsequent chapters where more thematically salient, and I will explore the last here. 'The dead line' describes living or dead bodies suspended in a liminal state for months or years. In this society, EEG flat line is used to mark time of death, but none the less a harrowing blurring of life and death ensues. This story draws explicitly on Gaylin's language of 'neomorts' and the 'bioemporium' to describe a set-off space for bodies classified as neurologically dead. Well beyond the procurement measures that actually came into being in the 1970s and since, this fiction imagines a world in which bodies with flat-line EEG are kept for years in a state called 'Maintenance', for blood and organ extraction, antibody manufacture, and a medical experimentation incubator to examine the effects of injected tumours, toxins, and infections. In this imagined world, the neomort 'is now – and will continue to be – neither alive nor dead' (p. 107), and neither are the loved ones they leave behind.

The torment of seeing a loved one in such prolonged undeath drives the first-person narrator to madness. He has watched his wife undergo surgical extractions and experimentation for nearly eighteen months, and has come to feel that he, too, occupies a liminal space between life and death. He dreams or hallucinates that he wakes in confined darkness, extricates a cigarette lighter, turns it on and sees he is in a silk-lined coffin. The silk catches fire and he starts to burn. The coffin opens and he realises he is in an embalmer's room, but the attendants do not seem to realise he is moving:

> I scream again, but no sound comes out.
>   They turn away.
>   I struggle up, out of the coffin. There is no pain. I claw off my clothing, baring my seared flesh.
>   See! I cry. I'm alive!
>   They do not hear.
>   I rip at my chest with smoldering hands, the peeled skin rolling up under my fingernails. See the blood in my veins? I shout. I'm not one of them! (p. 105)

In passages such as this, the story initially seems to root its horror in a contrast between living bodies and neomorts – 'I'm not one of *them*' – the third-person plural pronoun charged with the combination of revulsion and a sense of individual boundaries encroached upon. This seeming revulsion at '*them*', the neomorts, exemplifies Julia Kristeva's conception of the abject, that which simultaneously seduces and threatens the subject: 'It is ... not lack of cleanliness or health that causes abjection, but what disturbs identity, system, order ... The in-between, the ambiguous, the composite.'[44] Corpses, in particular, can confront the subject with 'that [which] I permanently thrust aside in order to live'; they are 'what life withstands, hardly and with difficulty, on pain of death ... [T]he corpse, the most sickening of wastes, is a border that has encroached upon everything'.[45] The abject impels subjects to actively differentiate themselves from such decay, from such threats to their own imagined integrity, and there are several hints, as above, that suggest that the narrator's driving impulse is an urge to get distance from his wife's ambiguous body. The story's opening line – described by Campbell as 'the most horrifying first line ever written' – sets up the reader's expectation that the protagonist feels not only revulsion at his wife's body but also hatred, resentment, or sadistic cruelty.[46] He declares, 'This morning I put ground glass in my wife's eyes' (p. 99).

As the story progresses, however, the threatening referent of 'them' shifts, to become instead the medical practitioners and hospital administrators. We realise that the protagonist, driven mad by grief and strain, has all along been paradoxically mutilating his wife's body to try to *stop* the bioemporium mutilating her any longer. The most malevolent 'them', in this narration, is the administration. When he meets a woman whose husband may become condemned to 'Maintenance', he warns her:

> 'He will be used around the clock to manufacture an endless red tide for transfusions ... His veins will be a battleground for viruses, for pneumonia, hepatitis, leukemia, live cancers. And then his body will be drained off, like a stuck pig's, and a new supply of experimental toxins pumped in, so that he can go on

producing antitoxins for *them* ... He will begin to decay inside ... *They* will take him organ by organ, cell by cell. And it will take years. As long as the machines can keep his heart and lungs moving ... And when he's been thoroughly, efficiently gutted – or when his body has eaten itself from the inside out ... They will begin to strip the skin from his limbs, from his skull, a few millimetres at a time. For grafting and re-grafting ...' (pp. 107–8, emphasis added)

The menacing referent of the third-person plural has become the institution, a force the narrator senses is voracious and mechanical: 'There is a machine outside my door. It eats people, chews them up and spits out only what it can't use, it wants to get me, I know it does, but I'm not going to let it' (p. 109). Yet he eventually realises his efforts are doomed:

It's no use. It will never be enough.
   They will never be done with her.
   When I go to the hospital today she will not be there. She will already have been given to the interns for their spinal taps and arteriograms, for surgical practice on a cadaver that is neither alive nor dead. She will belong to the meat cutters, to the first year med students with their dull knives and stained cross sections. (p. 109)

Ultimately, the only resistance he can mount is to steal her body and decay together:

I will search the floors and labs and secret doors of the wing, and when I find her I will steal her silently away; I will give her safe passage ... I will take her to a place where even *they* can't reach, beyond the boundaries that separate the living and the dead ... And there I will stay with her, to be with her, to take refuge with her among the dead. I will tear at my body and my corruption until we are one in soft asylum. (p. 109, emphasis added)

In lyrical confusion, this passage slides between life, death, a state beyond both, and a state combining both. It captures the agony of the protagonist's suspended experience and his slide into madness and a helpless longing to escape an institution's processes.

Institutional transfer horror of the 1970s influenced many works in subsequent decades. Other texts develop *Coma*'s approach of imagining not only individual doctors but the wider medical organisation itself as vulnerable to corruption. Stephen Kanar's *The J Factor* (2000), for example, has the tagline 'The business of medicine has taken a deadly turn', and imagines a near-future society in which medical institutions' corporate profit influences International Organ Replacement Corporation (IORC), which assigns organs on the basis of a person's Justification Factor or J-factor.[47] Another novel in the *Coma* tradition, Tess Gerritsen's *Harvest* (2003), suggests that physicians' own financial precarity opens them to corruption, notably the burden of student loans incurred during training. Financial gain is even more overt in the 2012 A&E TV adaptation of *Coma*, in which the Institute is a site not only for organ theft but also for medical experimentation, forced insemination, and foetal tissue theft, and doctors in Susan's own family are implicated. This vision is of highly commodified healthcare inflected with preoccupations of its historical moment, as Luckhurst notes: a veritable 'medical-industrial complex … inextricably interwoven with insurers, donors, venture capitalists and brokerage firms, reflecting the intensive commodification of American health care'.[48] The mini-series presents institutional exploitation as disturbingly resilient, the prime mover escaping punishment and moving to China where she establishes a new institute and solicits her former colleagues to join her. The film ends with the implication that other doctors may be tempted.

In addition to medical thrillers, science fiction has also explored corporate profit and transfer. Private hospitals may heal the wealthiest while treating the marginalised as disposable organ banks, and the device of imprisoned clones is used to rich effect in several such texts, simultaneously implicating the callous and privileged originals and demeaning the cloned body (in line with a long tradition in Western culture which denigrates 'copies', as I discuss elsewhere).[49] Greg Egan's short story 'The extra' (1990), for example, imagines a future world in which a wealthy man keeps a stable of clones to supply tissue and organs damaged in his hedonistic lifestyle.[50] These victims are not only incarcerated but also deliberately cerebrally mutilated. Equally bleak is the society of Michael Marshall Smith's novel *Spares* (1995), in which clones are imprisoned *en masse*, naked, 'Living in tunnels waiting to be whittled down … while mangled and dissected bodies stumped around them … a butcher's shop where the meat still moved occasionally, always and forever bathed in a dead blue light'.[51] As well as conveying the bodily damage to the clone, *Spares* conveys the damage done to the clones' capacity for interaction and fellowship. They have 'no family. They're like dead code segments, cut off from the rest of the programme and left alone in darkness' (p. 45). Consigned to a 'farm' (p. 42) and unable to speak, the clones are repeatedly likened to non-human animals. This factory farming of the human reminds us of the suffering of non-human animal bodies in contemporary agribusiness.[52]

Corporatisation of the medical is also foregrounded in the 2005 film *The Island*, directed by Michael Bay.[53] So indebted to *Parts: The Clonus Horror* that it led to a copyright infringement settlement, this film opens with a dystopian sealed environment of 25,000 apparent survivors of an unspecified earlier ecocatastrophe. A regular lottery is held to identify lucky people to go to 'the Island', ostensibly the last pathogen-free zone. In fact, the inhabitants are all clones, individually commissioned by wealthy outsiders to serve as sources for organs or pregnancy surrogates. The clones live highly regulated lives, their food prescribed, urine scanned, sleep REM cycles monitored, and male and female clones restricted from 'proximity'. When two clones escape and seek help from one of their originals, the original tries to turn them in but his clone successfully impersonates him. The clones infiltrate and bring down the organisation. As in *Clonus* and *Coma*, much of the drama hinges on vulnerable figures moving through corridors and peripheral infrastructural spaces, decayed industrial basements, and sterile white corridors. The project is wholly corporate and commercial, the US government reduced to an investor (the Department of Defense contributes millions). As in the earlier works, private profit and state investment are combined, but here private medicalised profit has moved entirely out of state control.

Spectral finance and bleeding bodies: transfer horror and the secondary life of finance

As discussed in my Introduction, spectral and supernatural imagery has long been invoked to describe the workings of capital, and since then the later permutations of capitalism have continued to gather a highly Gothic lexicon.[54] Imagery of ghosts and supernatural creatures has gathered around finance's abstractions before Marx, as in Voltaire describing stock-market traders as vampiric, and the imagery has only intensified as commodities have taken increasingly abstract and virtual forms. Brian Jarvis observes:

> An increasing number of transactions take place in a 'shadow banking' system. Neoliberal deregulation has permitted the proliferation of a network of financial organizations and arcane instruments which operate outside national boundaries and are largely unmonitored: off-shore accounts, stealth investments, hedge funds ... The evolution of shadow banking and other forms of cyberfinance confirms Marx's affirmation that capital tends to become increasingly autonomous and to dematerialise (from hard currency, gold and silver standard, to paper and now digital money).[55]

In these anticipatory modes of finance, futurity itself becomes commoditised, abstracted, split, and resold. Lisa Adkins points out that in this new 'time of money', it is the *flow* of finance rather than direct wage labour that now creates the most profit.[56] These financial networks are hard to represent. Fredric Jameson suggests we need to find imagery for such 'a network of power and control too difficult for our minds and imaginations to grasp ... the whole new decentered global network of the third stage of capital'.[57] In this way, Steve Shaviro reads the supernatural giant humanoid monster-moths of China Miéville's *Perdido Street Station* as a nightmarish representation of the way capital's functioning has morphed into 'something absolutely inhuman and unrecognisable ... Cthulhu rather than ... *Dracula*'.[58] The texts of this present chapter do not try to represent such baffling systems, yet they may be read as dramatising the violence of commodity abstraction and the insatiability of capital expansion.

American transfer economies are, after all, deeply enmeshed in capitalist structures and financial futurity, not least in the way that biotechnological intervention and care delivery can occur within corporate frameworks influenced by shareholder logics. An additional example of creative capitalist thinking around transfer, though, is the idea of a 'futures market' in organs. The economist Henry Hansmann suggests that 'the right to harvest a person's organs upon death' could 'be purchased from him while still alive'.[59] Future rights could be sold and resold and Hansmann praises the invisible web of transactions that would ensue, insurance companies selling the 'futures' on to specialist companies. Futures markets are, of course, even more spectral than transactions of manufactured commodities. The texts in this chapter can be read not only as anxious but also as *speculative*, making visible the brutality concealed in the spectralising, deferred logics of neoliberal late capitalism. There is not much ghostly about these visceral visions of predatorial harvest.

Corporate transfer Gothic is not only confined to transactions in which human material becomes commodity, but includes work in which transfer becomes associated with finance's intricate secondary forms. Beyond the initial transaction of a sale, harvest horror may invoke mortgages, repossession, inherited debt, and futures trading. Richard Engling's novel *Default on a Body* (1989, rev. 2001), for example, imagines a society in which people sign 'Human Resource Loans' in which their own bodies become collateral for loans: 'each of the participants – banks, doctors, and collectors – covered the legality of their specific contribution, and there was no one left to prosecute'.[60] In Sheri Tepper's sf novel *Sideshow* (1992), unpaid debt is bequeathed, and debtors are obliged to pay with their own bodies if they have no other resources. At its extreme, all organs are sold except the brain and some nervous system tissue, disaggregated across multiple boxes.[61] Indebtedness and corporeal vulnerability also structure the horror musical *Repo! The Genetic Opera* (2008) which imagines a society in the grip of a private corporation, GeneCo.[62] Set in 2056, the film imagines a world in which an epidemic has led to widespread organ failures, and GeneCo offers replacements which it gruesomely repossesses if purchasers fall behind on hire purchase agreements.

The body horror in the latter texts is inextricably entangled with a secondary financial structure of capital: the credit agreement. Whilst these texts' movement into a horror register often accompanies the moment of surgical extraction, dread is, if anything, a more dominant element, in that these texts dwell on the implications that these financial frames have for those trapped within them. The intricate secondary forms of late capitalist finance have a narrative impetus. A mortgage must be paid, default may lead to repossession, inherited debts must be fulfilled, a factory must obtain raw materials with which to generate profit, and these demands work directly on these subjects' bodies. When protagonists are aware of these economic scripts, they are in the grip of a narrative crisis, desperate to avert a story that is being written by vast forces beyond them.

From another perspective, however, the shock and intensity of fictional representations of predatorial harvest may actually compromise their efficacy in refracted, deferred, or symbolic exploration of these issues. To explain this dynamic, I will draw on a strand within Donald Joralemon's cultural studies discussion of efforts to find a middle ground between legalising all tissue sale and purely altruistic models. Joralemon notes that part of the success of the so-called 'intermediary' models lay in the fact they had extreme models against which to be contrasted. Acceptability of these models of 'rewarded donation', he suggests, 'is in no small measure linked to the rhetorical claim of moderation made possible by the expression of far more extreme proposals'.[63] This insight also has relevance for any critics who might wish to read Gothic representations of organ commodification as intrinsically subversive of oppressive structures. Extreme fantasies of transfer Gothic can normalise less outrageous (but still highly problematic) scenes of organ predation, inflected in more subtle ways by the workings of capital.

In sum, then, the victims of this chapter's fantastic texts are harmed not by a single villain but by systems of erasure, tormented not only by the will of individuals but by the consequences of a particular blend of corporate and state medicalisation within particular political economies. Apprehensions around institutional processes are symbolically rendered through descriptions of the architectures of these sites. It can be argued that these texts render 'spectral economies' of late capitalist finance viscerally immediate, extrapolating how the intricate abstractions and choreographies of finance impact a commercialised human body, and, similarly, that these texts reflect on the insatiability of capital, the need for ever-expanding resources. These fictions are certainly 'anxious' in that they respond to dread over a milieu in which bodies were perceived to be increasingly vulnerable to being raided for organs due to medical and legal changes, but they are also speculative, in trying to represent and unmask economic processes. These texts imagine people in emergent webs of profit, those capitalist processes both overt and obscured.

Notes

1 W. Gaylin, 'Harvesting the dead', *Harper's* (September 1974), 23–9 (p. 26).
2 Ibid, p. 26.
3 G. Haggerty, *Gothic Fiction / Gothic Form* (University Park: Pennsylvania State University Press, 1989), p. 20; E. Sedgwick, *The Coherence of Gothic Conventions* (New York: Methuen, [1980] 1986), p. 38.

4 M. Foucault, *Birth of the Clinic* (London: Routledge, [1963] 1989); W. Bynum, *History of Medicine* (Oxford: Oxford University Press, 2008); R. Porter, *Madness* (Oxford: Oxford University Press, 2002); R. Luckhurst, *Corridors* (London: Reaction, 2019).

5 M. Willis, K. Waddington, and R. Marsden, 'Imaginary investments', *Journal of Literature and Science*, 6:1 (2013), 55–73; K. Waddington, 'Death at St Bernard's', *Journal of Victorian Culture*, 18:2 (2013), 246–62.

6 A. Frank, 'Generosity, care, and a narrative interest in pain', in D. Carr, J. Loeser, and D. Morris (eds), *Narrative, Pain, and Suffering* (Seattle: IASP, 2005), pp. 289–300 (p. 298).

7 A. Clarke, L. Mamo, J. Fishman, J. Shim, and J. Fosket, 'Biomedicalisation', *American Sociological Review*, 68 (2003), 161–94 (pp. 162n3, 166–7).

8 D. Hamilton, *A History of Organ Transplantation* (Pittsburgh, PA: University of Pittsburgh Press, 2012), pp. 169–70.

9 S. Lederer, *Flesh and Blood* (Oxford: Oxford University Press, 2008), p. 6.

10 B. Fantus, 'Cook County's Blood Bank', *Modern Hospital*, 50:21 (1938), 57–8.

11 Lederer, pp. 91–2.

12 Ibid, pp. 94ff., xii.

13 Ibid, p. 72.

14 Hamilton, p. 249.

15 H. Davidson, 'Transplantation in the brave new world', *Mental Hygiene*, 5 (1968), 467–8 (pp. 467–8).

16 Hamilton, p. 399.

17 C. Waldby and R. Mitchell, *Tissue Economies* (Durham, NC: Duke University Press, 2006); H. Zwart, 'The donor organ as "object *a*"', *Medicine, Health Care and Philosophy*, 17:4 (2014), 559–71 (p. 564); M. Cooper, *Life as Surplus* (Seattle: University of Washington Press, 2008).

18 Waldby and Mitchell, p. 22.

19 L. Sharp, *Strange Harvest* (Berkeley: University of California Press, 2006), pp. 13, 27.

20 S. Carney, *The Red Market* (New York: William Morrow, 2011), pp. 11–12.

21 Sharp, *Harvest*, p. 27.

22 S. Kaufman, *And a Time to Die* (Chicago: University of Chicago Press, 2005), p. 89.

23 World Medical Association, 'Declaration of Sydney on the determination of death and the recovery of organs', 22nd World Medical Assembly, Sydney, Australia (August 1968), www.wma.net/policies-post/wma-declaration-of-sydney-on-the-determination-of-death-and-the-recovery-of-organs/ [accessed 21 June 2019]; A. Manara, P. Murphy, and G. O'Callaghan, 'Donation after circulatory death', *British Journal of Anaesthesia*, 108 (2012), supplement 1, i108–i121 (p. 112).

24 A. Joffe, J. Carcillo, N. Anton, *et al.*, 'Donation after cardiocirculatory death', *Philosophy, Ethics, and Humanities in Medicine*, 6.1 (2011), 1–20 (p. 10); cf. C. Goodman, C. Worrall, U. Chong, S. Kallinis, and M. Rockwood, *The Organ Donation Breakthrough Collaborative* (Washington, DC: US Department of Health and Human Services, 2003), docplayer.net/5153165-The-organ-donation-break through-collaborative-best-practices-final-report.html [accessed 6 June 2018].

25 H. Chimowitz and R. Sade, 'Benefits and harms to organ donors', *The American Journal of Bioethics*, 15:8 (2015), 19–20.

26 J. Bion, P. Nightingale, and B. Taylor, 'Will the UK ever reach international levels of organ donation?', *British Journal of Anaesthesia*, 108 (2012), Supplement 1, i10–i13 (p. 11).

27 G. Agamben, *Homo Sacer*, trans. D. Heller-Roazen (Stanford: Stanford University Press, [1995] 1998).

28 T. Lemke, *Biopolitics* (New York: NYU Press, 2011), pp. 61–2.

29 M. Lock, *Twice Dead* (Berkeley: University of California Press, 2002). Neurological criteria for death – whole-brain death in the US, and brain-stem death in the UK – took time to be defined and codified into law, and significant national differences in conception and implementation continue to apply. See Chapter 1 for discussion.

30 'Growing shortage of organs worrying doctors', *New York Times* (5 December 1967), www.nytimes.com/1967/12/05/archives/growing-shortage-of-organs-worrying-doctors-heart-transplant.html [accessed 13 August 2018].

31 *Night of the Living Dead*, dir. by G. Romero (Image Ten, 1968).

32 R. Luckhurst, 'Biomedical horror', in J. Edwards (ed.), *Technologies of the Gothic in Literature and Culture* (London: Routledge, 2015), pp. 84–98 (p. 91).

33 R. Cook, *Coma* (Boston, MA: Little Brown, 1977). Further references are in parenthesis.

34 C. Belling, 'The living dead', *Perspectives in Biology and Medicine*, 53:3 (2010), 439–51 (p. 448).

35 *Coma*, dir. by M. Crichton (Metro Goldwyn-Mayer, 1978); *Coma*, dir. by M. Salomon (A&E TV mini-series, 3–4 September 2012).

36 Belling.

37 Belling, p. 443.

38 'ICU', *Webster's New World Medical Dictionary*, 3rd edn (Boston, MA: Houghton Mifflin, 2008), online [accessed 29 June 2019].

39 K. Marshall, *Corridor* (Minneapolis: University of Minnesota Press, 2013).

40 Luckhurst, *Corridors*, p. 274.

41 *Parts: The Clonus Horror*, dir. by R. Fiveson (Group 1 International Distribution Organization, 1979). *Parts* was preceded by other 1970s works envisioning a remote warehouse of unwilling living donors. John Boyd's novel *The Organ Bank Farm* (1970), for example, imagines a farm where people who were autistic or otherwise neurodivergent were incarcerated for harvest. J. Boyd, *The Organ Bank Farm* (New York: Bantam, [1970] 1972).

42 J. Hejinian, *Extreme Remedies* (New York: Harper Collins, 1974). Subsequent references are in parenthesis.

43 D. Etchison, 'The dead line', 'Calling all monsters', and 'The machine demands a sacrifice', in *The Dark Country* (New York: Berkley, [1982] 1984), pp. 99–110, 93–8, 81–92. Subsequent references are in parenthesis in the text. For Campbell's comment, see R. Campbell, 'Introduction', in D. Etchison, *The Dark Country* (New York: Berkley, [1982] 1984), pp. xi–xii (p. xii).

44 J. Kristeva, *Powers of Horror*, trans. L. Roudiez (New York: Columbia University Press, [1980] 1982), p. 4.

45 Ibid, pp. 3–4.
46 Campbell, p. xii.
47 S. Kanar, *The J Factor* (New York: Bantam, 2000).
48 Luckhurst, 'Biomedical horror', p. 93.
49 S. Wasson, 'Love in the time of cloning', *Extrapolation*, 45:2 (2004), 130–44.
50 G. Egan, 'The extra', in J. Dann and G. Dozois (eds), *Clones* (New York: Ace, [1990] 1998), pp. 55–73.
51 M.M. Smith, *Spares* (London: Harper Collins, [1996] 1998), p. 45. Subsequent references in parenthesis.
52 Mercy for Animals, 'Extreme confinement and abuse' (2019), mercyforanimals. org/the-problem [accessed 1 July 2019].
53 *The Island*, dir. by M. Bay (Dreamworks, 2005).
54 K. Marx, *Capital*, vol. 1 (London: Penguin [1976] 1990); S. Shapiro, 'Transvaal, Transylvania', *Gothic Studies*, 10:1 (2008), 29–47 (pp. 30, 44n2); S. Shapiro, 'Material Gothic', *Gothic Studies*, 10:1 (2008), 1–3; H. Giroux, *Zombie Politics and Culture in the Age of Casino Capitalism* (New York: Peter Lang, 2011); D. McNally, *Monsters of the Market* (Brill: Leiden, 2011).
55 B. Jarvis, 'Fall of the hou$e of finance', in B. Cherry, P. Howell, and C. Riddell (eds), *Twenty-First Century Gothic* (Cambridge: Cambridge Scholars' Publishing, 2010), pp. 19–38 (p. 21).
56 L. Adkins, *The Time of Money* (Stanford: Stanford University Press, 2018).
57 F. Jameson, 'Postmodernism, or the cultural logic of late capitalism', *New Left Review*, 146 (1984), 53–92 (pp. 79–80).
58 S. Shaviro, 'Capitalist monsters', *Historical Materialism*, 10:4 (2002), 281–90 (p. 285).
59 H. Hansmann, 'The economics and ethics of markets for human organs', in J. Blumstein and A. Sloan (eds), *Organ Transplantation Policy* (Durham, NC: Duke University Press, 1989), pp. 57–85 (p. 62).
60 R. Engling, *Body Mortgage* (New York: Penguin, 2001), p. 9.
61 S. Tepper, *Sideshow* (Gollancz, [1988] 1992]). In a transhumanist vein, some characters actively choose the transformation to leave organic bodies behind.
62 *Repo! The Genetic Opera*, dir. by D. Bousman (Twisted Pictures, 2008).
63 D. Joralemon, 'Organ wars', *Medical Anthropology Quarterly*, 9:3 (1995), 335–56 (p. 346).

3

Clinical labour and slow violence: transnational harvest horror and racial vulnerability at the turn of the millennium

According to legend, in the sixth century CE Saints Cosmas and Damien miraculously replaced the diseased leg of a white Christian man with the leg of an Ethiopian man, recently deceased. In medieval and Renaissance art the latter man is usually a mystery. Mark Alice Durant says, 'While the biographical record of Cosmas and Damian has been preserved and embellished over the centuries ... nothing ... is known of the life of the Ethiopian ... He is a shadow, a dark mirror to reflect the European imagination.'[1] In one fourteenth-century depiction of this surgery, for example, the cadaver is in a box to one side, featureless and undistinguished, while in others the dead body is discarded on the floor, or absent entirely. In a 1547 carving by Isidre Villoldo, however, the Ethiopian man is alive, his face contorted, reaching for the stump where his leg should be (Figure 6).

The cultural work these images performed at the time differs from meanings viewers may find in them today. The legend would have been understood as illustrating core Christian doctrinal positions such as the resurrection of the body, and a willingness to sacrifice the flesh for salvation, and the images are often surrounded by depictions of Cosmas and Damian themselves dismembered in martyrdom.[2] I invoke these images here, however, in the spirit of conscious anachronism. Looking at it specifically from today and for today, this image captures a horror which may be oddly invisible. Today, too, a language of miracle gathers around transfer, but inequalities characterise donor pools and access to transplant. These inequalities are part of the long legacy of colonial, settler, and chattel slavery, tragedies far from finished. Capitalism has always been a world system, its local manifestations resting on the labour and suffering of Black and Indigenous People of Colour elsewhere in nations and across the globe and these exploitations were interconnected.[3] This chapter considers texts set in India, the UK, and North America, each of which engages with inequalities around transfer access and vulnerability to procurement, informed by legacies of colonisation and chattel slavery. Read at a figural level, these texts also symbolise systematic exclusions, structural violence, and slow violence, as Rob Nixon defines it, violence in which time itself is a force of ruination.[4]

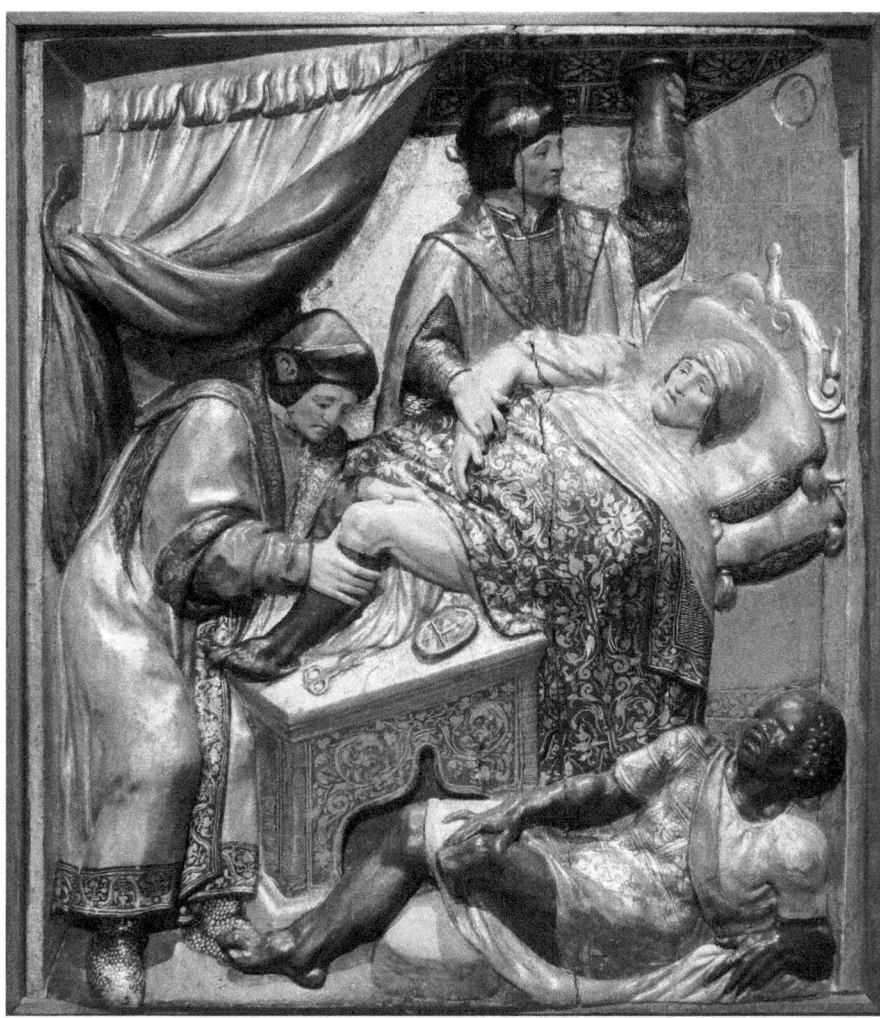

Figure 6 Isidro de Villoldo, *Milagro de San Cosme y San Damián* (c. 1547), © Museo Nacional de Escultura, Valladolid. Photo: Javier Muñoz y Paz Pastor CE0362.

'How does one mourn the interminable event?' asks Christina Sharpe in her passionate lamentation of the ongoing legacies of Atlantic chattel slavery.[5] I am concerned with 'economies of abandonment', in Elizabeth Povinelli's phrase, in which the wellbeing of some is predicated on the suffering of others, and a 'necropolitics' in Achille Mbembe's terms, where some are sentenced to 'new and unique forms of social existence in which vast populations are subjected to conditions of life conferring upon them the status of living dead'.[6] The texts of this chapter explore how certain bodies are still not represented at moments where they need to be, marginalised within healthcare environments in ways both overt and subtle.

As described in my Introduction, this book resists the assumption that exploitative transfer should be understood only as occurring in non-Western locales. There is substantial Western media enthusiasm for the kinds of stories that Lawrence Cohen has called 'Villavakkam gothic', stories of exploitative organ purchase in India, purchase which reached such a pitch that some villages earned the grim sobriquet *Villavakkam* ('kidney village').[7] Yet this media appetite is not always matched by attention to transfer-related inequalities within, for example, the UK and the US. Media coverage is also less attentive to the way in which many lives are rendered unequally precarious in other ways. This chapter considers fantasies not only of transfer across national lines but also of intra-national transfer as represented in imaginative work from India, the UK, and North America at the turn of the millennium, specifically work which represents societies as preying on people marked out as racially 'other' from a dominant group. The texts of all three settings are informed by the legacies of colonialism, extractive trade, and slavery.

In line with Glennis Byron's conception of the globalgothic, in these texts strategies of gothic representation are 'globalised – reproduced, consumed, recycled', even while globalisation's processes themselves are 'gothicked – made monstrous, spectral, vampiric'.[8] Ciara Kierans and Jessie Cooper warn, 'transplant medicine has served to underwrite privilege and power by exposing already marginalised populations to new forms of biotechnical intervention'.[9] Critics have observed that transnational trade in human organs literalises Gothic narratives of dismemberment and vivisection.[10] Film and urban legend can invert this trajectory: the Brazilian film *Turistas* (2006) makes young white tourists victims of an organ-theft ring motivated by vengeance for American medical and sex tourism, and an urban myth from the 1990s imagined an American businessman falling prey to kidney theft while travelling.[11] Such fantasies defensively invert real trends in the flow of organs and tissue, the neocolonial predation of transnational trafficking.[12]

Frameworks of neocolonial periphery-to-centre flow must, however, be complemented with attention to intra-national flows and diasporic dimensions of transfer, both in organ trafficking and in transplant tourism. Transfer inequalities involve permutations of debatable 'voluntarity', economic pressures, and healthcare marginalisation, all within environments of long-term structural ruination, ambiguous agencies, and predatorial entities both local and global. Critics (including myself) have already explored such texts as offering a hallucinatory mimesis of surgical catastrophe.[13] Deepening that reading, this chapter examines additional work that may be achieved with *registers* of horror. Specifically, I suggest that a shift into tropes and forms characteristic of gothic, horror, and dystopian science fiction can help to represent extended temporalities in two ways: slow violence on a systemic scale, as well as an unwilling supplier's *durée* in the aftermath of procurement. I am concerned with the prolonged enduring of vulnerability in time, within neoliberal and necropolitical frameworks of clinical labour. In many cases, suppliers in these precarious conditions are selling not just tissue but a wounding that endures over *time* – the extended duration of (non)recovery, and even, sometimes, a permanent wounding of their worlds.

Whilst forced organ procurement may sound fantastical, many local oral narratives imagine children and other vulnerable people preyed on for organs. The United Nations' Bellagio task force found that 'these stories of violations to bodily integrity are ... "metaphorically true, operating by means of symbolic substitutions"', conveying threats to the 'bodily integrity of the poor'.[14] The local narratives – and these fictions – work on symbolic levels to dramatise how certain populations are precarious or rendered 'ungrievable' within dehumanising public imaginaries.[15] However, I am not only reading these fictions symbolically. I am wary of the danger of 'narrative prosthesis', reading particular bodies as symbolic of generalised states and in the process erasing specificity of subjects so embodied.[16] Fictions of exploitative sale may also echo very real inequalities and vulnerabilities within transfer process, certain groups having unequal access to transplant and/or being disproportionately subject to harvest. The very metaphor of 'harvest' risks dehumanising donors and implying that the surgical procurement is a natural and destined reaping (see Chapter 5). Here, I use it deliberately to emphasise the horror of that very dehumanisation.

I will analyse imaginative representations of predatorial harvest within three turn-of-the-millennium contexts: India, Britain, and North America. These sites' transfer economies differ, but each text engages a supplier's pre- and post-surgical *durée*, and communicate structural and slow violence. In each case I wish to complicate exoticising stories of dysfunctional transfer economies as wholly distant from American or European contexts.

'Intricate crimes': predatorial harvest and victim agency

Effective immunosuppression transformed tissue mobilities on a global scale. Cyclosporine was approved for non-experimental use in humans in multiple countries during the 1980s. Since it overcame major incompatibilities it opened the way to large-scale unrelated living donation, initially for kidneys but later for other paired organs or lobes. Cohen observes, 'Cyclosporine *globalizes*, creating myriad biopolitical fields where donor populations are differentially and flexibly materialized', and the routes in which such tissue was mobilised were well-grooved.[17] Nancy Scheper-Hughes observes, 'The global traffic in organs follows the modern routes of capital and labour flows, and conforms to the usual lines of social and economic cleavage. *In general*, the organs flow from South to North, from poor to rich, from black and brown to white, and from female to male bodies.'[18] Biomedical industries more widely, too, are inflected by past structures of violence and other legacies of marginalisation, reproducing and exacerbating existing structures of health inequality.[19] Ethnographic studies trace intricate networks of pressure within local and particular milieux of transfer, intra-national processes and flows, diasporic dimensions of tissue mobilities, organ trafficking, and transplant tourism.[20]

Melinda Cooper and Catherine Waldby coin the term 'clinical labor' to describe situations in which bodies are incorporated into biomedical industry, such as some forms of organ or tissue sale or pharmaceutical experimentation. 'Clinical labour' is by definition of asymmetrical benefit to corporation and subject, bioindustrial organisations profiting while the subject's wellbeing is risked or harmed. Extended temporalities are central to the violence endemic in these asymmetrical structures, in that 'much clinical labour consists precisely in the *endurance of risk* and exposure to non-predictable experimental effects that may be actively harmful, rather than therapeutic'.[21] As Charis Thompson observes, 'the biotech mode of (re)production does not alienate one's labour from one's person so much as alienate one's body from one's person'.[22] Clinical labour can echo economic, political, social, and environmental asymmetries.

The question of who owns tissue can be hotly contested, as seen in the case of *John Moore* v *Regents of the University of California* (1990).[23] Moore fought to have rights recognised to his cancer cell tissue that had been developed into a profitable immortal cell line. When it comes to transplantation, almost every country in the world has laws against selling solid organs (with the notable exception of Iran), and multiple international resolutions and guidelines condemn such transactions, including The Council of Europe Convention on Human Rights and Biomedicine (1997) and the Declaration of Istanbul (2008), at which representatives from multiple nations established guidelines to reduce the risk of exploitative organ markets.[24] Yet sale continues, either illegally or in ways that incorporate illegally acquired material into ostensibly legally compliant transfer. As mentioned in my Introduction, I use the terms 'harvestee' or 'supplier' rather than seller, since, as Martin Gunnarson and Susanna Lundin note, suppliers may not actually receive promised payment, and the ideologically charged term 'seller' implies both a certain agency and a product separate from a self.[25]

Arguments have been made in favour of a market in human organs.[26] Janet Radcliffe-Richards, for example, argues that 'There are probably millions of people in the world who would be better off for a properly conducted, properly rewarded, properly followed-up kidney sale', and she suggests that some people in America during the sub-prime mortgage crisis might have been eager to sell a kidney to retain their house.[27] Such framings reinforce the neoliberal virtue that people should take responsibility for their own security. Valorisation of self-reliance also characterises defences of buyers as righteous and suppliers as in economic straits due only to poor life choices.[28] Justifications can draw on the dangerous binary of 'agent not victim', to use Gudrun Dahl's term, in which 'victimhood and agency are made each other's opposites', so that 'any presence of agency can disqualify a person from victim status', but organ trades can be 'intricate crimes' in which agency and victimhood are not exclusive.[29] Every instance of organ sale occurs within webs of social and economic force, often longstanding. The agent-not-victim binary is central to neoliberal efforts to normalise exploitative harvest. Radcliffe-Richards unwittingly illustrates the influence of the binary when she says, 'sellers themselves are usually willing, even eager, participants in the exchange. No doubt they are encouraged and often misled by enterprising brokers, *but* we know that there are many who actively volunteer, and seek out the opportunity.'[30] The compound conjunction 'but' sets those who 'actively volunteer' in a different category from those who are misled. Here victimhood and agency are implied to be somehow incompatible, yet the degree to which such choice might be 'free' under severe economic pressure has been brought into question by the United Nations Bellagio Task Force and others, as previously discussed.[31]

Neoliberal justifications for legalising organ trade also typically fail to take account of the way that supplying organs often permanently damages impoverished suppliers physically, emotionally, and interpersonally. Evidence to date indicates that free markets exacerbate the radical corporeal vulnerability of impoverished and marginalised organ and tissue suppliers.[32] Furthermore, the very presence of a market changes dynamics. For example, Cohen describes how, when illegal organ brokers became active in an impoverished part of Chennai, moneylenders became more aggressive in demanding repayment of debts since households now had an additional way of raising those funds.[33] Ethnography, with its attention to idiosyncratic details of particular phenomena in a demarcated space and time, can engage these kinds of subtlety. As Veena Das says, 'What anthropologists can offer to bioethics is the means for overcoming the seductions of a highly abstract contrast theory because it can be shown that what appears ethical at the level of an abstract discourse can be productive of violence at the levels of local communities'.[34] Without implying that ethnography can give unmediated access to direct experience, a core value of ethnographic work on organ and tissue sale is, as Cohen says, the 'refusal to allow us any remove from the bodies and lives of poor donors and sellers'.[35]

Literary scholars, too, can strive to notice how imaginative texts challenge agent-not-victim simplicities. Writing in a Gothic mode – invoking confinement, corporeal vulnerability, and strange temporalities – may render vivid a complex *durée*, unpacking some of the affective and systemic subtleties of particular instantiations of tissue mobility.

'Slow violence' and 'machines of social death': horror representations of a durative present

Describing lacunae attendant on neoliberalism, Elizabeth Povinelli identifies three habits of thought that normalise its violence: focusing on the tense of 'future anterior' that elides present and near-future suffering; noticing catastrophic violence at the expense of ongoing hidden violence in the present; and accepting that the welfare of some is inextricably dependent on the suffering of others.[36] Povinelli calls instead for attention to dispersed, protracted violence of quasi-events, neither spectacular nor ever quite completed, and to represent these horrors in terms of a *durative present*. Povinelli's work chimes with a profusion of recent scholarship on the affective dimensions of dispersed and gradual violence. Nixon's formulation of 'slow violence', for example, describes environmental, social, and structural suffering wrought over time by decisions both distant and local, 'occur[ing] gradually and out of sight … an attritional violence that is typically not viewed as violence at all'.[37]

One of the most diabolical products of systems is the naturalisation of exclusion, making the violence seem common sense. In the face of such erasure, a core challenge is to represent the exclusion – both its processes and the experience. Nixon asks, 'In an age when the media venerate the spectacular … how can we convert into image and narrative the disasters that are slow moving and long in the making?'[38] and Povinelli asks, 'How do scholars find the right distance or the right scale from which to sketch the "slow rhythms" of this lethal violence?'[39] Critics analysing such subtle deathwork have repeatedly had to have recourse to representational innovation. Biehl, for example, reluctantly develops the idea of the ex-human, to convey a lacerated state of being, yet he is wary of this coinage, since the term 'might generate a distance and thus unintentionally participate in discursive regimes that ultimately miss the paradoxes and dynamism involved in letting the Other die … A human form of life that is no longer worth living is not just bare life—language and desire continue.'[40] To counter such abstraction, Biehl and Povinelli create new forms of ethnography.[41] Whilst less formally innovative than those ethnographic strategies, horror, gothic, and speculative fiction may be vivid, affective, and effective in imagining transfer predation and the systems that could support it, and eliciting visceral responses from readers or viewers. These cultural artefacts may help to imagine a durative present of horror, its spaces of exclusion, hidden logics, and the agonies of its subjects, even if the representations are inevitably incomplete and partial.

'To mourn you piece by piece': Manjula Padmanabhan's *Harvest* and turn-of-the-millennium Indian tissue economies

Manjula Padmanabhan's play *Harvest* (1997) has a complex transnational provenance.[42] Written as the winning entry for an international competition hosted in Greece in 1997, the play was performed in Athens in 1999 and then in India, Canada, the US, Australia, and the UK, adapted to radio in the UK, translated into German, and adapted to screen in Hindi.[43] The play's representation of the aftermath of predation can be read as an indictment of millennial markets of clinical labour on the Indian subcontinent, in which bioindustry profits while subjects are risked through organ and tissue sale, pharmaceutical experimentation, or surrogacy.[44] I will consider how the play represents not only the violation of economically coerced surgery but also the extended duration of preoperative and postsurgical time.

The 1990s saw Indian exposés of trafficking in kidneys, liver lobes, and corneas from living suppliers.[45] Multiple sites earned the grim sobriquet *Villavakkam* (kidney village), and the demographics of donor pools varied, as I will shortly discuss. Most beneficiaries were wealthy foreign purchasers, although there was (and is) also significant domestic need, due to scarcity of dialysis units.[46] In 1994, Parliament passed the Transplantation of Human Organs Act (THOA) which decreed that living donors must be near-relatives of recipients. THOA applies to central territories, and other states followed with their own versions.[47] Authorisation Committees rapidly developed a norm of approving petitions for exception to close relatedness, but, provided the appearance of relatedness is performed, organ and tissue sale still flourishes. Thus in practice, as Lawrence Cohen observes, the laws 'had the effect of limiting foreign consumption of the poor's organs while increasing wealthy domestic and diasporic consumption'.[48] In the light of these shifts, Monir Moniruzzaman warns that 'Domestic organ trade, which perhaps comprises the majority of organs being trafficked worldwide, also ought to be examined in depth, as opposed to [only] global organ trafficking'.[49] This broadening of scrutiny is far from alleviating Western powers from responsibility, however: the domestic and diasporic tissue economies that have emerged continue to be marked by legacies of earlier exploitation, as well as shaped by economic inequalities ensuing from multinational pharmaceutical corporations' search for profit, and foreign investment in private hospitals that profit from transplants. Corporate profit imperatives are also at play in other ways in this national milieu. As in the US, transplantation signifies 'marketable modernity', the reputational value of a new transplant ward enhancing other streams of medical profitability.[50] Sales continue.[51]

Contemporaneously with Padmanabhan's writing of *Harvest*, some transplant surgeons silenced queries about donor welfare by quoting neoliberal philosophy.[52] Yet whilst research in the West has consistently indicated no long-term damage to living kidney donors from their donation, within these contexts the sale of a kidney overwhelmingly tends to increase financial vulnerability by permanently diminishing health, earning capacity, and mental and social wellbeing. Ethnographic research in turn-of-the-millennium Chennai found that household debt was almost always the primary motivator for selling a kidney, debts gleaned from paying for food, rent, medical expenses, and the money earned was typically spent on repaying debts and buying more food and clothing.[53] In addition to the sale's money being quickly used up for necessities, the surgery reduced earning capacity and it did not recover with passage of time.[54] Ethnographic research in other South Asian contexts has also yielded evidence of psychological suffering and social stigma.[55]

Set in the future in 2010, fifteen years after the time of writing, Padmanabhan's play sets the entirety of its action in a humble urban apartment. It is home to Om, a young man; his wife Jaya, Om's mother 'Ma', and sometimes Om's brother Jeetu, with whom Jaya is having a clandestine affair. The household is in crisis, Om struggling to find employment after losing his post as a clerk. He signs up with InterPlanta, an intermediary that matches wealthy organ buyers from distant countries with people from 'Donor World' willing to sell their organs. 'Donors' and their families are monitored by the purchaser through a 'contact module' installed in their home, and are confined and controlled, with even their food being regulated.

The purchaser initially seems to be a young American woman, Ginni. Over the course of months, Om and his mother grow accustomed to Ginni's surveillance and internalise some of her values, but Jaya and Jeetu remain unpersuaded. Finally, guards come to take Om, but take Jeetu instead, and when he returns his eyes have been replaced with a prosthesis which he experiences as torture. Ginni reappears on the contact module and demonstrates that she can transmit images directly to his mind, and he agrees to go with her for further harvests to escape the torture device. After he leaves, the bizarre InterPlanta strategy is fully revealed. 'Ginni' is actually 'Virgil', an elderly American man. He explains to Jaya that InterPlanta seeks out young couples to raid the men for organs and ultimately to occupy his entire body, and then use the women for reproduction: 'We look for young men's bodies to live in and young women's bodies in which to sow their children' (p. 86).

It is useful to contextualise Padmanabhan's play in terms of other stories of transplantation foregrounded in India in the 1990s and turn of the millennium, particularly in media reports and cinema. Whilst exposés of 'organ bazaars' were scandalous, media coverage celebrated transplantation surgical success within a framework of national pride, the medical advances presented as underscoring India's modernity. Veena Das has shown, for example, that, although the nation's first heart transplant was full of ambivalence for the donor kin, media coverage elided that complexity.[56] Cinema of the 1990s also uses transplantation plots to celebrate Indian nationhood and communities, and particularly to valorise 'the familial order of giving eroded by selfish Western modernity'.[57] Padmanabhan's play contrasts with both these discourses.

Padmanabhan's play engages gender in ways that both echo and deviate from the gendering at play in the turn-of-the-millennium Indian markets on which it indirectly comments. Women were predominant in supplier pools in Chennai and men predominant in rural Tamil Nadu.[58] The play modifies the urban paradigm, with the intended 'supplier' being the male breadwinner. As such, the play engages rhetorics of impaired masculinity that circulate around nephrectomy. In his work with men in both north and south India, Cohen finds a recurring tension between a fantasy of selling a kidney and in the process regaining a masculine power to enrich a household and enable marriages, versus a masculine anxiety around a symbolic equation of nephrectomy and castration. Research in the 1990s with female suppliers in Chennai, too, consistently found that the aftermath of kidney sale was seen as more gravely affecting men's ability to work than women's.[59] In other words, selling a kidney simultaneously bolsters certain forms of imagined 'masculine' power, and diminishes it. Likewise, the play shows a tension between Om's authority as a breadwinner and his being the prospective supplier. All the characters assume that it is men who are needed for work, rather than women, and Om's mother also assumes that all the employers are men, and is surprised at the notion of a male worker based at home whose task it is to wait and care for his body in the service of another: Om's work is seen as feminised. Whilst the play's fantasy of suppliers being contained and monitored is fantastical, it has points of connection with elements of some gestational surrogacy practice or pharmaceutical experimentation.[60]

Applicants to InterPlanta are treated like raw material in a factory. Six thousand men strip naked, stand on conveyer belts and submit to machines that wash them and take blood samples: 'the line went on and on … slanting up, forever. All in iron bars and grilles. It was like being in a cage shaped like a tunnel … Ahead of me a man screams and cries, but we're in separate little cages now' (pp. 11–12). This mistreatment is presented as a blend of neocolonial exploitation and local complicity. Sujatha Moni describes the way that 'the "Indian" and "American" worlds are initially depicted through a discourse of binary division … precisely in order to reveal the effect of their deconstruction as the play progresses'.[61] The binary is complicated by the ultimate merging of Virgil and Jeetu, and by the way the guards and InterPlanta agents are presented as occupying transitional positions between 'DonorWorld' and recipients. The localisation of threat does not erase power imbalance, but makes it even more insidious, a coercive web of economic and social pressures.

A strand of commentary on the play praises Jaya for choosing to die rather than become an unwilling gestational surrogate. In this strand of criticism, other characters may be condemned for 'corruption and decay', while Jaya is celebrated for her resistance: 'Jaya is the first and only character in the play who can distinguish between … the illusion of freedom as easy and without cost, and true freedom bought with pain and risk'.[62] On the other hand, Om chose to enter an organ supply contract not solely in order to gain consumer delights but also to sustain the household's basic needs, and Jeetu did not choose to have his eyes removed and is legitimately in deep distress at the nonconsensually implanted prosthesis, that distress underpinning his agreement to undergo further harvest. Rather than see the play's message in terms of individual characters' moral choices and the nobility of self-annihilation, I am interested in the ways the play as a whole conveys a durative present for supplier and kin, in both the presurgical period and its aftermath.

Jaya describes Om's impending surgery with stark imagery:

> He's sold the rights to his organs. His skin. His eyes. His arse. Sold them! … What's the meaning of this nightmare! (*To Om*) How can I hold your hand, touch your face, knowing that at any moment it might be snatched away from me and flung across the globe! If you were dead I could shave my head and break my bangles – but this? To be a widow by slow degrees? To mourn you piece by piece? Should I shave half my head? Break my bangles one at a time? (p. 21)

Invoking traditional high-caste mourning rituals, Jaya conveys the horror of gradual dismemberment in clinical labour as well as the emotional endurance of both supplier and loved ones, the strain of living in the knowledge of imminent wounding. The play also dramatises tension that may be felt prior to surgery. Two scenes show Om fearing that people knocking at the door are guards come to take him for surgical extraction: 'Om (*looking suddenly grey*) You're right – it could be the guards!' (p. 49). Dread is made palpable with relentless, repetitive knocking and Om's visibly crumbling resolve. 'How could I have done this to myself?' (p. 51). He sinks to the floor, tries to hide in the refrigerator, curls into a foetal position (p. 53).

The play explores other emotions of the preoperative period in addition to anticipatory mourning. Om is conscious of stigma attached to the sale and urges secrecy, and these appeals resonate with the plight of other organ suppliers recorded in ethnographic research.[63] In a further hideous twist to the burden of preoperative endurance, the play shows particular emotions becoming mandatory. Ginni requires that all members of the family perform happiness in order to keep Om's organs in peak condition. Mispronouncing his name as a marker of her indifference, she declares, 'The Most Important Thing is to keep *Auwm* smiling. Coz [*sic*] if Auwm's smiling, it means his body's smiling and if his body's smiling, it means his organs are smiling. And that's the kind of organs that'll survive a transplant best – smiling organs' (p. 38). Arlie Hochschild has coined the term 'emotional labor' to describe remuneration for performing emotion, and here that labour is especially chilling since the required emotion is so grotesquely at odds with what is felt.[64] In a range of ways, then, the play represents the preoperative period, too, as painful emotional effort unfolding in time.

The fraught postsurgical duration, too, is conveyed in arresting terms. Jeetu's eyes have been taken and in their stead he received unwanted electronic implants. He tells Jaya:

> I'm in a place worse than death ... A bleached and pitted place. Scars and slashes against infinite blackness ... You're just a bunch of bright white lines, no nose, no eyes, no head, no skin. When you open your mouth to speak I see a gaping black hole ... Everywhere else, it's just a shapeless sparkling madness. And I can't turn any of it off, I can't blink. I can't sleep, I can't even cry. (pp. 66–7)

This scene is problematic in presenting a disability or impairment as necessarily a torment, yet the horror of the scene hinges less on the impairment and rather on the nonconsensual prosthetic cybernetic augmentation. This science-fiction image communicates the ongoing passage of time, every second an agony, a hallucinatory and fantastic description of postsurgical suffering to be endured minute to minute – daily life rendered permanently strange.

That pre- and postsurgical experience is also evoked in a haunting promotional image for a recent theatrical production of *Harvest*, a 2018 University of Texas at Dallas production directed by Shelby Hibbs. Designed by Taylor Guest, this poster represents the play with an image combining an extracted heart and a dwelling (Figure 7). The image communicates that it is not only the body that is severed in surgery but also the subtle intricacies of subsequent life – the relationships that play out within the domestic sphere, the workings of the everyday. The home is as mutilated as the heart. The play captures something of that prolonged enduring of both precursor time and aftermath. This violence is slow, and it is hard to see. Transfer economies may indeed be about mourning, piece by piece.

'Humanity is thrown away': Stephen Frears's *Dirty Pretty Things*

This chapter opened by challenging the tendency in media and academic discussion to present transfer predation as a function only of non-Western locales. The UK, North America, and European contexts, too, are deeply implicated in these tissue flows, not least through transplant tourism *to* other countries.[65] Rather than discuss transplant tourism, however – which again locates the predation fundamentally *elsewhere* than the recipient's home site – I will use the remainder of this chapter to problematise the distancing move that defensively situates predation as occurring elsewhere. I will examine North American and UK harvest horror, inflected by the transgenerational legacies of colonialism and slavery. As in Padmanabhan's play, these creative works present organ

Figure 7 Poster for *Harvest*, dir. by Shelby Hibbs. Designed by Taylor Guest. University of Texas at Dallas Theatrical Production, 2018. © Taylor Guest.

predation as hallucinatory mimesis, symbolic of wider structural oppression and slow violence in which Black and Indigenous People of Colour may be disproportionately precarious.

The primary protagonist of Stephen Frears's film *Dirty Pretty Things* (2002) is Okwe, a doctor who has immigrated to the UK from Nigeria as a result of political persecution.[66] He works as a minicab driver and a hotel nightman, and becomes friends with Senay, a Turkish woman seeking asylum. Okwe sees a human heart in a toilet, finds a man weeping with pain after a nephrectomy, and discovers that the hotel manager Juan pressures desperate immigrants into kidney sale. Senay herself agrees to sell a kidney in the hopes of a passport and visa to America, and Okwe warns her, 'Because you are poor you will be gutted like an animal ... They will take what they want and leave the rest to rot.'

Juan justifies his trade disingenuously: 'I sell the kidney for $10,000 so I'm happy. The person who needs the kidney gets cured so he's happy. The person who sold his kidney gets to stay in this beautiful country so he's happy. My whole business is based on happiness.' His language here echoes that of the real-life black-market organ broker who said, '"Think of me as a new version of the old-fashioned marriage broker. I locate and match up people in need".'[67] Both justifications ignore potential long-term effects of nephrectomy in contexts of cursory aftercare.

Human tissue sale has been illegal in the UK since the 1832 Anatomy Act which constrains the circumstances under which corpses could be sold and the uses to which they could be put. (The 1832 Anatomy Act was superseded by the Anatomy Act of 1984 and the Human Tissue Act in 2004.) That said, there have been controversial cases. In 1985, for example, a private London clinic was enmeshed in scandal when it was revealed that wealthy clients had travelled from India to London for transplantation, bringing impoverished unrelated donors with them for procurement and transplantation surgery at the UK clinic.[68] There continues to be a risk of such procedures, masked as altruistic donation.[69] Arenas other than transplantation, too, have seen controversies over uses of tissue, notably the scandal of Alder Hey Children's Hospital. In 1999 this hospital in Liverpool was found to have taken tissues and organs from dead children without parental knowledge, selling some to pharmaceutical companies to underpin development of profitable drugs.[70] In various ways, the thriller plot of Frears's film can be read as commenting on a range of fraught forms of corporeal profitability.

The film also, however, uses predatorial harvest as a symbol of other kinds of physical and emotional exploitation operating on transnational scales within the UK. Numerous scenes present characters, documented or undocumented, in vulnerable positions, their labour underpinning wealth-creation for others while their own bodies and minds are at terrible risk, and these inequalities are deeply informed by transnational cruelties. London is a 'post-imperial' city, in

Jane Jacobs's terms, a metropolis shot through with traces of its imperial past, both in its 'grand monuments' and in the way that imperialist 'operations and ideologies ... shaped urban spaces of deprivation'.[71] *Dirty Pretty Things* does not describe a neat trajectory of migration from ex-colonies to the once-imperial centre, but rather responds to, as Laila Amine says, the way that 'people living in large British cities increasingly come from countries whose histories do not necessarily intersect with Britain's [colonial history]'.[72] Britain continues to be shaped by processes which Ann Laura Stoler has called 'imperial debris', in which 'imperial formations persist in their material debris, in ruined landscapes and through the social ruination of people's lives', and these legacies inform the power asymmetries that characterise the interactions between the film's charac- ters and the wealthier people they serve.[73] This asymmetry is drawn sharply in the line of dialogue that gives the film its name. Juan declares: '*Strangers* come to hotels to do *dirty* things. In the morning it's our job to *make things pretty again.*'

Throughout the film, sexual violation becomes a metonym for forms of cor- poreal exploitation that can ensue from these asymmetries. Emily Davis notes that 'Nearly every character in the film is under threat of penetration' including Okwe, who kneels before his manager's penis at the minicab firm (examining him for STDs, but the scene initially frames it for the viewer to expect fellatio), and Senay (forced to fellate her boss at the illegal sweatshop, and later coerced into having sex with Juan).[74] For characters to reach a place where they can be safe from violence and sexual exploitation they need certain kinds of capital, and its possession is precarious. Even when legally resident, characters remain vulnerable. Those seeking asylum are especially at risk. Frears explains, 'people granted asylum are given money, but they're not given enough to live on, so ... they ... take jobs illegally. They're immediately open to being exploited in sweatshops and hotels and places like that.'[75] As Okwe's friend Guo Yi says, without legal status 'you have nothing, you are nothing'. The screenplay writer Steve Knight recalls, 'I thought the idea of a human heart in the toilet would be emblematic of the fact that a lot of people with talent who happen to migrate are wasted – their humanity is thrown away'.[76] Citizenship does not neutralise these asymmetries. Juliette, a Black British citizen, is triply marginalised due to her ethnicity, her class position, and her role as a sex worker. As she says, 'I don't exist, do I?'

As in the texts I discussed in Chapter 2, these economic and social precar- ities are expressed through Gothicised spaces. The characters move through alleyways, labyrinthine workplace access passages, underground car parks, sweatshop warehouses, and a morgue. The spaces are confining, confusing, and disciplinary; we also see CCTV footage monitoring housekeeping staff entering the hotel. Personal space is rare, with Okwe sleeping on Senay's couch or in the morgue where Guo Yi works. Indeed, most of the film's settings are non-places, in Marc Augé's terms, spaces which 'cannot be defined as relational, or historical or concerned with identity'.[77] The disorientation is intensified by a deliberately decentred representation of London that refuses the usual establishing shots of famous landmarks, instead offering, as Rebecca Prime says, 'a collection of disconnected, impersonal spaces, an unfamiliar cinematic city … The absence of establishing shots means that it is difficult to get your bearings, to construct any sense of cohesive space'.[78] These confining and disciplinary spaces have a cumulative impact. We see the characters move through and submit to these sites daily, navigating constraints, descending, waiting, enduring. The film communicates states of social marginalisation and corporeal vulnerability, stemming from a combination of diminished state protections and increased state threat. In the thriller plot, exploitative harvest entangles with the exploitations of migrant mobilities. Through repetitive traversing of carceral sites, the film conveys not only moments but durations of peril.

Bodies 'in service, plundered': African-American harvest horror

For the remainder of this chapter, I will discuss North American texts of harvest horror. These works are informed by the intersection of medicine with the transnational violence of slavery, and its contemporary social, political, and economic legacies. Medicine and slavery were entangled from the start, with doctors helping to value enslaved persons for sale, maintaining working capacity, and using enslaved persons for medical research.[79] In 1838, for example, the South Carolina *Charleston Mercury* included an advertisement placed by a Dr. T. Stillman, seeking living human subjects: 'To PLANTERS AND OTHERS. – Wanted, fifty Negroes, any person, having sick Negroes … and wishing to dispose of them, Dr. S. will pay cash.'[80] James Marion Sims developed the gynaecological speculum through unanaesthetised surgeries on African-American slave women.[81] In the twentieth century, the Tuskegee Study from 1932 to 1972 notoriously prevented 399 African-American men from receiving treatment for syphilis.[82] African-American women were coercively sterilised in state-run programmes, most notoriously in North Carolina which performed over 7,500 non-voluntary sterilisations between 1929 and 1977 in a project that researchers have called 'racially biased and genocidal'.[83] At the New York State Psychiatric Institute from 1993 to 1996, one hundred boys, predominantly African-American and Hispanic, were injected with toxic fenfluramine to test whether violent behaviour might be triggered by particular neurochemicals.[84] Given such histories, it is unsurprising that legends of 'night doctors' or 'student doctors' emerged, predatorial figures that prowl at night to seek victims for medical experimentation.[85]

When early markets in blood and tissue emerged, in so far as African-American people were disproportionately affected by both poverty and incarceration, there was a disproportionate risk of their being affected by clinical labour, including blood sale and incentivised tissue yield. Economic and social inequalities influenced blood supplier pools, and some surgeons targeted their search efforts accordingly.[86] (Today, too, some blood plasma companies target the economically marginalised.)[87] Prisoners were targeted for blood and other tissue in return for parole or reduced sentences. Incarcerated men were 'donors' in 1920s experimental testes transfer conducted at San Quentin prison near San Francisco. Surgeon Leo Stanley took testes from African-American, Japanese, and Mexican inmates for transplantation into white men, and consent was incentivised with sentence reduction or parole leniency. The most profitable transformations of tissue, however, have been cell lines developed from cancer cells for research, and here, too, African-American suffering has been central. The extraordinarily influential HeLa cell line was developed from the cells of Henrietta Lacks, an African-American woman who died of cervical cancer in 1951. Her cells were harvested without her knowledge and developed into a profitable cell line while her family endured poverty.[88]

Virulent racist discourse emerged in response to both blood and organ transfer. Stanley's racist commentaries on his experiments, for example, claimed that African-American tissue enhanced white recipients' sexual virility and humour. While Stanley saw transfer as beneficial to white recipients, others saw transfer as a threat. After Karl Landsteiner's 1900 discovery of blood typing, several countries (including Nazi Germany and America) saw efforts to map serological types on to racial categories, and in the 1950s research into sensitisation through transfusion was recruited to renewed calls for desegregating blood supply. Blood banks labelled blood for donor's race, textbooks encouraged differentiating between 'colored' and 'white' blood, and in 1941 the American Red Cross banned African-American donors from donating blood. After outcry, the Red Cross agreed to resume, but specified that 'negro blood' must be kept and used separately from Caucasian donations. The US blood supply was not desegregated until 1950, and even after that some states passed laws to extend it, arguing that African-American donors were more likely to carry infectious disease or that transfusion would corrupt white racial 'purity'. A Mississippi congressman claimed that white parents feared that 'negro or Japanese' blood would 'crop out in their children' after transfusion, an Alabama congressman described constituents' panic at interracial transfusion, and a South Carolina congressman said he would rather die than receive African-American blood.[89]

In the light of this history, transfer horror can be seen as partially symbolic of the slow violence of exploitation and exclusion across a range of spheres, and indeed this chapter argues exactly that. Yet such transplant horror is not only symbolic, as a 1968 case at the Medical College of Virginia shows. This early US attempt at heart transfer used the heart of Bruce Tucker, an African-American man, without informing his family he was in hospital, seeking consent, or waiting the twenty-four hours then mandated by law before treating his body as 'unclaimed'. In the ensuing trial, the Tuckers' attorney, L. Douglas Wilder, argued (unsuccessfully) that 'the hospital pulled the plug because he was poor and black'.[90] When the state of Virginia was considering a law that would permit cadaveric organ procurement without kin consent, Wilder invoked the legends of night or student doctors, warning 'They're not going to be taking the hearts of any white mayors … If this bill passes, it's going to be so that black mothers will tell their children, "Don't go walkin' down by the Medical College at night or the student doctor's gonna get you".'[91] The editor warned of 'hearts being taken under conditions that remind [people] of ghoulish movies'.[92] Media coverage of Christiaan Barnard's second successful heart transplant in South Africa also influenced discourse around African-American vulnerability to harvest. The heart was taken from Clive Haupt, who was classified under the racist regime of the time as 'Coloured', and transplanted to Philip Blaiberg, who was classified as 'white'.[93] The American magazine *Ebony* commented on the irony of this transfer in a 1968 editorial:

> Haupt's heart will ride in the uncrowded train coaches marked 'For Whites Only' instead of in the crowded ones reserved for blacks. It will pump extra hard to circulate the blood needed for a game of tennis where the only blacks are those who might pull heavy rollers to smooth the courts … Many black people in the United States and South Africa fear hospitals because they believe that white doctors use black patients only for 'experimentation' and that doctors may 'hurry death'.[94]

The turn-of-the-millennium context of the following fictions also saw certain African-American bodies disproportionately subject to procurement and even potentially to some controversial antemortem procedures, due to structural inequalities that characterised contexts of organ procurement at that time and place. Brain-death procurement relies on catastrophic neurological damage, such as from intra-cranial haemorrhage or head injury, and the dominant causes vary by region and historical moment. An economic and social distance existed between many cadaveric donors and recipient at that period, with a majority of donors being younger and dying due to external trauma including gunshot wounds, and recipients often older and at risk of death from long-term chronic illness.[95] In societies where socioeconomic disadvantage shapes patterns of death, then, at some sites, some groups will be disproportionately represented in cadaveric donation. Furthermore, the last decade of the twentieth century saw a new procurement method emerge, 'controlled non-heartbeating donation', now called Donation after Circulatory Death. This practice involves withdrawing life support from patients who are dependent on it but who are not brain-dead. I discuss the controversies around early versions of the practice in Chapter 1. Notably, in the 1990s, the University of Pittsburgh began surgery two minutes after asystole, although life has been shown to return spontaneously up to five minutes after heartbeat ceases, and some patients were subjected to painful ante-mortem procedures including groin lymph node removal and harmful drugs.[96] Lesley Sharp was told by one medical practitioner that 'some teams who work in "high crime areas" – where patients are likely to be people of color and poor – may even initiate organ preservation techniques before family consent has been obtained'.[97] The Pittsburgh team were driven by a desire to improve transplan-tation practice, yet it is also necessary to consider how biomedical innovation may inadvertently exacerbate vulnerabilities attendant on existing precarity.

US procurement officials record lower consent rates for cadaveric donation from donors they classify as 'African-American' than from those they classify as 'white'. However, this oft-repeated statement conceals multiple inequalities within the fields of transplantation, particular in terms of access. Research shows that African-American patients are less likely to be deemed viable recip-ients for transplant, less likely to be referred for evaluation, less likely to be thoroughly evaluated, and less likely to have their names submitted to waiting lists.[98] Furthermore the very concept of 'race' has directly affected match pro-tocols, which have been documented to disadvantage prospective recipients who are not classified white. The genetic grounds for categorising any person as a particular race are tenuous, as Elisa Gordon observes: '"Races" do not empirically exist because not *one* set of phenotypic or genetic traits is con-sistent within or distinctive of any group called a "race" ... [Yet] transplant studies still assume a correspondence between clines and "race".'[99] Kierans and Cooper observe that, 'in the transplant literature, what are highly complex variations are typically represented in simplified ... racial terms'.[100] Inequalities for ethnic minorities from matching protocols became so marked that both the US and the UK were obliged to revise their algorithms.[101] Such inequalities in medical care have parallels in ways in which African-American patients receive analgesia and hospice care at different rates from others.[102] Wider health arenas, too, are fraught with health inequalities, functions not of genetic histories but of economic, social, and environmental marginalisation.[103] The rate of diabe-tes, for example, with all its consequences for heart disease and kidney failure, may be twice as high. Ailments are diagnosed and treated differently among groups with different economic, social and cultural capital.[104] In other words, structural forces can wound bodies into transplant need. Sharpe warns, 'The semiotics of the slave ship continue ... in everyday life in the form of the prison, the camp, the school'.[105] To that list can be added the hospital, where treatment may not be equal.

I will discuss four texts from the twentieth century and turn of the millen-nium which present African-American bodies vulnerable to radical corporeal violation within the increasing corporatisation of the biomedical field: Charles Gardner Bowers's short story 'The black hand' (1931) and Dennis Etchison's

'The machine demands a sacrifice' (1972, 1984), both of which I then contrast with Walter Mosley's short story 'Whispers in the dark' (2001) and Nalo Hopkinson's novel *Brown Girl in the Ring* (1998).[106] While the former pair tend to reinforce dangerous erasures of African-American subjectivity, the latter texts challenge such erasure and conduct 'wake work', in Sharpe's terms, both mourning African-American suffering in the ongoing wake of the slave ship's bow, and embracing the wakefulness of creative resilience.

Bowers's 'The black hand' adapts the hand transfer trope popularised in Arthur Cheney Train's novella *Mortmain* (1907) and Maurice Renard's novel *Les mains d'Orlac* (1920), which I discuss in Chapter 4.[107] Bowers's story imagines a hand transplant from an African-American prisoner to a white man who lost a hand due to infection. The surgeon tells the prospective recipient that the donor will consent in return for $10,000 for his family and 'an impressive burial' (p. 911). The donor is anaesthetised, his hand amputated and he is executed while under sedation. The narrative's focus, however, is on the transplant and the recipient. A detailed description of the surgery is followed by a psychiatric report on 'patient no. 5026', which describes how the recipient artist's work becomes 'grotesque', he becomes psychotic and begins to murder African-American men. The report-writer closes by stating that the recipient must have had hitherto-undiagnosed psychological instabilities.

The characters in Bowers's story express overtly racist views – '"it is not very pleasant to know that you are using the arm that has murdered an unarmed man, *still worse* to realise that the arm is black' (pp. 910–11) – without any narrative voice correcting the racism, and the story as a whole implies that the transfer made the recipient homicidal. The text conflates perceived racial otherness and criminal transgression, and abjects the incarcerated African-American supplier. At certain moments, the story struggles to maintain its racist premise. The doctor advises the artist, 'For some strange reason his blood types perfectly with yours', and implies that this indicates shared ancestry (p. 911). While under-informed of the mechanics of tissue matching, this line undercuts the sense of a distinction between the two bodies. In addition, the text's formal choices open up spaces of challenge to its premise. The shift in genre – from third-person narration to the scientific detachment of a psychiatric report – can work in two ways. On the one hand, the horror of the story lies in the implication that the psychiatric report is mistaken and there is a link between the transplant and the recipient's homicidal psychosis. On the other hand, the psychiatric report has intradiegetic authority, and it explicitly states that the murderousness stems from recipient instability, rather than the transfer. Both conceptually and formally, the story cannot wholly maintain its toxic premise. Yet the story does nothing to consider the interiority or plight of the African-American donor or supplier. He is not named or described, and his few remarks appear only via indirect speech. The recipient, by contrast, has a name, a medical history, and direct speech, and is the subject of the attentive gaze of two doctors, a surgeon, and a psychiatrist. In multiple ways, then, both in characterisation and narrative form, the story reinforces, and is complicit in, racist attitudes of its era.

Predation on African-American bodies also features in Etchison's 'The machine demands a sacrifice' (1972, rev. 1984), and this story, too, arguably reinforces rather than challenges problematic tropes of transfer. This story imagines a near-future United States in which 'independent units' resembling ambulances trawl highways seeking road traffic accidents, offering emergency care, and harvesting organs from the dead. The third-person narration takes the perspective of Jaime, a new recruit under a veteran, Jesse. The narrative centres on Jaime's discovery that the business preys on African-American victims. They find a car with a family whose father/husband has undergone a medical crisis. Jesse persuades the man's wife to hand over her credit card for emergency care and they take the man into their van. Jaime sees the man is still alive but Jesse sets the dissection machines over his living body regardless, in a hideous unanaesthetised vivisection. Jesse pushes the eviscerated corpse into a body bag, dumps it on the pavement, and throws the woman's credit card at her while she and her children sob.

The 'machine' of the story's title includes the factory processing of living flesh and the wider social and structural violence within which the murder occurs. Jesse justifies his actions with reference to the Vietnam War, describing how in this fictional world front-line troops were maintained with the bodies of the dead through organ transplants:

> '"Got to keep the war machine running!" they told us. Then there wasn't enough. We finally had to get our own casualties. The NCOs told us to get what we needed off our own. They wouldn't let us take nothing off the whites. We got some of the brown brothers together ... We made sure there were always enough of 'em. Then they started transing stateside. Right away there were too many patients, not enough donors ... So when we got on the outs, we went into business ... We wasn't the only ones.' (pp. 90–1)

In its shocking imagining of racial inequalities escalating to deliberate slaughter, condoned by a government in combat theatres and then domestically implemented by private contractors, this brutal story critiques racist systemic structures. The story's narrative structure and perspective, however, reinforce related symbolic violence, and repeat erasures and objectifications of African-American suffering. The 'formless encapsulated remains' are dumped 'like a giant slug caught on the cement' (p. 90), and, despite the horror of the vivisection scene, no interiority is given to the victim or his bereaved family. Furthermore, the narrative movement of the piece revolves around *Jaime's* burden of having witnessed the murder. As the story closes, Jesse is still talking, but 'Jaime did not hear him. He was back on the dark street, waiting, but she [the wife] would not stop. She would not stop screaming' (p. 92). The African-American victim and bereaved kin are treated as suffering objects rather than subjects, their suffering a catalyst for horror experienced by a witness. In other words, horror is not used to describe the subjective experience of long-term structural exclusion and slow violence.

The next stories I discuss, however, do exactly that. Hopkinson's novel *Brown Girl in the Ring* (1998), and Mosley's short story 'Whispers in the dark' (2001) are near-future North American speculative fictions from the turn of the millennium, and they give their suppliers or donors voice and, to some degree, agency. Hopkinson is Trinidadian-Canadian and Mosley is African-American. These texts should be understood in terms of a tradition of African-American writing around enslavement and bodily commodification, which continue to be powerful themes, as in Jordan Peele's recent horror film *Get Out* (2017).[108] Like Etchison's story, these texts present African-American subjects as vulnerable to corporeal violation within predatorial socioeconomic networks. Yet these later works also convey African-American experiences and interiorities, representing 'multiple black identities, varied black experience', as bell hooks advocates.[109] These texts also challenge particular assumptions in biomedicine, particularly the ideal of autonomous individuality.

Suffering, torture, and constraint are long-running themes in African-American Gothic, as Maisha Wester has shown.[110] Whilst eighteenth- and nineteenth-century British and American Gothic overwhelmingly tend to reinforce fictions of racial otherness, some writers use Gothic tropes, intertextualities, and narrative conventions not only to invert that model but to subvert such binaries altogether.[111] As Wester says, Gothic can be used to 'destabiliz[e] the entire notion of categories and boundaries',[112] and to quote Hopkinson herself, building on Audre Lorde, 'In my hands, massa's tools don't dismantle massa's house – and in fact, I don't want to destroy it so much as I want to undertake massive renovations – they build me a house of my own'.[113] In that spirit, African-American speculative fiction has grappled with commodification and enslavement as well as imagining more hopeful futures. Afrofuturism, in particular, uses science fiction forms to visionary ends. The concept has seen an explosion of elaboration in the decades since Mark Dery's formulation of the term in 1994, as 'Speculative fiction that treats and addresses African-American concerns in the context of twentieth century technoculture – and, more generally, African-American signification that appropriates images of technology and a prosthetically enhanced future'.[114] The very act of imagining a future is creative rebellion, as John Jennings says: 'Afrofuturism is imagining ourselves in the future, which is pretty audacious … seeing how we're not supposed to have one'.[115] Such visions for the future can be both utopian and diagnostic of present-day injustice. Similarly, Sharpe has called for writing that will dwell 'in the wake' in two senses: the wake of the slave ship as it continues its work of systematic oppression and death, and wakefulness, defiant and creative: 'To be in the wake is also to recognise the ways that we are constituted through and by continued vulnerability to overwhelming force, though not *only* known to ourselves and to each other *by* that force'.[116]

Mosley's short story 'Whispers in the dark' (2001) is influenced by incarceration becoming an increasingly profitable industry in the twentieth- and twenty-first centuries, disproportionately affecting African-American men.[117] As Noah De Lissovoy notes, 'policing practices, sentencing guidelines, and post-incarceration disenfranchisement unequally … [affect] people of color'.[118] The corporate prison-industrial complex relies on bodies as raw material for profit. Mosley's story imagines a near-future America in which nation-states have merged with corporations and have extreme control over people's lives. The story describes the struggles of an impoverished African-American family fighting to keep their grandson and nephew Popo. His mother died, and now he lives with his grandmother Misty and uncle Chill, a loving substitute father. Popo's intellectual promise is such that the state and education corporation wish to take him for 'elite education', but Chill refuses. He weeps and declares, '"I love that boy more than I love anything … I will not let them take him. I will not let them white people and them people wanna be white turn him into some cash cow or bomb builder or prison maker. He will find his own way an' make up his own mind"' (p. 176). They cannot hold the state and corporations at bay without money to pay for Popo's education, yet as an ex-convict Chill's earning capacity has been damaged by post-incarceration disenfranchisement.

The first description of Chill emphasises his history of suffering within violence: 'The pale and jagged scar on his jaw' speaks of 'violence and rage in the young man's life' (p. 165). He is a physically 'powerful man', but, by the story's close, Chill has comprehensively sacrificed his strong body. He goes away for unspecified work for six weeks, and then 'a private ambulance drove up the … dirt driveway … Chill was there under a thin sheet … his eyes were covered with … gauze. The form his legs made under the sheet was straight and motionless' (p. 177). Chill sold his eyes, legs, spinal nerves, genitalia, and other organs in return for six million dollars, which in this world of hyperinflation will buy a modest house and an educational computer uplink for Popo. (Selling an organ to fund a child's education is a common reason cited by suppliers of kidneys in illegal markets in a global context, so this story is grimly not as farfetched as it may sound.)[119] Chill explains:

> 'My eyes were a perfect fit for a Swiss banker's son who lost his in a ski accident. But when I was there they had an emergency. It was a Russian general needed the nerve in the spine where he could use his legs. They offered two

million for that … One thing led to another and I got outta there wit' six million. They transferred the whole thing into my name 'fore I went under the knife.' (p. 178)

The solution to funding a loved one's education that emerges in the course of the story is literally to sell one's body. The text can be read as symbolic of people eaten away by structural racism, regimes of incarceration, and the daily, grinding burden of life within a hostile society where 'living while Black' is a relentless quotidian strain and state forces are an explicit threat.[120] Claudine Rankine says, 'A sustained state of national mourning for black lives is called for in order to point to the undeniability of their devaluation. The hope is that recognition will break a momentum that laws haven't altered.'[121] Fictions such as these can seek to make systematic, slow violence more visible.

Mosley's imagining of Chill's sacrifice is also important in rectifying a gap in some discussions of the biopolitics of incentivised transfer. Giorgio Agamben's figure of the *homo sacer* has been used to describe how victims of exploitative harvest are rendered bare life, but, as Cohen notes, the model is insufficient in that it misses a sacrifice that does indeed occur at the moment of predatorial harvest: the sacrifice of the *supplier* for loved ones, for a household which needs the money they can earn with their body and pain: 'What is exceptional in these situations is less one's reduction to a zone of indistinction … but a more articulated zone in which one trades in one's bare life – kidneys, other biomatter – in order to remain a political subject of sacrifice and love'.[122] Crucially, Mosley's story does recognise such sacrifice, and invests imaginatively in contemplating the context for the character's choice. Whilst Etchison's text treats the African-American victim as an object with no name or interiority, Mosley foregrounds Chill's experience and emphasises the devotion that drives his choice. The story is heart-breaking not only in that such a sacrifice occurs but in that the protagonist feels it inevitable. As with Mark Fisher's concept 'capitalist realism', it seems that one cannot even imagine a way out of this horror.[123]

The story can also, however, be read in a more surprising way. Chill's sacrifice is repeatedly described as giving him peace and satisfaction. He 'smiled in a way that Misty hadn't seen since he was a child' (p. 178), and he reassures them that 'Everything's fine now' (p. 179). Accepting this reading relinquishes the assumption that happiness requires (the illusion of) 'autonomy', an illusion which disability studies rightly challenges.[124] At the same time, the story does not let us flinch from the brutality of Chill's paid wounding. The text requires we simultaneously contemplate both the generosity of elective sacrifice, either symbolic or literal, and the atrocity of societies that necessitate and normalise it.

Hopkinson's novel *Brown Girl in the Ring* (1998) is similarly rich in ambiguities. Set in an imagined near-future Canada, it describes inner-city

Toronto as devoid of state control for twelve years. People living in central Toronto use barter, catch wild game, and improvise healthcare including traditional Caribbean practices. Socialised medicine has given way to privatised care, and the only medical care for the uninsured comes from outsider paramedic 'vultures'. 'The price for established medical care was so high that only the desperately ill would call for help. If you saw a vulture making a house call, it meant that someone was near death' (p. 8). In the suburbs, insurance coverage is more widespread and medical care more sophisticated. There, transplantation is common using porcine xenografts, but these are becoming controversial. The nation's Premier needs a heart transplant, but due to her electorate's change in attitudes cannot accept a pig's heart. Her team decide to obtain a heart in inner Toronto and ask mob boss Rudy to find a compatible 'donor' and arrange their death. In parallel, the story focuses on the protagonist Ti-Jeanne, a Trinidadian-Canadian woman who lives in inner Toronto with her grandmother Gros-Jeanne. They use traditional Caribbean healing practices alongside Western methods of healing. Ti-Jeanne has inherited the capacity to commune with spirits, although she initially rejects this talent. Under pressure from Rudy, Jeanne's ex-boyfriend kills her grandmother, to yield a heart for Uttley's transfer, and Rudy then tries to capture Ti-Jeanne and imprison her spirit as a *duppy* bowl puppet under his control. It is revealed that Rudy is Ti-Jeanne's grandfather and that he has already done this to his daughter, Ti-Jeanne's mother, years before. Ti-Jeanne escapes by working with the spirits and saves her mother's life and her own. The heart transplant leads to a merging of consciousness between Uttley and Gros-Jeanne, and the latter's wisdom henceforth shapes the political development of the society.

As a whole, the novel is positive about organ transfer. It closes with the Premier, her personality now combined with the protagonist's benevolent grandmother, deciding to establish presumed consent for cadaveric donation. Yet the novel is highly critical of two strands of the practice: unequal access to transplantation and the impact of insensitive cadaveric donation management on bereaved loved ones. Ti-Jeanne screams as she is deprived of the chance to mourn over her grandmother's body.

> 'Mami! Oh God, Mami!' She crawled over to her grandmother's body, reaching to touch. Hands pulled her away, dragged her to her feet …
>
> 'Please stay out of our way, miss. That woman is a bio-material donor.' … The words came faster, like a litany: 'Angel of Mercy Hospital offers its condolences for your loss and thanks you and your family for making this life-giving donation of your loved one's biomaterial. Your address has been entered into the hospital's data banks and you will be compensated for your donation. Good day.'
>
> … They had to pull her away, prevent her forcibly from entering the ambulance with Mami's body … The doors slammed shut, hollowly … 'Mami!' Ti-Jeanne

wailed. 'Oh God, Mami; I sorry!' She ran after the ambulance, screaming, begging, crying ... She stood in the road, howling, wailing, until her breath was gone and her desolate eyes were swollen nearly shut. (pp. 152–4)

The callousness here is a function of an insensitive procurement process in which the needs of the bereaved are dismissed.

The novel also uses predatorial harvest as metaphor for complex temporally extended burdens: specifically, the experience of enduring the structural oppression of slow violence of economic, environmental, and social harms, and the weight of such transgenerational trauma marring a family and community. Exemplifying the strategy for which bell hooks calls, Hopkinson offers a richly specific and gendered protagonist position.[125] In this regard, tissue predation occurs *within* the city as well, and indeed within the protagonist Ti-Jeanne's own family. Rudy misuses Caribbean spiritual traditions to torture female descendants, in violence that is intrafamilial and gendered. Stories of female bodies wounded by a black patriarch have a powerful tradition in African-American women's writing. Wester and Sharpe analyse similar fictions as marking the ongoing transgenerational trauma of enslavement and sexualised violence. Sharpe has coined the term 'monstrous intimacies' to describe 'the long psychic and material reach' of those tortures, 'their projection onto and erasure from particular bodies, and the reformulation, reproduction, and recirculation of their intimate spaces', over generations.[126] Similarly, Wester observes that these horrifying representations can be informed by 'subjugation and violation of women's bodies and psyches', particularly when African-American women are represented solely as mothers or heterosexual partners, their interests subsumed to the restoration of masculine pride.[127] Hopkinson's representations of torture in this novel go further than describing extreme visceral torment. They also describe transgenerational repetition, familial violation informed by past systemic horrors. Crucially, Hopkinson does not frame Rudy as a mere traditional single villain but frames his actions in the context of a predatorial wider society. Esther Jones notes:

> To emphasise the systemic nature of evil, as opposed to attributing it to Rudy's singular villainy, Hopkinson brackets the narrative within the previously described social and political context ... [T]he story opens with a 'business meeting' between Rudy and an emissary from the Angel of Mercy Hospital, these characters serving as intermediaries to provide a few degrees of separation between the socially legitimised power class making demands and the lowest rung of society who function as the supply.[128]

Intrafamilial struggle over tissues and organs, skin, eyes, and hearts is also a nightmarish intensification of situations where living donation may become coercive within families, sometimes in gendered ways. Ethnographers have shown how privatised contexts of healthcare and neoliberal formulations of personhood shape particular capacities for work productivity, sometimes with gendered implications for donation.[129] Pressures to donate or sell can be, at times, disproportionately exercised across the bodies of women, who may be sacrificed to support husbands or offspring in a disturbing echo of traditional female roles in the reproduction of labour value – replenishing other workers through their own bodily sacrifice.[130]

Ultimately, Hopkinson draws on Trinidadian spiritualism to challenge conventional medical thinking around transfer itself. It initially seems that the transplant is failing due to graft-host disease, a rare condition in which immune defences within the transplanted material attack the host. The experience is described from the perspective of the recipient. She feels a presence taking over her body and mind, and panics at the prospect of her identity being annihilated:

> Uttley began to feel a numbness spreading out from her chest with each beat of the heart: down her arms, through her trunk and legs. Bit by bit, she was losing the ability to control her own body. The heart was taking it over. Uttley became alarmed, had tried talking to the alien organ. 'Please,' she said. 'This is my body. You can't take it away from me.' But the creeping numbness spread up her neck. She was now completely paralyzed. All she could do was wait for it to reach her brain. She had known that when that happened, she would no longer be herself. Unable to move, unable to save herself, she had felt her brain cells being given up one by one. Then blackness. Nothing. (pp. 236–7)

This description of paralysis and dread of impending annihilation is alarming, but heralds a blessed metamorphosis. When Uttley wakes, she is aware of herself as now two-in-one. Within herself she can see 'In every artery, every vein, every capillary: two distinct streams, intertwined' (p. 237). Donna McCormack points out that the novel draws on Yoruba and Caribbean traditions of Myalism, in which two spirits can occupy the same body. As such, the novel offers a 'decolonisation of epistemologies that were demonised and outlawed by colonial law', 'challeng[ing] the biomedical school of selfhood used in transplant therapy, which insists on a strict distinction and separation between living recipient and deceased donor'.[131] This work contrasts with the metaphors of immunological warfare that dominate transplant science and which are themselves being challenged by emerging work on microchimerism, as I discuss in my introduction and Chapter 4. Esther Jones points out that the novel 'confers dignity on multiple modes of knowledge production'.[132] Drawing on these non-European frameworks of knowledge respects other traditions of knowing.

Hopkinson's novel both engages with aspects of contemporary tissue economies and uses surgical extraction and transplantation as metaphors for complex social processes. The novel condemns the sociopolitical and economic exclusion that blights this imagined future Toronto bereft of effective socialised medicine, in which procedures like transplantation are reserved for the suburban wealthy. The inequality between the suburbs and inner city is starkly described: 'Imagine a cartwheel half-mired in muddy water ... rusted through and through. When Toronto's economic base collapsed, investors, commerce, and government withdrew into the suburb cities, leaving the rotten core to decay. Those who stayed were the ones who couldn't or wouldn't leave. The street people. The poor people' (pp. 3–4). Hopkinson offers a haunting vision of an imagined future closer to the US, in that it features largely privatised rather than socialised medicine. As such, readings of the novel can also be enriched by recent work on African-American experience within the United States' healthcare systems. Cheryl Mattingly's *Paradox of Hope* (2010) uses the spatial trope of the 'clinical borderland' to describe profound structural inequalities and racism endured by African-American parents and children in a particular hospital. The study participants forge a form of hope that does not deny suffering, one which Mattingly describes through Cornel West's language of 'blues hope', a stance of agency that none the less recognises catastrophic constraints and oppressions.[133] These fictions, too, hold hope and grief in tension, neither denying nor romanticising profound precarity.

The legend of the Miracle of Saints Cosmas and Damien has been retold and revised over centuries. Natasha Trethewey's poem 'Miracle of the black leg' describes how that legend changes over time, but one thing remains constant: 'the story beneath this story ... what remains each time the myth changes':

> What knowledge haunts each body,
> what history, what phantom ache? One man always
> low, in a grave or on the ground, the other
> up high, closer to heaven; one man always diseased,
> the other a body in service, plundered.[134]

The texts of this chapter imagine insidious, often invisible work of structural ruination in which some are invisibly sacrificed for others. Those unknowable, personal sacrifices, people choosing to bleed *from love*, should haunt those of us not under those knives. Neither literature nor ethnography can capture unmediated experience, nor can they communicate the structural legacies that inform that experience, but perhaps, at times, both may succeed in offering a sense of slow violence – so elusive to representation, even while its impact on bodies and environments is brutally material in every sense. The surgical incisions at the heart of these texts are pale corollaries of slower lacerations.

Notes

1 M. Durant, 'The Ethiopian's leg', *Saint Lucy*, saint-lucy.com/essays/the-ethiopians-leg/ [accessed 12 August 2018].

2 L. Barkan, 'Cosmas and Damian', in S. Youngner, R. Fox, and L. O'Connell

(eds), *Organ Transplantation* (Madison: University of Wisconsin Press, 1996), pp. 221–51.

3 L. Lowe, *The Intimacies of the Four Continents* (Durham, NC: Duke University Press, 2015).

4 R. Nixon, *Slow Violence and the Environmentalism of the Poor* (Cambridge, MA: Harvard University Press, 2013).

5 C. Sharpe, *In the Wake* (Durham, NC: Duke University Press, 2016), p. 19.

6 E. Povinelli, *Economies of Abandonment* (Durham, NC: Duke University Press, 2011), pp. 4, 29; A. Mbembe, 'Necropolitics', trans. L. Mentjes, *Public Culture*, 15:1 (2003), 11–49 (p. 40).

7 R. Chengappa, 'The great organs bazaar', *India Today* (31 July 1990), 60–7; L. Cohen, 'Where it hurts', *Daedalus*, 128:4 (1999), 135–65 (p. 137, emphasis added).

8 G. Byron, 'Introduction', in G. Byron (ed.), *Globalgothic* (Manchester: Manchester University Press, 2013), pp. 1–10 (p. 5).

9 C. Kierans and J. Cooper, 'Organ donation, genetics, race and culture', *Anthropology Today*, 27:6 (2011), 21–4 (p. 12).

10 K. Ancuta, 'The return of the dismembered', in L. Blake and A. Soltysik Monnet (eds), *Neoliberal Gothic* (Manchester: Manchester University Press, 2017), pp. 83–103.

11 *Turistas*, dir. by J. Stockwell (2029 Entertainment, 2006); 'Kidney theft', *Snopes*, www.snopes.com/fact-check/youve-got-to-be-kidneying/ [accessed 13 August 2018].

12 H. Zwart, 'Transplantation medicine', *Subjectivity*, 9:2 (2016), 151–80 (p. 175).

13 Ancuta; L. Blake and A.S. Monnet, 'Introduction', in L. Blake and A. Soltysik Monnet (eds), *Neoliberal Gothic* (Manchester: Manchester University Press, 2017), pp. 1–18 (p. 9); S. Wasson, 'Butcher's shop', in S. Wasson and E. Alder (eds), *Gothic Science Fiction, 1980–2010* (Liverpool: Liverpool University Press, 2011), pp. 73–86.

14 D. Rothman, E. Rose, T. Awaya, *et al.*, 'The Bellagio Task Force report', *Transplantation Proceedings*, 29:6 (1997), 2739–45 (p. 2744); cf. V. Campion-Vincent, 'Organ theft narratives', *Western Folklore*, 56:1 (1997), 1–37; 'Organ theft narratives as medical and social critique', *Journal of Folklore Research*, 39:1 (2002), 33–50; 'On organ theft narratives', *Current Anthropology*, 42:4 (2001), 555–8.

15 J. Butler, *Precarious Life* (London: Verso, 2004).

16 D. Mitchell and S. Snyder, *Narrative Prosthesis* (Ann Arbor: University of Michigan Press, 2000); M. Davidson, 'Concerto for the left hand', *PMLA*, 120:2 (2005), 615–19.

17 L. Cohen, 'The other kidney', *Body and Society*, 7:2 (2001), 9–29 (pp. 11–12).

18 N. Scheper-Hughes, 'Commodity fetishism in organs trafficking', in N. Scheper-Hughes and L. Wacquant (eds), *Commodifying Bodies* (London: Sage, 2002), pp. 31–62 (p. 45), emphasis in original.

19 K. Sunder Rajan, *Biocapital* (Durham, NC: Duke University Press, 2006).

20 M. Crowley-Matoka, *Domesticating Organ Transplant* (Durham, NC: Duke University Press, 2016); C. Kierans, 'Biopolitics and capital', *Body and Society*, 21:3 (2015), 42–65; B. Parry, 'Domesticating biosurveillance', *Health and Place*, 18:4 (2012), 718–25.

21 C. Waldby and M. Cooper, *Clinical Labor* (Durham, NC: Duke University Press, 2014).

22 C. Thompson cited in S. Franklin and M. Lock, 'Animation and cessation', in S. Franklin and M. Lock (eds), *Remaking Life and Death* (Santa Fe, NM: School of American Research Press, 2003), pp. 3–22 (p. 8).

23 C. Waldby and R. Mitchell, *Tissue Economies* (Durham, NC: Duke University Press, 2006).

24 F. Delmonico, 'The declaration of Istanbul on organ trafficking and transplant tourism', *Indian Journal of Nephrology*, 18:3 (2008), 135–40; M. Gunnarson and S. Lundin, 'The complexities of victimhood', *Somatechnics*, 5:1 (2015), 32–51 (p. 33, 47n3); D. Budiana-Saberi and S. Columb, 'A human rights approach to human trafficking for organ removal', *Medicine, Health Care, and Philosophy*, 16:4 (2013), 897–914 (pp. 897–8).

25 Gunnarson and Lundin, p. 47n1.

26 'Have a heart', *Investor's Business Daily* (9 December 2011), A12; L. Andrews, 'My body, my property', *Hastings Center Report*, 16:5 (1986), 28–38 (p. 32); L. Cohen, 'A futures market in cadaveric organs' *Transplantation Proceedings*, 25 (1993), 60–1; J. Cherry Mark, *Kidney for Sale by Owner* (Washington, DC: Georgetown University Press, 2005); J. Stacey Taylor, *Stakes and Kidneys* (Aldershot: Ashgate, 2005).

27 J. Radcliffe-Richards, *The Ethics of Transplants* (Oxford: Oxford University Press, 2012), p. 57.

28 Gunnarson and Lundin, pp. 40–5; D. Smith, 'Hospitals in South Africa charged over kidney transplant trafficking', *The Guardian* (16 September 2010), www.theguardian.com/world/2010/sep/16/hospitals-south-africa-kidney-transplant-scam-charged [accessed 20 October 2018].

29 Gunnarson and Lundin, pp. 34–3; G. Dahl, 'Sociology and beyond', *Asian Journal of Social Science*, 37:3 (2009), 391–407.

30 Radcliffe-Richards, p. 50, emphasis added.

31 Rothman *et al.*

32 Gunnarson and Lundin, p. 32; Cohen, 'Where it hurts', p. 151; Cohen, 'The other kidney'; M. Goyal, R. Mehta, L. Schneiderman, and A. Sehgal, 'Economic and health consequences of selling a kidney in India', *Journal of the American Medical Association*, 288:13 (2002), 1589–93; M. Moniruzzaman, '"Living cadavers" in Bangladesh', *Medical Anthropology Quarterly*, 26:1 (2012), 69–91 (p. 83).

33 Cohen, 'Where it hurts', p. 152.

34 V. Das, 'The practice of organ transplants', in M. Lock, A. Young, and A. Cambrioso (eds), *Living and Working with the New Medical Technologies* (Cambridge: Cambridge University Press, 2000), pp. 263–87 (p. 283).

35 Cohen, 'Where it hurts', p. 147.

36 Povinelli, pp. 4, 29.

37 Nixon, p. 2.
38 Ibid, p. 3.
39 Povinelli, p. 152.
40 Biehl, pp. 317–18.
41 Povinelli, p. 133.
42 M. Padmanabhan, *Harvest* (London: Aurora Metro, [1997] 2003). Subsequent references are in parenthesis in the text.
43 H. Gilbert, 'Manjula Padmanabhan's *Harvest*', *Contemporary Theatre Review*, 16:1 (2006), 123–30 (p. 124n2).
44 Waldby and Cooper.
45 D. Hamilton, *A History of Organ Transplantation* (Pittsburgh, PA: University of Pittsburgh Press, 2012), p. 409; R. Baru and P. Nanda, *Trading of Organs* (Delhi: Voluntary Health Association of India, 1993).
46 Campion-Vincent, 'Organ theft narratives', p. 8.
47 L. Cohen, 'Operability, bioavailability, and exception', in A. Ong and S. Collier (eds), *Global Assemblages* (Malden: Wiley-Blackwell, 2005), pp. 79–80 (p. 81).
48 Cohen, 'Other kidney', p. 11.
49 Moniruzzaman, p. 71.
50 Cohen, 'Where it hurts'.
51 N. Bhalla, 'Top Indian hospital says duped into removing kidneys for organ traffickers', *Reuters* (6 June 2016), www.reuters.com/article/us-india-traffick ing-organs/top-indian-hospital-says-duped-into-removing-kidneys-for-organ-tr affickers-idUSKCN0YS1Z9 [accessed 3 February 2018].
52 Cohen, 'Where it hurts', pp. 151, 149.
53 Moniruzzaman; Cohen, 'Where it hurts', p. 151; Goyal *et al.*, p. 1589–91.
54 Goyal *et al.*, p. 1591.
55 Moniruzzaman, pp. 69–70.
56 Das, p. 273.
57 Cohen, 'The other kidney', p. 18.
58 Cohen, 'Where it hurts', p. 140.
59 Cohen, 'The other kidney', p. 29.
60 K. Schanbacher, 'India's gestational surrogacy market', *Hastings Women's Law Journal*, 25:2 (2014), 201–20; D. Deomampo, 'Transnational surrogacy in India', *Frontiers*, 34:3 (2013), 167–88; Sunder Rajan, *Biocapital*.
61 S. Moni, '"In bits and pieces"', *Journal of Postcolonial Writing*, 50:3 (2014), 316–28 (p. 318).
62 A. Ramachandran, 'New world, no world', *Theatre Research International*, 30:2 (2005), 161–74 (pp. 166, 170).
63 Moniruzzaman, pp. 78–80.
64 A. Hochschild, *The Managed Heart*, 3rd edn., (Berkeley: University of California Press, 2012).
65 J. Babik and P. Chin-Hong, 'Transplant tourism', *Current Infectious Disease Reports*, 17:4 (2015), 1–6; F. Ambagtsheer, D. Zaitch, and W. Weimar, 'The battle for human organs', *Global Crime*, 14:1 (2013), 1–26; B. Winter, A. Odedra, and S. Green, 'A questionnaire based assessment of numbers, motivation and medical

care of UK patients undergoing liver transplant abroad', *Travel Medicine and Infectious Disease*, 14:6 (2016), 599–603.

66 *Dirty Pretty Things*, dir. by S. Frears (BBC, Celador and Jonescompany, 2002).

67 Scheper-Hughes, 'Commodity fetishism', p. 42.

68 Hamilton, pp. 398, 519n74.

69 A. Sharif, 'Directed altruistic kidney donors from overseas mask transplant tourism', *The Lancet*, 385:9973 (21 March 2015), 1074.

70 S. Squier, *Liminal Lives* (Durham, NC: Duke University Press, 2004), p. 175; J. Laurance, 'Alder Hey "sold" body parts to drugs firms', *Independent* (27 January 2001), 2.

71 J. Jacobs, *Edge of Empire* (London: Routledge, 1996), p. 73.

72 L. Amine, 'A house with two doors?', *Culture, Theory and Critique*, 48:1 (2007), 71–85 (p. 73).

73 A. Stoler, 'Imperial debris', *Cultural Anthropology*, 23:2 (2008), 191–219 (p. 194).

74 E. Davis, 'The intimacies of globalization', *Camera Obscura*, 21:62 (2006), 33–73 (p. 53).

75 Cited in C. Lucia, 'The complexities of cultural change', *Cineaste*, 28:4 (2003), 8–15 (p. 11).

76 J. Goldsmith, 'Dirty Pretty Things', *Creative Screenwriting*, 11:1 (2004), 56.

77 M. Augé, *Non-Places*, trans. by J. Howe (London: Verso, [1992] 1995), pp. 77–8.

78 R. Prime, 'Stranger than fiction', *Post Script*, 25:2 (2006), 56–66 (p. 62).

79 S. Lederer, *Flesh and Blood* (Oxford: Oxford University Press, 2008), p. 69.

80 *Charleston Mercury* (12 October 1838), cited in W. Goodell, *American Slave Code in Theory and Practice* (New York: American and Foreign Anti-Slavery Society, 1853), pp. 86–7.

81 H. Washington, *Medical Apartheid* (New York: Harlem Moon, 2006), p. 2.

82 S. Reverby, 'Rethinking the Tuskegee Syphilis Study', *Nursing History Review*, 7 (1999), 3–28 (p. 3).

83 G. Price and W. Darity, 'The economics of race and eugenic sterilization in North Carolina', *Economics and Human Biology*, 8:2 (2010), 261–72 (p. 261).

84 P. Hilts, 'Experiments on children', *New York Times* (15 April 1998), www.nytimes.com/1998/04/15/nyregion/experiments-on-children-are-reviewed.html [accessed 7 July 2017].

85 G. Fry, *Night Riders in Black Folk History* (Chapel Hill: University of North Carolina Press, [1975] 2001), pp. 171–82.

86 M. Telischi, 'The evolution of Cook County Hospital Blood Bank', *Modern Hospital*, 50 (1938), 57–8.

87 Organ sale was criminalised in the US in 1984 with the passage of the National Organ Transplant Act. It remains legal to profit from selling sperm plasma, eggs, and blood marrow in the US, though financial recompense may be framed as reimbursement for time, for example, rather than for the material specifically. Hamilton, p. 399; H. Shaefer and A. Ochoa, 'How blood-plasma companies target the poorest Americans', *The Atlantic* (15 March 2018), www.theatlantic.com/business/archive/2018/03/plasma-donations/555599/ [accessed 10 August 2018].

88 R. Skloot, *The Immortal Life of Henrietta Lacks* (London: Macmillan, 2010);

'The Lacks family', *TheLacksFamily.net*, www.lacksfamily.net/ [accessed 26 July 2017].

89 Lederer, pp. xii–xiv, 107–29, 169.

90 Ibid, p. 172.

91 'Heart snatch case', *Afro-American* (10 June 1972), 4.

92 Ibid, p. 4.

93 Mindful of the optics, Barnard took care for the first heart transplant to avoid Black-to-white transfer, and indeed one of the white donor's kidneys was transplanted to a Black recipient. M. Lock, *Twice Dead* (Berkeley: University of California Press, 2002), p. 81.

94 'The telltale heart', *Ebony* (March 1968), 118–19 (p. 118). In the South African context, there is evidence that both before and since Apartheid some bodies were harvested for organs without family consent, and, after the African National Congress came to power in 1995, the new government imposed a temporary moratorium of transplantation. See N. Scheper-Hughes, 'Bodies for sale', in N. Scheper-Hughes and L. Wacquant (eds), *Commodifying Bodies* (London: Sage, 2002), pp. 1–8; Campion-Vincent, 'Organ theft narratives as medical and social critique'; N. Scheper-Hughes, 'The global traffic in human organs', *Current Anthropology*, 41:2 (2000), 191–224.

95 M. Lock, *Twice Dead*, p. 86.

96 M. Rady, J. Verheijde, and J. McGregor, '"Non-heart-beating," or "cardiac death" organ donation', *Journal of Hospital Medicine*, 2:5 (2007), 324–34; R. Fox, 'An ignoble form of cannibalism', in R. Arnold, S. Youngner, R. Schapiro, and C. Spicer (eds), *Procuring Organs for Transplant* (Baltimore, MD: Johns Hopkins University Press, 1995), pp. 155–64.

97 L. Sharp, *Strange Harvest* (Berkeley: University of California Press, 2006), pp. 70–1.

98 A. Epstein, J. Ayanian, and J. Keogh, 'Racial disparities in access to renal transplantation', *New England Journal of Medicine*, 343 (2000), 1537–44.

99 E. Gordon, 'What race cannot tell us about access to kidney transplantation', *Cambridge Quarterly of Healthcare Ethics*, 11:2 (2002), 134–41 (pp. 135–7).

100 Kierans and Cooper, p. 136.

101 M. Cecka, 'Significance of histocompatibility in organ transplantation', *Current Opinion in Organ Transplantation*, 12:4 (2007), 402–8; X. Su, S. Zenios, H. Chakkera, E. Milford, and G. Chertow, 'Diminishing significance of HLA matching in kidney transplantation', *American Journal of Transplantation*, 4:9 (2004), 1501–8; R. Johnson, S. Fuggle, L. Mumford, J. Bradley, J. Forsythe, C. Rudge, *et al.*, 'A new UK 2006 national kidney allocation scheme for deceased heart-beating donor kidneys', *Transplantation*, 89:4 (2010), 387–94; Kierans and Cooper.

102 C. Smith and O. Brawley, 'Disparities in access to palliative care', *Health Affairs Blog* (30 July 2014) healthaffairs.org/blog/2014/07/30/disparities-in-access-to-palliative-care/ [accessed 17 August 2019]; R. Tait, J. Chibnall, and J. Anderson, 'racial/ethnic disparities in the assessment and treatment of pain', *American Psychologist*, 69:2 (2014) 131–41; R. Dickason, V. Chauhan, A. Mor, E. Ibler, S. Kuehnle, D. Mahoney, E. Armbrecht, and P. Dalawari, 'Racial differences

in opiate administration for pain relief at an academic emergency department',
Western Journal of Emergency Medicine, 16:3 (2015), 372–80.

103 P. Mohai and R. Sata, 'Racial inequality in the distribution of hazardous waste',
Social Problems, 54:3 (2007), 343–70; N. De Lissovoy, 'Conceptualizing the
carceral turn', *Critical Sociology*, 39:5 (2013), 739–55 (p. 743).

104 Washington, p. 3; C. Rouse, *Uncertain Suffering* (Berkeley: University of
California Press, 2009); C. Mattingly, *The Paradox of Hope* (Berkeley: University
of California Press, 2010); K. Wailoo, *Dying in the City of the Blues* (Chapel Hill:
University of North Carolina Press, 2001).

105 Sharpe, *In the Wake*, p. 21.

106 C. Bowers, 'The black hand', *Amazing Stories*, 5:10 (1931), 909–11, 923;
D. Etchison, 'The machine demands a sacrifice', in *The Dark Country* (New York:
Berkley, [1972] 1984), pp. 81–92; N. Hopkinson, *Brown Girl in the Ring* (New
York: Grand Central, [1998] 2012), pp. 3–4; W. Mosley, 'Whispers in the dark',
in S. Thomas (ed.), *Dark Matter* (New York: Aspect, [2001] 2004), pp. 162–82.
Subsequent references are in parenthesis.

107 A.C. Train, *Mortmain* (New York: Charles Scribner, 1907); M. Renard, *The
Hands of Orlac*, trans. I. White (London: Souvenir, [1920] 1981); *Orlacs Hände*,
dir. by R. Wiene (Berolina, 1924).

108 *Get Out*, dir. by Jordan Peele (Universal, 2017).

109 b. hooks, 'Postmodern blackness', *Postmodern Culture*, 1:1 (1990), www.africa.
upenn.edu/Articles_Gen/Postmodern_Blackness_18270.html, para. 12.

110 M. Wester, *African-American Gothic* (Basingstoke: Palgrave, 2012).

111 H. Malchow, *Gothic Images of Race in Nineteenth-Century Britain* (Stanford:
Stanford University Press, 1996); Wester, p. 2.

112 Wester, p. 2.

113 N. Hopkinson, 'Introduction', in N. Hopkinson (ed.), *So Long Been Dreaming*
(Vancouver: Arsenal, 2004), pp. 7–9 (p. 8).

114 M. Dery, 'Black to the future', in M. Dery (ed.), *Flame Wars* (Durham, NC: Duke
University Press, 1994), pp. 179–222 (p. 180).

115 T. Henry, 'Afrofuturism and the power of black imagination', *NBC News*
(2 December 2015), www.nbcnews.com/news/nbcblk/power-black-imagination-
can-you-dig-it-n408201 [accessed 30 June 2017]. Cf. Y. Womack, *Afrofuturism*
(Chicago: Lawrence Hill, 2013); W. Imarisha and a. m. brown (eds), *Octavia's
Brood* (Oakland: AK Press, 2015), pp. 3–6.

116 Sharpe, *In the Wake*, p. 16.

117 L. Wacquant, *Punishing the Poor* (Durham, NC: Duke University Press,
2009); M. Marable, I. Steinberg and K. Middlemass (eds), *Racializing Justice,
Disenfranchising Lives* (New York: Palgrave, 2007); M. Alexander, *The New Jim
Crow* (New York: New Press, 2010).

118 De Lissovoy, pp. 741–50.

119 Scheper-Hughes, 'Global traffic'; 'Bodies for sale'.

120 R. Robinson, 'We can't trust police to protect us from racist violence', *The Guardian*
(21 August 2019), www.theguardian.com/commentisfree/2019/aug/21/police-
white-nationalists-racist-violence [accessed 21 August 2019]; B. Patterson, '11

more things you can't do while Black (or Brown)', *Mother Jones* (9 May 2018), www.motherjones.com/crime-justice/2018/05/11-more-things-you-cannot-do-while-black-starbucks-nordstrom-rack-1/ [accessed 11 August 2018].

121 C. Rankine, 'The condition of Black life is one of mourning', *The New York Times* (22 June 2015), www.nytimes.com/2015/06/22/magazine/the-condition-of-black-life-is-one-of-mourning,.htm [accessed 12 January 2018], para. 27.

122 Cohen, 'Operability', p. 83.

123 M. Fisher, *Capitalist Realism* (Ropley: Zero Books, 2009).

124 A. Finger, *Past Due* (London: Women's Press, [1990] 1991); R. Garland-Thomson, *Extraordinary Bodies* (New York: Columbia University Press, 1997); B. Hughes, 'Fear, pity and disgust', in N. Watson, A. Roulstone, and C. Thomas (eds), *Routledge Handbook of Disability Studies* (London: Routledge, 2012), pp. 67–77.

125 hooks, para. 12.

126 C. Sharpe, *Monstrous Intimacies* (Durham, NC: Duke University Press, 2010), p. 4.

127 Wester, p. 164.

128 E. Jones, *Medicine and Ethics in Black Women's Speculative Fiction* (Basingstoke: Palgrave, 2015), p. 102.

129 Crowley-Matoka; Kierans.

130 N. Hodson, 'The gender kidney donation gap' (18 July 2018), *Dosís*, medhumdosis.com/2018/07/18/feature-the-gender-kidney-donation-gap-where-are-all-the-male-kidneys/ [accessed 19 July 2018]; D. Zimmerman, S. Donnelly, J. Miller, D. Stewart, and S. Albert, 'Gender disparity in living renal transplant donation', *American Journal of Kidney Disorders*, 6 (2000), 534–40; N. Biller-Andorno, 'Gender imbalance in living organ donation', *Medicine, Health Care and Philosophy*, 5:2 (2005), 199–204; P. Khajehdehi, 'Living non-related versus related renal transplantation', *Nephrology Dialysis Transplantation*, 14:11 (1999), 2621–4.

131 D. McCormack, 'Living with others inside the self', *Medical Humanities*, 42:4 (2016), 252–8 (pp. 253, 252).

132 Jones, p. 93.

133 Mattingly; C. West, 'Strength in the blues', *The Monarch Review* (9 September 2012), www.themonarchreview.org/cornel-west-strength-in-the-blues/ [accessed 15 August 2018].

134 N. Trethewey, 'Miracle of the black leg', *Thrall* (Boston, MA: Houghton Mifflin, 2012), pp. 9–12 (p. 11).

4

Possession? Uncanny assemblage and embodied scripts in tissue recipient horror

Gaspare Tagliacozzi's sixteenth-century work on skin transfer established the metaphor of 'graft' in transfer discourse.[1] Horticulture not only provided the language for the process but also informed Tagliacozzi's technique, including keeping the graft located for a long period to enable its fixing and dividing connection points between tissues. Yet there is an ominous ambiguity in the botanic metaphor when applied to transfer practice. Botanic 'grafting' is a technique of plant propagation in which a 'host' plant has a cutting from another plant attached to it, the 'scion'. The grafted material thrives and the host dwindles.[2] Fantasies of human allograft, too, can inspire a sense of the transferred tissue having usurping power over the host. Who is the transfer for? – the root stock or the scion?

This chapter examines texts which imagine dead donor transfer tissue changing recipients.[3] These fantasies may draw on the sciences of heredity and genetics, the language of gift exchange, and the supernatural concepts of possession and curse. At their extreme, fantasies of cadaveric organ receipt can dramatise Gothic's preoccupation with alienation from the body. David Punter says, 'Gothic tests what it might be like to be a shell … a shell which has been filled to the brim with something that looks like ourselves but is irremediably other … Thus it is we ourselves who are cast as the ghost, the spectre, the "revenant".'[4] Tropes finding new forms here include possession, paranoia, and the return of the past.

'Possession' transfer Gothic is invariably influenced by contemporaneous discourses of otherness, notably of race, class, and gender. What also emerges from these fictions, however, is the sense that maintaining a boundary between recipient and received tissue might be injurious to the recipient's recovery, and that all human tissue, *including the recipient's own pre-transplant's body*, may be uncanny. I open by discussing the emotional and imaginative work that may accompany transfer for a recipient. I then examine fictions of blood, hand, and face transfer from the nineteenth and early and mid-twentieth century from a range of British and European contexts. I will contextualise the works within their particular moment, but this chapter's analysis is not only historicist for I wish also to approach these works anachronistically, as offering figures for recipient experience since the onset of the transplantation era. These works can be seen as coincidentally foreshadowing – in fantastical and poetic terms – elements that have come, decades later, to be pertinent to some recipients' experience and which can be exceptionally challenging to communicate. Several researchers of transfer recipient experience have observed that, in qualitative interviews, the 'intangibles' and 'embodied interaction' of emotional expression and body language complicate reassuring verbal or statistical data, but these intimate and troubling data are difficult to express or capture.[5] As in my previous chapter, there is a challenge to find ways to represent suffering that occurs over a long duration. In several cases, these early fictions foreshadow conceptual and affective work that attends transplantation. I then examine millennial works which imagine accepting strangeness rather than resisting it, and which also trouble the convention that illness narrative should achieve 'coherence' or a reaffirmation of an enriched self.

Each text in this chapter resists the trend in transplant commentary to downplay any sense of the received tissue as alien or to elide recipients' imaginative work or distress. The texts figure recipient experience variously in terms of mutual enfleshment across shared tissue, possession by multiple non-human forces, and an evacuation of self and agency altogether, in crises both affective and ontological. Ultimately, the works unsettle not only a distinction between self and other but also the idea of transplantation surgery as a time-bounded event, rather framing it as an ongoing process which includes recipients' imaginative labour. In such instances, a Gothic mode may, as Barry Murnane says, 'articulate the abject moments of embodiment that is suppressed in the medical construction of the body. Thus, it may well become a more realist mode than we had ever imagined.'[6] Recipients may need to forge a new story of a self both enabled and undone by medical intervention.

The imaginative work of tissue incorporation

Whilst possession Gothic is fantastical, some recipients do fear that transfer may change them.[7] Margareta Sanner, for example, describes a recipient who initially refused heart transplant in case it diminished her own love objects, and mentions recipients who felt unease at the possibility that a differently gendered donor might compromise their own gender identity, and others who felt disturbed by desires perceived to be ego-alien.[8] In cadaveric donation, the continuation of the receiver's story is literally dependent on the ending of another's, but there is also a sense in which a receiver may feel that she and her donor share a future, in so far as the donor's life persists within her own. That intuition may become Gothic at moments where the recipient intuits a threat, a sense of fatality. The tissue transferred may feel soaked in story, in a script, as much as in blood.

Recipients are discouraged from dwelling on thoughts of the donor's death, the transferred tissue or their changed self. With some national variations, donors are often anonymised and recipients encouraged to see transferred tissue as analogous to a machine's spare parts.[9] Lesley Sharp notes, 'Transplant recipients who openly express the sense that another person dwells within them may well acquire medical labels that draw on monstrous imagery, such as "Frankenstein syndrome"'.[10] For such practitioners, a book such as this, emphasising morbid imagery, must seem perverse. Relatively few organ recipients feel the extreme form of this distress. In one survey of 47 heart transplant recipients in Vienna, for example, only 6 per cent of heart recipients felt their personality had been changed by the received tissue.[11] Yet research also suggests that recipients' emotions can be more complex than current medical frameworks may recognise.

The Toronto-based project Process of Incorporating a Transplanted Heart (PITH) has researched recipient experience since 2006. In a recent report analysing video interviews with recipients, for example, the interdisciplinary researchers found that participants' embodied communication reveals the organ incorporation process to be far more fraught than either qualitative or quantitative studies had previously suggested. All twenty-five interviewed transplant recipients had been confirmed as stable in psychological assessment both prior to and after the transplant, but 80 per cent of the video recordings of the interviews displayed intense distress. 'Slumped posture, agitated hand gestures, and above all, tearfulness' predominated, in videos that the researchers, including transplant clinicians, found 'genuinely shocking': 'It was as though the essence of heart recipients' feelings of changes to their embodied selves was beyond words, needing instead corporeal expression to convey the potent mix of hope, anxiety, dysphoria, loss and wonder ... It isn't that the clinical data are "wrong", but it can be deeply misleading about recipients' phenomenological experiences.'[12] Similarly, Matilda Almgren *et al.* found that 88 per cent of the heart transplant recipients they interviewed experienced distress, and subsequent focus-group work by Jennifer Poole *et al.* found that this included 'issues of bereavement and loss around the autonomous self ... [and] grief for their "old" hearts and the donor family', yet '[t]his ... disenfranchised grief ... is pain not recognised by current social and political norms. Consequently, patients may try to keep quiet, disallowing themselves the outward mourning that may be cathartic ... [M]ultiple and complicated forms of grief ... visit these patients.'[13] Rhonda Shaw finds similar emotion in her qualitative interviews with tissue recipients in New Zealand, in which emotion and body language were often freighted with distress. '[T]ears flowed in well over half of the interviews' in 'an outpouring of emotion', blending grief for the donor, a longing to reciprocate, and weariness over ongoing immunosuppression and medical monitoring. One participant says, particularly of her grief over the unknown donor's untimely death, 'you come away [after the surgery] and you're never the same again. You never wake up and feel the same ever again. You never do because, you know, it just changes you. It's this deep sadness in you.'[14]

The Gothic framework of this chapter is an invitation to validate such difficult aspects of recipient experience. The PITH researchers observe, 'there is a clear need to revamp clinic practice to enable recipients to express their embodied experiences, without fear of ridicule, or being thought ungrateful or psychiatrically disturbed'.[15] Such an insight connects with calls to heed disruptive forms of illness narrative and to respect the ambivalence of patient experience. Certain affective proprieties tend to prevail in terms of what is seen as appropriate patient response. Within the context of late capitalisms, a patient has a particular 'sick role' (to update Talcott Parsons's 1951 term), and central to neoliberal formulations of correct patienthood is internalising responsibility for managing one's own health through self-surveillance and lifestyle practices.[16] This can include affective imperatives. A 'positive attitude', ranging from faith in a future cure to positivity in daily self-management, is held up as both enhancing health and morally laudable; as I say elsewhere, there is a 'positivity imperative – to be hopeful, a warrior, a survivor, a meaning-finder'.[17] Yet transfer recipients, like other patients, may also experience ambivalence or more negative emotions. Surgery itself may sometimes be experienced as a violation, even if also deeply desired, and afterwards there may be emotional adjustment around imagined relationship with the tissue, and lifelong immunosuppression and medical monitoring may at times be a burden, albeit gratefully sought.[18] This is the realm of the 'new chronic' in Eric Cazdyn's terms, in which cure is not hoped for, but (highly profitable) management is.[19] As Arthur Frank says, triumphal survivorship discourse may have no place for '[l]oss and ongoing sadness, recognition of how disease can diminish life'.[20] This chapter resists cultural pressures to elide transfer recipient affective and ontological complexity, and to that end I consider how a Gothic mode may engage disturbing dimensions of the imaginative labour of tissue incorporation.

Recipients may draw on a range of cognitive and emotional strategies to come to terms with their changed embodiment. Some avoid thinking about the donor; others consciously identify with imagined donor qualities; and others describe taking a care-taking attitude towards the organ and, metonymically, towards the donor.[21] Despite medical efforts to downplay difference and to encourage recipients not to 'dwell' on it, evidence suggests that it is not necessarily always a drawback if the recipient continues to feel the transferred tissue is 'other'. In fact some recipients have found that successful post-transplant life requires coming to terms with that otherness, letting the tissue remain an Other presence but adopting a caring rather than apprehensive stance towards it. Foetal imagery features in some such recipients' descriptions of their new experience of embodiment. Margaret Lock, for example, quotes recipients saying, '[S]ometimes I feel as if I'm pregnant ... but there's another life inside of me, and I'm actually storing this life ... It's weird', 'I even call it my baby! I take so much care, I feel protective', and Francisco Varela feels his transplanted liver 'as a small sphere, as if I'm carrying an infant'.[22] These metaphors convey, as Catherine Waldby says, an intuition of the organ as a 'semi-autonomous life within', as well as a duty of care.[23] A poem by J. Reed, which opened this book, captures tender and ominous possibilities for this imagined relationship: 'My blood has adopted a child / who shuffles through my chest / carrying a doll'.[24]

Waldby calls such meshings a form of 'intercorporeality', adapting an earlier use of the term by Gail Weiss. Waldby notes that pregnancy is intercorporeal in 'the crucial double sense that it involves both a material confusion of bodies, a material indeterminacy and that it makes a relationship ... [B]iomedical intercorporeality also has this double sense. A material confusion of bodies through the exchange of fragments produces various kinds of relationality.'[25] This relationality may take many forms, from a concorporeality of two selves harmoniously coexisting, to more entangled interconnections.[26] To articulate some of the latter, stranger, possibilities of relationality, two different philosophical concepts can be invoked: Jacques Derrida's concept of 'absolute hospitality', and Gilles Deleuze and Félix Guattari's concept of 'assemblage'.

Derrida describes 'the absolute *arrivant*, who is not even a guest. He surprises the host – who is not yet a host or an inviting power – enough to call into question, to the point of annihilating or rendering indeterminate, all the distinctive signs of a prior identity'.[27] The receiver must accept the incomer entirely, including the risk that they may change what they have previously understood as home. Margrit Shildrick notes the applicability of this theory to tissue transfer:

> the recipient must recognise that when she accepts the living organ of another, she can neither claim it as a right nor expect that it will become a comfortably integrated part of herself. Given the lifelong persistence of the difference of the other's DNA, she must willingly accommodate the unknown other within – even though that otherness may prove fatal ... if her body's rejection of the alien material succeeds, she will die. And again Derrida's take on hospitality has preceded such a risk ... To give an unreserved welcome ... is an inherently insecure move ... This is a form of hospitality ... that owes nothing to the comfort of homogeneity or stability.[28]

Unpredictable (will the graft succeed? What consequences might the transplant have for side effects and future life?) yet implacably *there*, the transplant requires a recipient to welcome without certainty. This Derridean framework does not deny the otherness of the tissue, but insists upon that otherness.

The concept of assemblage emerging from the work of Deleuze and Guattari may also speak to a recipient's position. As discussed in my Introduction, assemblages are impermanent blends of materials and forces, tangible and not, impermanent and subject to entropy. Assemblages are 'living, throbbing confederations', in Jane Bennett's terms, 'not governed by any central head: no one materiality or type of material has sufficient competence to determine consistently the trajectory or impact'; she argues for 'a conception of self ... as an impure, human–nonhuman assemblage'.[29] Life itself can be seen in terms of 'a non-personal vitalist force that exceeds the unique interests and experiences of each individual'; after all, as Shildrick points out, 'each deceased donor body will provide on average organs and tissues for around seven recipients', demonstrating the 'crosscutting power of connectivity and assemblage'.[30]

There are many ways, then, to frame the corporeal intermeshing that characterises the post-transplant recipient body. The researchers of PITH suggest that

> The postoperative recipient knows that something fundamental has changed, that their sutured bodies speak to a different mode of being-in-the-world, and they want support in thinking through how to live well in a hybrid body ... To insist, as current practice does, that the pretransplant subject will live on essentially unchanged is profoundly restrictive of alternative narratives ... that might better express this human experience.[31]

Most of the texts I examine in this chapter do not offer support in thinking through how to 'live well in a hybrid body'. Rather, they usefully dramatise *failures* of such imaginative adaptation, showing that it is perilous to cling to the illusion of discrete individuality.

Uncanny bodies and narrative opacity: vectors of donor influence and the pre-transplant strange

What causalities of donor influence, what logics, may be deployed within possession transfer Gothic? Three of the most common are the mysterious agency inhering in a gift, the transfer of genetic material, or transfer-associated infection.

Anthropological studies have explored how gifts may bear a sense of a lingering connection with the donor, along with a burden to reciprocate, and the most famous exploration of this link is Marcel Mauss's research on mid-twentieth-century Trobriand Islander society. Mauss argues that, here, the obligation for individuals to reciprocate gifts stemmed from the way that gifts are perceived to retain something of those who gave them. He uses the

Maori term *hau* to describe this quality and argues that 'the thing received is not inactive ... the *hau* follows after anyone possessing the thing'.[32] Receivers must reciprocate in kind, but, even if they do, they can never equal the fact that the original gift inaugurated the exchange network. Subsequent gift theory has emphasised that givers have control.[33] As Eytan Bercovitch says, one can discern an 'agent in the gift'.[34]

The conception of 'gift' that circulates in patient-facing discourse, by contrast, emphasises altruistic donation as a 'no strings attached' event.[35] Medical documentation may depersonalise transferred tissue – diluting the *hau*, as it were – by referring to the transplanted organ as 'the material', omitting mention of donors from most patient-facing communications, and depersonalising and even dehumanising the donor through symbolic substitutions, such as comparing transplant to the growth of plants or to replacing spare machine parts.[36] The one exception to this is the thank-you letter recipients may be encouraged to write to bereaved donor kin. The letter directly challenges the depersonalising framework, and those who write them often describe these letters as difficult to write, and a sense of the impossibility of reciprocation.[37] In a real sense tissue *does* retain markers of the 'giver' – a very material *hau* (immunological markers, genetic material and more). Margaret Lock describes the 'lingering animism' that recipients may feel about the tissue they receive, and, in the case of cadaveric organ donation, any such sense of lingering presence is particularly unnerving since the 'giver' is dead. Mauss's words take on a whole new resonance in the context of Gothic fictions of tissue transfer possession: 'the *hau* follows after anyone possessing the thing'.[38]

Tissue itself, too, may feel charged with threat. In fact, the immunological threat stems from the recipient's body, rather than the donor tissue (the exception being Graft-versus-Host disease, rare except in bone marrow transfer, in which transferred immune defence cells attack recipient tissue). That being said, GvH, infection, and the migration of genetic material are all plausible ways that transfer tissue itself might impact the recipient body. Some recipients fear that genetic transmission may rewire the rest of their body or personality in some unspecified way, and, while there is no evidence of that, donor genetic material does migrate elsewhere.[39] In Alaska, for example, a recipient of a bone marrow transplant committed a crime, and the DNA found at the scene implicated his living donor who was in jail at the time.[40] Tissue may also bear infection, and representations of that risk are often associated with dominant prejudices of an era. In my previous chapter I discussed racist commentary on mid-twentieth-century blood transfusion, and later in the century anxieties over HIV gave rise to 'bizarre proposals (including a blood bank containing only blood donated by certified virgins)'.[41]

Yet iatrogenic genetic chimera and tissue-borne infection also remind us that bodies are always already strange prior to transplant, including in terms of infection and genetics. A side effect of immunosuppression is the release of infections stored in the recipient body, hitherto held in check by the body's immune system. In the process, it unmasks the way that pre-transplant bodies already hold quantities of potentially harmful alien material. More benevolently, research on the microbiome indicates that much non-identical material within the human body is vital for life.[42] Furthermore, 'our' own genetic material is hardly a readable or unthreatening text either. Readability is admittedly the impression given by what might be called the 'genetic imaginary', the constellation of ideas and fantasies that circulate around genetic knowledge.[43] Media coverage of the Human Genome project describes 'breaking the code' and declares 'Biologists seek the words in DNA's unbroken text', and contemporary commercial gene-sequencing companies like 23andme ask 'What is your DNA story?', explicitly invoking past narratives from ancestral DNA, and future narratives as suggested by statistical predictions of predilection to develop certain diseases or conditions.[44] Media representations of DNA as text can overstate genomic predictive power as something closer to fate, with the difference that a human trajectory is scripted by microscopic cellular proteins rather than supernatural entities.[45] In the case of genetic inheritance, that cryptic agency is partially a function of inherited genetic code. The title character of Robert Louis Stevenson's 'Olalla', in which vampirism is genetically transmitted, represents heredity in terms of malevolent ancestors acting on her body in the present: '"The hands of the dead are in my bosom; they move me, they pluck me, they guide me; I am a puppet at their command"'.[46]

Faced with this panoply of strangeness in both transferred tissue and recipient body, embodiment may become uncanny. The uncanny is typically defined in terms of emotional unease or a crisis of certainty. Ernst Jentsch, for example, sees the *Unheimlich* as hingeing ambiguous vitality, the tendency to 'infer … that things in the external world are also animate'.[47] Threatening animism is also part of Freud's later description of the *Unheimlich* (translated 'uncanny' by his English translator James Strachey, but more accurately 'unhomely'). Unlike Jentsch, however, Freud explains the uncanny effect ensuing not from uncertainty over life or death but from the return of repressed memories or desires too taboo or overwhelming to be admitted to consciousness, or a regression to earlier childhood 'surmounted beliefs' of an animate world. In the process of such return, the familiar becomes strange.[48] Anthony Vidler says that Freud's uncanny describes 'the fundamental property of the familiar to turn on its owners, suddenly to become defamiliarized, derealized, as if in a dream'.[49]

Crucially, Freud's uncanny involves a sense of narrative opacity. He introduces the concept by recalling an experience he had in an Italian town, during which he kept unwittingly returning to the sex workers' quarter despite consciously trying to avoid it. After the third return he is overcome by 'a feeling ... which I can only describe as uncanny'.[50] This description of the uncanny, as I say elsewhere, involves 'feeling helpless in the grip of a narrative we cannot recognise or shape. We sense a malevolent design behind events/ an encounter/an object, but we are shut off from knowing that meaning' (even if, as Freud's intrapsychic model suggests, that unknowable agency is unconscious desire).[51] In other words, when we are in an uncanny state, we do not know the story we are in, but we sense there *is* a secret script, one beyond our control and perhaps our comprehension.

Freud's psychoanalytic rationale for the uncanny is less persuasive to many of us today. I suggest, however, that elements of Jentsch's earlier approach – the uncanny as an effect of an uncertainty over living or dead – might be fruitfully combined with one particular strand of Freud's discussion in a way that can help us talk about some transfer recipient affect. Approaching the uncanny as an *experience of narrative opacity* may be useful for articulating some transfer recipients' experience. There is admittedly a sharp disjunction between psychodynamic hermeneutics and those which emphasise assemblage, 'absolute hospitality', or intercorporeality, since the latter three approaches emphasise materiality, boundary blur, and network. Yet if we loosen the term from its psychodynamic frame (since Freud was not the first to define it, and does not have the final word), and redefine the uncanny as an experience of mysterious threat and narrative opacity, it is useful language for describing some transfer recipients' affective response. If the new form of hybridity is experienced as an unwanted destabilising of self, then the intuition of assemblage or intercorporeality may indeed lead to the sense of being in the grip of a cryptic narrative governed by opaque agencies. Whilst the language of the 'weird' and the 'eerie' emphasises the radical otherness and unknowability of a nonhuman agency,[52] the language of the uncanny is imbued with a sense of strange kinship and familiarity, even while conveying that the intuited controlling agency is opaque and out of the subject's control.

As it happens, Freud himself illustrates the uncanny with reference to a short story about harvest horror: E.T.A. Hoffmann's short story 'The sandman' (1817), which centres on the horror of the excision of eyes.[53] In Freud's reading, however, the uncanniness of the disembodied eyes is not intrinsic to the tissue, but stems rather from the repressed fear that he argues the excision symbolises (castration). By contrast, possession transfer Gothic *literalises* the threat of the excised material. The transferred material is feared as itself effecting change in the recipient. Similarly, tissue transfer Gothic also often identifies the recipient's pre-transplant body as already cryptic and uncanny, encoded with its own genetic story. In other words, both the received tissue and the original body are rife with agencies generating scripts that subjects cannot control and may not even be able to discern. Material has agency. Tissue is the locus of horror.

'Seething' forces and 'fantastic melancholy' in early fantasies of blood and hand transfer

Blood transfusion was a significant component of iconic nineteenth-century Gothic, and an important precursor for later transfer horror. As William Hughes has observed, blood 'may signify at various times notions of family, race, religion, and gender ... Diluted or depleted it may signify simultaneously personal lassitude alongside racial, familial, or moral decline and degeneration.'[54] Popular media celebrated transfusion successes but also reported some transfusion recipients feeling grief for their lost 'purity'. The Italian singer Enrico Caruso, for example, lamented 'I'll have no more my pure Italian blood. What now am I?'[55] Anxieties over compromised body boundaries were intensified by the way that, in addition to the symbolism of the fluid itself, nineteenth-century technologies of transfusion were profoundly intimate. Until twentieth-century developments in plastics technology, transfusion required 'direct transfusion' surgically connecting donor and recipient blood vessels, 'ma[king] it difficult to ignore the social and material realities of the individual bodies and bloods involved'.[56] That intimacy also sat uneasily with the way that nineteenth-century blood transfusion was often gendered, typically involving male relatives to women afflicted by blood loss in childbirth.

Gendered apprehensions often overlap with fear of racial contamination in early transfusion Gothic. Bram Stoker's novel *Dracula* (1898), for example, features a blood transfusion scene which echoes typical nineteenth-century gendering of the scenario; Lucy Westenra receives blood transfusions from three of the male heroes who love her. Several twentieth-century romantic films, too, feature characters donating tissue or blood to another, demonstrating deep devotion and normalising transfer within heteronormative sentimentality.[57] This implication is also present in *Dracula*, the doctor van Helsing declaring, 'this so sweet maid is a polyandrist!' and half-jokingly describing himself as a 'bigamist' for also donating his own.[58] In *Dracula*, however, the suggestion of reproductive conjunction is presented as appalling. The transfusion turns out to benefit the novel's monster, who then drinks their blood from Lucy, and the vampire is coded in terms evocative of anti-Semitism or a 'foreign' form of criminal degeneracy. His threat to the Englishmen – "'your girls whom you love are mine already, and through them you and others shall be mine'" – has been analysed in terms of late nineteenth-century unease over racial 'purity' and the decline of Empire.[59] Anxieties over blood transfer abound in media and fiction of the period, and I will single out one in particular for further scrutiny: Frank Kinsella's novel *The Degeneration of Dorothy* (1899). This text is paradigmatic in using possession tropes and representing transfer as a threat to racial purity, but it also engages in important ways with the emerging science of heredity in ways that complicate a simplistic trope of possession.

Dorothy, a virginal, privileged Englishwoman, receives a blood transfusion from a Spanish man.[60] After her transfusion, she changes from being demure and busy with charitable works to being callous and promiscuous, and abandons her husband to go with her blood donor (now lover) to Spain. She also chooses flamboyant dress designs and begins attending a Catholic church, and her singing voice changes from 'a silvery sweetness' to 'crimson velvety voluptuousness' – well might the narrator say she 'changed in a great many ways' (pp. 92–6)! The surgeon Dr Archbell laments, "'Like Frankenstein, I have through the agency of science, literally created a monster, that may fill my life and that of others with regret and remorse'" (p. 201). This 'monstrosity', in Archbell's telling, is a function of blood crossing racial and gendered lines. The transfusion is explicitly described as contamination: "'the germ-laden blood of this Spaniard carried into … a young, sensitive girl'" (p. 202). Like Stoker's *Dracula*, this text communicates racist apprehensions over blood changing a recipient, and by extension fear of women's unbridled sensuality opening a nation's bloodline to imagined corruption.

In addition, however, the novel does something more unexpected: it does not ultimately locate the cause of Dorothy's change in the transfusion alone. Archbell, the medical authority in the novel, declares that the transfusion was only a catalyst. The 'real' source of her change, it transpires, lies in heredity. Dr Archbell tells Dorothy's father:

> 'The inherited traits of her grandmother … were … held in subjection in Dorothy by all the sterling, upright traits inherited from you … [After transfusion, t]he disturbing, vile-germed life fluid … permeating every portion of Dorothy's physical being … at once *acted upon, and in conjunction with*, those inherent and latent inclinations which before had lain altogether dormant … a million seething, dominating germs are all through the great life streams of the body … [T]he germs of the degenerated blood … have, *through the operation of her latent sympathetic atavism*, taken full possession … (pp. 202–3, emphases in original)

Here, Dr Archbell draws on late nineteenth-century conceptions of biological inheritance, including Charles Darwin's idea that hereditary material was shed in 'minute granules … dispersed throughout the whole system'.[61] Notably, the form of 'possession' described in this extract is not a single malevolent entity controlling a victim, nor is it the 'Legion' demonic collective imagined in the Christian New Testament (Matthew 8: 28–34). This possession is a web of a 'million seething' forces, including 'germs' and unspecified structures of heredity. Other narratives of seeming tissue transfer possession, too, may position donor as threat only to complicate the binary of threatening alien tissue versus 'pure' original self, by showing the recipient body to be always already in the grip of malevolent scripts – specifically, scripts which unsettle assumptions of individual autonomy. Possession transfer Gothic is sometimes less about a horror of a firm boundary transgressed than about revealing that body and subject were never stable but always porous, permeable, other.

A similar unease characterises several fictions of hand transfer, one of the most widespread tropes of transfer recipient horror. Too numerous to list comprehensively, such works hinge on a hand or arm transfer, often from a murderer, which seems to change the recipient.[62] Hands need not, of course, be transplanted to be strange: a vast body of horror imagines hands turning against their owners or becoming animated by an alien will.[63] Neurological research, too, has identified 'phantom limb' syndrome – the lingering felt presence of a lost limb – and 'alien hand syndrome', in which a person cannot consciously control their own hand yet the hand moves purposefully seemingly of its own will.[64] It makes sense that hands are a particularly charged locus for transfer horror for they are so often assumed to be a primary tool for human acting on the world, a means to grasp, to write, to reach, and to act (though such cultural equations of hands and agency are of course problematic in that they risk diminishing the agency of people who may have an amputated hand or upper limb).

The following works try to grapple, in an extreme form, with ontological and affective aspects of tissue incorporation. I will explore three early fantasies of hand transfer from 1907 to 1924. Each initially seems to portray the recipient developing homicidal impulses, but ultimately shows these changes to be illusory. Such anti-climax and refutation of the supernatural is of course a long-established Gothic device and, narrated thus, it may sound as though the main impact of these works is to debunk recipient dread. Yet since these works emphasise the recipient's frame of mind, that final debunking does not dilute the impact of their (failed) efforts to come to terms with ontological and affective challenges attendant on tissue incorporation. The tendency I identify in these is not necessarily generalisable across later adaptations, in which hands may indeed seem to be animated by a supernatural presence. I am interested in this early cluster specifically because, although these do not ultimately ascribe the hand transfer a supernatural consequence, they none the less present recipient experience in terms of horror and dread.

The title of Arthur Cheney Train's novella *Mortmain* (1907) means 'dead hand' in French.[65] Train was friends with the hand surgeon Robert Abbe who performed hand reconstructions and experimented with limb graft in animals.[66] The title character, Sir Richard Mortmain, sustains a severe injury. Under anaesthesia he hallucinates that he has had a hand transfer from a clerk who was paid for it but died after the surgery. In his fantasy, Mortmain deteriorates psychologically, and is framed for a murder performed by the hand's original owner. He wakes and discovers he had no transplant.

The work's primary impact lies in the emotive description of perceived changes after transfer. Mortmain feels body dysmorphia at the contrast between the two hands, and is repelled by the new one:

> unmistakeably it was not his own. He never laid the two together – never let his eyes fall upon the vicarious fingers if he could avoid it, for inevitably a sickening sensation of repulsion followed … [T]he new one was broader and hairy … There were too many pores!
>
> He loathed the thing, tell himself as often as he would that it was nothing but a mechanical device to supplement Nature. (pp. 44–5)

Mortmain tries to erase the hand's otherness by seeing it as mechanical rather than organic, but he feels he is becoming easily angered, and 'On the slightest provocation the fingers … would curve and clutch, and a fierce longing seize him to compass the extinction of life' (p. 46). 'At night he would dream … that he was fastened to some miserable convict, shackled by the wrist in such a way that somehow they two had grown together', and, as the dream closes, he merges with the other figure, and sees 'his own wretched shape writhing at the other end of their mutual arm' (p. 48). The dream of the 'mutual arm' confronts him with the fact of the material connectedness of donor and recipient, and it is in this that his horror lies.

Mortmain inspired other fictions including Maurice Renard's novel *Les mains d'Orlac* (*The Hands of Orlac*) (1920).[67] I will analyse a 1981 English translation by Iain White which invites comparison with the near-contemporaneous late 1970s harvest horror texts which I discuss in Chapter 2. Like those, the novel comments on hospitals as sites of capitalist industry, 'resembl[ing] factories. Under the scalpel, living flesh is treated there like wood under the plane or steel under the rolling mill' (p. 59). Yet whilst that metaphor seems to parallel those 1970s horror texts' focus on corporate and profit-driven settings, this 1920s text is generally more preoccupied with the individual struggle of the recipient.

The virtuoso pianist Stephen Orlac loses both hands in a railway accident, and a surgeon replaces Stephen's hands with hands from a prisoner executed for murder. Stephen is aware of his hands' provenance, while his wife Rosine is not. The first part of the novel is described from Rosine's perspective, and presents her dismay at Stephen's post-surgical strangeness. Like the protagonist of *Mortmain*, Stephen struggles with guilt and a sense of having been changed by the procedure. The couple seem to be haunted by a ghost and menaced by a gang urging Stephen to commit murder, and he is blackmailed by a person who claims to be the dead man returned. Eventually it emerges that the blackmailer is an imposter, and furthermore that the man from whom Stephen's hands were taken was innocent. Stephen's fantasies of his new hands' murderously changing him were unfounded. The novel ends abruptly after that revelation.

The Dr Cerrel of *Orlac* is partially inspired by the Nobel-prize-winning Alexis Carrell, a luminary of transplantation history. Whilst Carrell was celebrated in the US, he had a rather more ambiguous reception in France. In 1913, for example, one print publication represented him alongside images of chimeric bodies and occult trappings.[68] Campion-Vincent observes that the 'surgeons (part supernatural heroes, part executioners) are heirs to the ambivalent fictional characters of the sacrificial priest and the butcher'.[69] *Orlac's* Dr Cerrel embodies similar ambiguities, on the one hand 'a white-clothed superman' (p. 30) inventing astonishing grafting techniques, and on the other hand eliciting ambiguous responses from his peers. A fellow doctor observes, "That reputation of his … there's something that's not quite wholesome about it" (p. 27). Yet Cerrel is not the driver of malevolence. As with *Mortmain*, the novel's horror is a function of the *recipient's* affective state.

Post-transplant, Stephen finds the imaginative work of incorporation devastating in three ways, experiencing fear over contamination by the hand's difference, melancholy for his lost capacity, and an obsession with trying to remove the hand's otherness. He becomes preoccupied with the criminality of the transferred hand and, by extension, with theories of the way criminality may be embodied. He reads Cesare Lombroso's works of criminal anthropology and newspaper reports on the donor's crimes, and increasingly comes to suspect his hand has muscle memory of strangulation. Stephen is disconcerted not only by criminality but also by class difference. When he meets the seeming-donor he is troubled by his class-crossing, his "'air of a workman with artistic pretensions … [T]the way he speaks … at one moment it's commonplace, the next it's almost dandified … He's frightening'" (p. 276). More sympathetically, Stephen grieves his lost capacity to play. Rosine sees him sit and listen to a gramophone recording of one of his own old performances:

> The piano seemed distant, distant, immured in the depths of an unimaginable cavern … [F]rom the enormous convolvulus flower that exhaled sounds rather than odours the clamorous spectre of a time that was dead and gone burst ceaselessly forth. The Stephen of former times was making himself heard to the Stephen of today, like one of the dead come, quite openly, to haunt one of the living. Oh! The melancholy, the fantastic melancholy of that invention that freezes sounds. (p. 93)

Similarly, Stephen describes the gramophone discs as 'funerary tablets' (p. 94). His melancholy becomes materialised in the audio technology of the gramophone, both the physical presence of the machine and the aural quality of the recordings.

Stephen's response to fear and grief is to try to annihilate the fact of his new hybridity. He becomes obsessed with treatments to increase the hands' resemblance to his original hands, having them treated for hours with electrical and manual techniques in a 'therapeutic mania' (p. 97). Another character later tells him:

> 'Your one thought was to make ... *naturalise* those interlopers, those refugees, those necessary parasites as *Orlac's hands*! ... You tormented them so as to make them lose all recollection of their former owner, to appropriate them to yourself and fashion them in the likeness of your own dead hands!' (p. 253, emphasis in original)

In this extraordinary passage Orlac's version of tissue incorporation is condemned as pathological *because* it seeks to erase the otherness of the received tissue. In a highly Derridean move, Orlac's erasure of otherness is presented as a lamentable violence, injurious to both parties.

An even more complex and moving reflection on the work of tissue incorporation can be gleaned from Robert Wiene's film adaptation, *Orlacs Hände* (1924), an Austrian silent horror melodrama released in English as *The Hands of Orlac*.[70] Drawing on techniques made famous in Wiene's Expressionist masterpiece *The Cabinet of Dr Caligari* (1920), this film is less overtly fantastical but retains moments of disorienting cinematography and striking *mise en scène*.[71] The film translates Renard's plot into the context of postwar Germany. Although Paul Orlac is not a soldier, many elements of the film echo the experiences of those returning from war, as Anjeana Hans observes. Both the real soldiers and the fictional Paul write yearning letters home but return to find a changed world of socioeconomic upheaval, transformed gender dynamics, a sense of betrayal by the older generation who sent them to war, and a split self stemming from becoming killers in war.[72]

The film's plot resembles that of Renard's novel. The pianist Paul Orlac and his wife Yvonne are devastated after a railway accident destroys his hands. After a hand transfer from an executed murderer he begins to fear he is becoming murderous. As in Renard's version, his fears prove unfounded, and he is being manipulated by a criminal pretending to be the donor; furthermore, it also emerges that the donor was innocent, so Paul does not have a murderer's hands. Yet the film and novel differ in important respects. Whilst Renard's Stephen is tortured by the feared criminality of the hands, he is also deeply preoccupied by the loss of his virtuoso ability to play the piano. Wiene's Paul, by contrast, is most tormented by the knowledge of the hands' guilt and his consequent conviction that he should no longer touch another person, including his wife.

Loving touch is central to the film. It opens with a letter from Paul to his wife, saying he looks forward to seeing her on his return home from a performance: 'my hands will glide over your hair – and I will feel your body beneath my hands'. Hands are central for Paul not only in his capacity as a virtuoso pianist but also for human and erotic connection. He receives a letter that tells

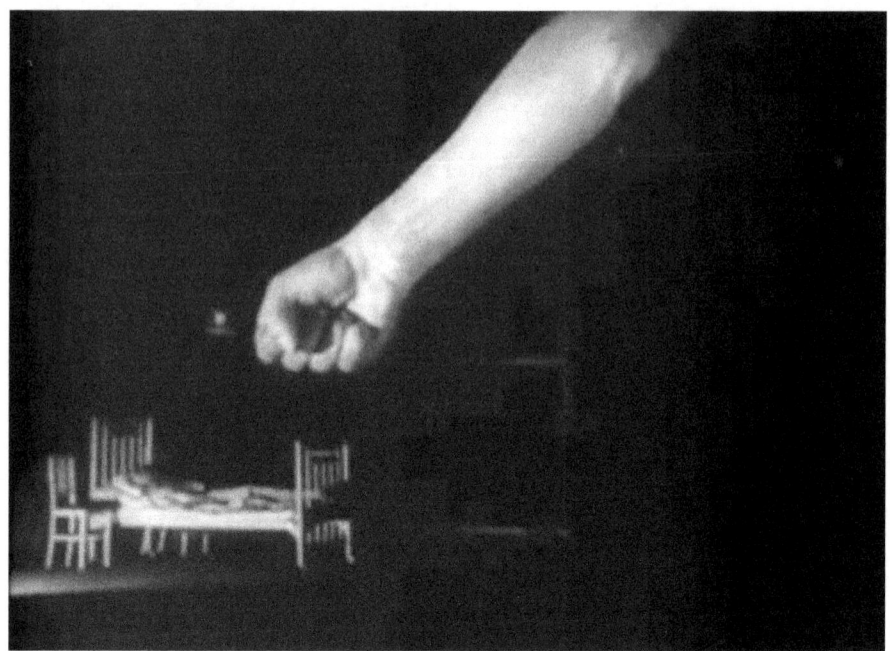

Figure 8 The fist descends. Still from *Orlacs Hände*, dir. by Robert Wiene
(Berolina, 1924).

him he has the hands of a convicted murderer, the doctor confirms this is true.
Paul vows, 'These hands will never be allowed to touch another person', and
collapses in despair. He begins experiencing the compulsion to kill and feels
himself pulled and controlled by the hands.[73] The impact of this dread is intensified by the way the actor Conrad Veidt also portrayed a somnambulist under
malevolent control, in Wiene's *Cabinet of Dr Caligari*. At night he dreams of the
hands controlling him, menacing him (Figure 8). At one point, Paul declaims in
despair to the absent donor that the desire to kill 'comes from you – along the
arms – until it reaches the soul. ... Damned, cursed hands!' Paul pleads with
his surgeon to remove the hands, but the surgeon refuses.

Deeply sympathetic, Conrad Veidt's performance conveys agony and
estrangement through passionate movement, curving, tensing, and reaching
in eloquent postures (Figure 9). Much of the film presents Orlac in stark isola-
tion, illuminated by chiaroscuro effects amid black surrounds and extended in
postures bespeaking despair and dread. In his expressive, silent performance,
Veidt offers corporeal expression for a range of emotions that may be associated
with tissue transfer, including revulsion, fear, and, ultimately, acceptance. This
bodily expressiveness reaches a powerful culmination in his reaction when he
learns that Vasseur was innocent. Orlac brings the transplanted hands to his

Figure 9 Despair. Still from *Orlacs Hände*, dir. by Robert Wiene (Berolina, 1924).

heart and face and kisses them in an act of tenderness. In the film's closing scene, he again embraces his wife. In the same way that Shildrick *et al.* argue that the corporeal nonverbal communication of recipients may express significant affective challenges in coming to terms with transplant, so too does this film offer deeply moving embodied expression to communicate fear, yearning, and acceptance around recipient experience.

'[B]aleful ceremonial ritual': Georges Franju's *Les yeux sans visage*

The world's first successful face transplant was performed on Isabelle Dinoire in France in 2005, and the fact that France was the first country to master this is arguably not a coincidence. French literature includes a rich lineage of fantasies of facial ruination and repair. Stefanos Geroulanos observes, 'from Alexandre Dumas's *Man in the Iron Mask*, Leroux's *Phantom of the Opera*, and Victor Hugo's *Laughing Man*, the post-WWI obsession with the *gueules cassées* – the facial mutilées of trench warfare – and all the way to the groundbreaking 2005 facial graft ... the replacement of a face ... has been a theme so significant as to amount to a national obsession'.[74] Geroulanos suggests that this preoccupation may partly have a linguistic cause. Whilst the word *face* is occasionally used in French, the more common term is *visage*, and the term denotes, as Geroulanos observes, 'both the physical front of the face and the character of the person who carries or wears it ... [T]he face is the site that bears the tension between expression and interiority.'[75] In that framing, an injured face may be read as implying an injury to selfhood and/or ability to be in human fellowship. (This is the kind of equivalence that disability studies seeks to challenge.)[76] The face and its ruinations is a pervasive theme of an abundance of post-First World War philosophy and art in France, often hinging on reveries around the loss of humanity of someone deprived of it or the ways the face mediates social connection.

Georges Franju's *Les yeux sans visage* (1958) (*Eyes without a Face*) is one of the most famous films of transfer horror.[77] I will summarise the plot reluctantly, for – as with Denis's film *L'intrus*, which I discuss later – the film's relevance to my discussion lies not so much in the narrative trajectory as in its disorienting atmosphere and treatment of time. The film begins with a woman (Louise) driving a car at night to drop a girl's wrapped corpse in a river. The next day Professor Genéssier, a pioneer in skin grafts, is giving a lecture when he is interrupted to come and identify the girl's body as his daughter Christiane. The police believe Christiane committed suicide out of despair at facial injuries sustained in a car accident, for which her father was responsible. In fact, Christiane is alive, and Genéssier and Louise kidnapped the dead girl and removed her face to attempt skin graft for Christiane; the harvestee then killed herself. As in *Mains d'Orlac*, ambivalence around Alexis Carrell influences the film's portrayal of a pioneering surgeon combining genius and menace. Genéssier traps stray dogs to torture in grafting experiments, keeping them in cellar cages like a 'suburban equivalent of ... Moreau's "House of Pain"', as Suzanne Biernoff wryly notes.[78] Parallels are established between these canine victims and the surgical patients, with Genéssier's erstwhile patient and assistant Louise wearing a wide collar-like choker to conceal her own scar and Christiane asking Louise to euthanise her like the animals. Driven to madness, Christiane stabs Louise and sets the dogs loose on the father. They destroy his face and she drifts into the forest surrounded by doves.

Summarising the plot evokes the bloody Grand Guignol tradition. Adam Lowenstein, for example, says that 'corpses multiply' and 'the daughter's resentment builds ... [to] murderous rage'.[79] Such a statement misses the film's restrained delivery, its melancholic register, and its preoccupation with the strange temporalities of waiting. These latter qualities are at the heart of my analysis. I want to draw out the way the film portrays both surgical time and a post-transplant melancholic suspense – a state less about possession by another agency than of *evacuation* of agency or self-possession.

Notorious for its extended scene of the surgical removal of a woman's face, the film is said to have led to seven people fainting when it was screened at the Edinburgh Film Festival in 1960. No music cushions the scene. The surgical

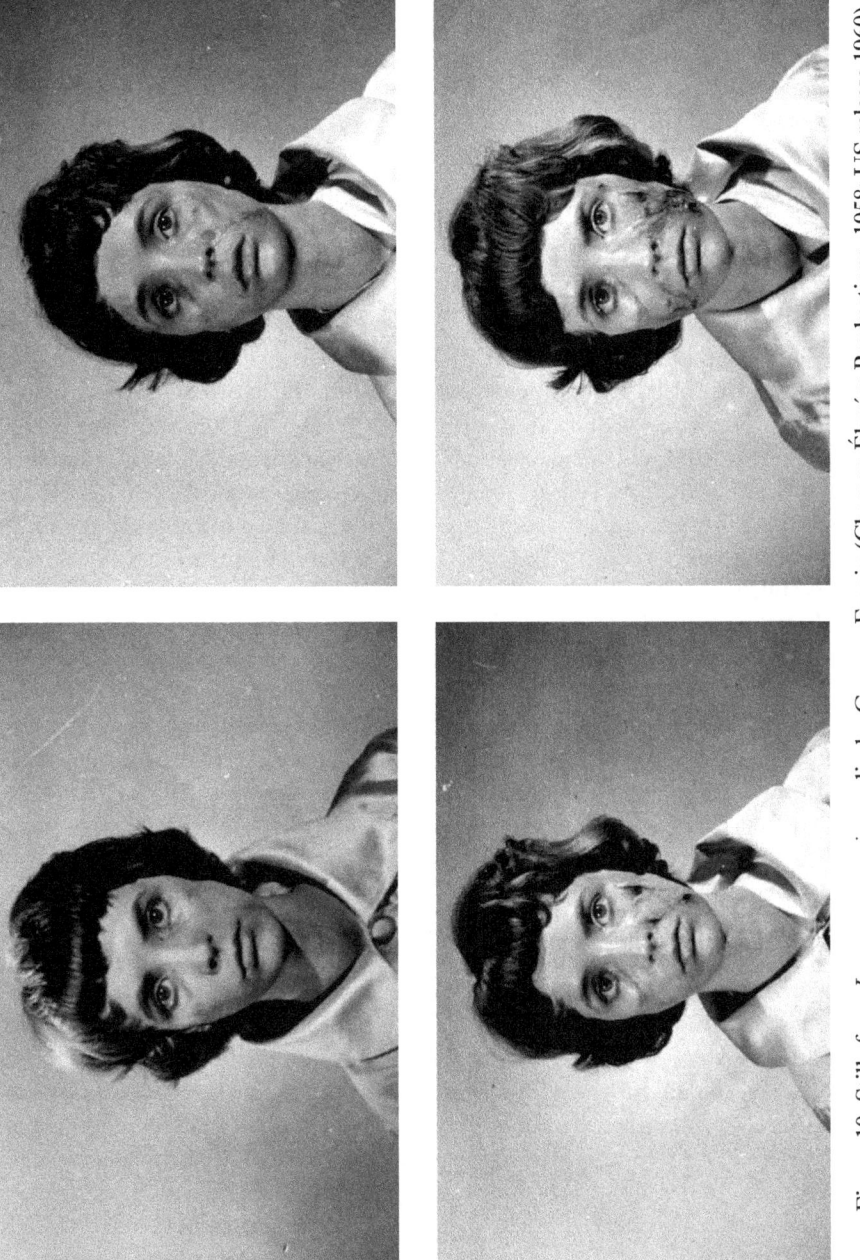

Figure 10 Stills from *Les yeux sans visage*, dir. by Georges Franju (Champs-Élysées Productions, 1958; US release 1960).

action is recorded in detail, the shining metallic tables holding supine women, the bright lights, masks, scalpel tracing skin, and, after long silent minutes of relentless, subtle movements, the pulling off of the face in a single strip. The scene 'leads us implacably on to the very limits of what our nerves can stand', as Jean Cocteau says.[80] What is central to the force of this scene, however, is not the gore of the final image but the stillness, silence, and extended duration that characterise the previous minutes. Duration and suspense make the scene excessive and startling, and these very qualities continue to be foregrounded throughout the film's exploration of the *post*-graft life of the recipient.

After the seemingly successful second face transfer, Christiane says, 'When I look into a mirror, I feel I'm seeing someone who looks like me, returning from far away'. Her return is equivocal and temporary. Her tenuous sense of self and her detachment from the (not yet 'her') new face is intensified by the knowledge of prior failure and the likelihood of further failure, and that grim prognosis is realised. The film captures that bleak trajectory in a series of clinical stills presenting the deterioration of the skin graft over the course of twenty days (Figure 10). Genéssier's captions record the process: 'spots of pigmentation appear', 'palpation reveals small subcutaneous nodules', 'necrosis of the graft tissue', 'The dead tissue must be removed'. The clinical language of his captions contrasts sharply with Christiane's defeated expression of bewildered vulnerability.

Christiane's masked presence on the screen is futuristic, fantastical; as Sinclair says, she is 'mesmerizing … an arsenic-powdered kabuki doll, with a tensile steel-skin fragility … Bandaged like a futurist chrysalis'.[81] She is bandaged to facilitate transformation but doomed never to reach it. To appreciate the impact of her on-screen presence, and indeed the rest of the dreamlike quality of the film, it helps to draw on Franju's philosophy of *le cinéma de l'insolite*. The 'cinema of the strange or unusual' is created by 'infusing an affective image with a significance that is felt but whose meaning is not perceived'.[82] *Elusive* significance is central to the concept. *Les yeux* engenders *insolite* through performance and camerawork that engender suspense without satisfying it. For example, Franju describes a shot in which he held the camera on an empty courtyard for an extra five seconds prior to a car entering the frame, and observes that the lingering is what 'made the spectator think to himself, well, if he's so insistent about it, he must have a reason. What reason? There's the uncertainty, the unknown … But on another level, of course, it boded nothing, since there was no message whatsoever.'[83] Christiane's slow movements around the house, walking up stairs and through rooms, are richly evocative of strangeness. Sinclair laments the film's 'funereal' pacing – 'all that plodding up endless staircases' – but I argue that is actually the point: the scenes have a deliberately slow, oneiric quality, a sense of 'baleful ceremonial ritual', in Franju's terms.[84] Elsewhere, Franju suggests that *le cinéma de l'insolite* can also be evoked by ruin, an edifice 'with no depth to it, now uninhabited, a hollow shell ... An emptiness that was once inhabited'.[85] Christiane herself is evacuated of agency rather than restored to it, living compliant within an oppressive system of restraints. These scenes construct a post-surgical melancholy, a suspenseful waiting (for graft rejection) and a stasis (a permanent imprisonment, a lack of hope).

I do not argue that *Les yeux* offers a mimetic representation of transplantation recipient experience, especially since the onset of immunosuppression has reduced the horror of tissue rejection. I do suggest that the film's fantasticality, its dreamlike evocation of post-transplant suspense and melancholy, is anachronistically valuable now in expanding our rhetorics of potential post-transplant temporalities and subjectivities: the intuition of the body made strange, the sense of a restored 'intactness' that feels not one's own, and the need to watch and fear for clues of graft failure. Whilst the film may be fantastical, these affects are not.

I will conclude this chapter by considering three texts from the transplantation era which build on these literary and cinematic lineages to represent autobiographical experiences of transplant. These works, too, deploy Gothic tropes and intertextualities to communicate challenging ontological and affective dimensions of recipient experience. In these cases, however, such representation may be marshalled in recipient *acceptance* of the fractures and contingencies of the post-transplant body.

Survival and violation: three millennial representations of tissue transfer

I will examine the autobiographical essays '*L'intrus*' (2000) by Jean-Luc Nancy, in Susan Hanson's 2002 translation, and 'Intimate distances' (2001) by Francisco Varela, and Claire Denis's film *L'intrus* (2004) inspired by Nancy's work.[86] Each explores recipient experience through images of distress, disorientation, and permanent wounding. In addition to grappling with emotional complexity, these works grapple with ontological challenges attendant on tissue receipt. These works use images of dismemberment and haunting to theorise both the visceral experience of their new embodiment and the way in which that experience challenges dominant cultural discourses of human bodies as individual, autonomous, and intact.

The two life-writing essays resist a widespread (but not universal) trend in illness writing, that the author reclaim a sense of self and their own agency amid the challenges of illness and the passivities attendant on much medical treatment. Rita Charon argues that writing illness narratives enables 'patients to give voice to what they endure and to frame the illness so as to escape dominion by it', and Ann Hunsaker Hawkins suggests that illness narratives 'restore to reality its lost coherence and ... create, a meaning that can bind it together again'.[87] Stories of survivorship, in particular, may show illness culmi-nating in new insights and an enriched sense of 'self'. Yet some kinds of illness experience – chaos, pain, passivity in the grip of medical interventions – may fit uneasily with such confidence in story-making agency and narrative con-solations. Access to a narratively coherent self is variable and often entangled with privilege.[88] Frank warns that some representations of distress 'cannot, and never will coalesce into a cohesive whole, as narrative traditions expect whole-ness', and that marginalising such stories can mean that some 'sound wrong at best and less than human at worst'.[89]

The texts I will discuss in the remainder of this chapter do not offer a sense of restored 'coherence'. My analysis is not structuralist and does not hinge on classifying texts within a particular taxonomy, but there are points of useful connection with Frank's categorisation of illness narrative. The following texts do not match the most widely valorised forms of illness narrative as identi-fied by Frank: the 'quest narrative' in which a person's experience of illness becomes a meaningful journey, or the 'restitution narrative' in which a benev-olent medical system restores a patient's health. Nor do they match the more ambiguous move of 'intransitive hope', being open to an unspecified beneficial transformation in future time.[90] A more pertinent category for my analysis is that of 'chaos narrative' (or more accurately *anti*-narrative), Frank's term for a mode in which pain, disorientation, and despair annihilate the ability to rep-resent the experience. There are dangers in identifying a chaos anti-narrative strand in literature or film since chaos is by definition unspeakable, but the con-cept may be useful in approaching narratives which lack meaningful sequence, 'untellable silence' alternating with urgent 'and then' repetitions, and lack the comforts of clear causality or a sense of progress.[91] In chaos, nobody is clearly in control, and the experience is one of confusion and distress.

With such writing in mind, Gothic studies can offer medical humanities scholarship strategies in examining literary and cinematic representations of helplessness and confinement. In practical terms, scholars in our field may have the following: experience of the narrative structures and forms of lan-guage that can express and/or tame harrowing experience; sensitivity to the way spaces may discipline bodies; and most of all, perhaps, a willingness to hear fear and despair. This latter willingness is no small thing – research has shown significant lack of appetite to hear such stories, including among healthcare practitioners.[92] When illness narratives do not end in such moves of coherence, hope, or healing there remains an ethical necessity to witness, both to validate the speaker and to correct the wider cultural temptation to privilege survivors' stories over those who do not – quite – survive.[93] As I say elsewhere, 'when certain kinds of ... self-story are deemed indispensable to a bearable human life, we risk marginalising those who cannot or will not take that stance'.[94]

Nancy describes his received heart as 'the intruder' who 'enters by force' (p. 1). Rather than forge a point of connection with the tissue, Nancy's memoir emphasises the otherness; in Derrida's terms, he is absolutely hospitable to the inassimilable.[95] Nancy figures this invasion in terms of a narrative clash. He is told his own heart was 'programmed to last to the age of fifty' (pp. 4–5). That genetically inscribed story is altered by the donor tissue and the medical technologies that envelop both bodies: 'what other program was to cross … my own, physiological, program?' (p. 2). Both Varela and Nancy emphasise that the received tissue retains something of the giver that will impact one's own story, indeed, something that *must* change one's story, since without it one would die. Yet neither limits 'intrusion' – or their Derridean hospitality – to the tissue itself. Recipient estrangement is also a function of a complex web of national administrative organisations, the abstractions of waiting lists, permissions, and the ongoing materialities of pharmacological and surgical intervention. 'From the first,' says Nancy, 'my survival is inscribed in a complex process woven through with strangers and strangeness' (p. 5), and Varela observes that 'the process oscillates between an intimate inside and a dispersed outside of donor, receiver and the "team"' (p. 261).

Nancy and Varela see their pre-transfer bodies as always already mysterious, flawed and ambiguous, and not straightforwardly autonomous. Rather than idealise a pre-transplant state, Nancy experiences his original genetic material as uncanny, in that it controlled a malevolent script of cardiac deterioration that would have killed him were it not interrupted by tissue governed by a different genetic narrative. Illness, too, makes the pre-transfer body strange. Nancy recalls, 'From the moment that I was told that I must have a heart transplant … There is simply the physical sensation of a void already open [*déjà ouvert*] in my chest … It was becoming a stranger to me, intruding through its defection … I was already no longer in me' (pp. 3–4). Varela, too, sees his body as 'foreign' before surgery, his liver 'gradually becoming alien as it ceased to function', and when a doctor tells him his liver is very sick, 'The statement made the silent organ suddenly un-me, threatening' (pp. 262–3). Embodiment is rendered strange by both the experience of physical frailty and by diagnostic declaration. In a further twist, immunosuppression reveals that the pre-transplant body was always occupied by infections, held temporarily in abeyance only to be unleashed after immunosuppression. Nancy realises, 'the most vigorous enemies are inside: the old viruses that have always been lurking in the shadow of my immune system – life-long *intrus*, as they have always been there' (Nancy, pp. 8–9).

Furthermore, in their determined embrace of strangeness, both authors frame transfer less as healing and more as (desired) violation. Surgery is eagerly sought but none the less shattering both experientially and physiologically. Subsequent immunosuppression and cancer treatment are also experienced as violent. When Nancy contracts cancer as a side effect of the immuno-suppression, he describes autologous stem cell transfer and chemotherapy: 'One emerges from this adventure lost. One no longer knows or recognizes oneself ... [O]ne is no more than a slackening, floating strangeness' (p. 11). Varela also describes psychological distress attendant on intense immunosup-pression, 'special suppressive drugs and massive doses of corticoid (leaving the mind disjointed, hallucinating, and with an obsessive compulsion to repeat certain inner discourses; nights spent in the corticoid desert are certainly a form of hell)' (p. 264). The destruction of all his immune cells is traumatic: 'As I felt the effect coming in a few minutes, my whole body was swept by an uncontrollable shaking, like an alien possession that left me (who?) in a limbo of non-existence; looking steadily into my wife's face the only reference point in a disappearing quagmire' (p. 264). Life-saving processes are paradoxically experienced as annihilatory.

Both writers, then, vividly communicate their sense of their contingent embodiment as brutally affected by both surgical and pharmacological inter-vention, but both go even further than this: neither writer depicts the violation as *ending*. Both present transplantation as an ongoing process involving the creation of a complex spatiality both inside and outside a body's ostensi-ble boundaries, of continuing penetration and openness. Neither represents recipient experience as merely an encounter of two entities. Instead, both describe post-transplant embodiment as a haunted assemblage, haunted not by a straightforwardly discrete presence of an other but rather by the sur-gical transfer and immunosuppressive processes that have occurred in the past and continue to play out within their bodies, play out in ways that make the always-already compromised boundaries of any embodiment explicit and unavoidable. Both writers resist presenting recipient experience in terms of repair. As Varela says of his own experience, 'Transplantation is never in the past ... It produces an inflexion in life that keeps an open reminder from the trace of the scar altering my settledness, bringing up death's trace ... The expression of it all ... eludes me, makes me face a twilight language' (p. 271). This is neither a past restored nor a future perfect. Each writer forges a subtly different 'twilight language' to describe this state. As I will show, for Nancy it is *béance*, a state of permanent openness. For Varela the most dominant trope is of the body being occupied *by* death as itself a force, a scar, a presence.

Nancy consistently figures the ontological and affective shock through imagery of opening, gaps, and disorientation. When he is told his heart is failing, he feels 'the physical sensation of a void already open in my chest' (pp. 3–4). As time passes this openness intensifies both literally and symbolically. The radical nature of the surgery (circulating blood outside the body, opening the thoracic cavity, severing the existing heart's connections, removing it, grafting in the new heart), 'imposes the image of a passage through nothingness, of an entry into a space emptied of all property, all intimacy – or … this space intruding in me: of tubes, clamps, sutures, and probes' (p. 7). Not as straightforward as two sets of tissue conjoining or even a cyborg hybridity, what Nancy is describing here is an assemblage that he experiences as challenging both affectively and ontologically. He enters a space engineered for the annihilation of borders – 'emptied of all property, all intimacy' – a space where boundaries are meaningless, or, equally astonishing, he becomes occupied *by* a space, 'this space intruding in me, of tubes, clamps, sutures and probes'. This occupying space is a stage engineered for penetration, a permanent stage for ongoing opening and stitching, a stage for breaching of barriers, for violation of the illusion of 'self' as self-possessed and discrete. The gaping open-ness intensifies as time continues:

> It is not that they opened me wide [*béant*] in order to change my heart.
>
> It is rather that this gaping open [*béance*] cannot be closed. (Each x-ray moreover shows this: the sternum is sewn through with twisted pieces of wire.) I am closed open. There is in fact an opening through which passes a stream of unremitting strangeness: the immuno-depressive medication, and others … I am the illness and the medical intervention, I am the cancerous cell and the grafted organ, I am the immuno-depressive agents and their palliatives, I am the bits of wire that hold together my sternum, and I am this injection site permanently stitched in below my clavicle. (pp. 10–13)

The ensuing embodiment – like all embodiment – is an assemblage. His life is both undone and made possible by permanent openness to intrusion.

In subsequent postscripts, Nancy describes outliving the expectations of the transferred heart's duration, and describes further intrusions (titanium rods in hipbone, a pacemaker, post-surgical infections, pharmaceuticals, and an implanted epicardic machine). In lieu of an official English translation, I will offer the French original and an informal translation.

> En fait, je le comprends de plus en plus, il y a plusieurs organismes: au moins le mécanique, le chimique, le nerveux, le sensoriel, et le viscéral. L'intrus me donne une perception plus déliée de cet assemblage qui fait «moi».[96]

> [In fact, and I understand it more and more, there are several organisms: at the very least a mechanical one, a chemical one, a nervous one, a sensory one, and a visceral one. The intruder gives me a looser perception of the framework that is 'me'.][97]

Throughout his commentaries, Nancy emphasises the strangeness of transplant and the strangeness of *all* life and cultural practice, as things of difference, connection, and graft:

> Le greffe d'un coeur n'est qu'une image – ou une manifestation – encore lointaine de ce qui en tout «être soi» (d'une personne, d'un pays, d'une langue, d'une pensée) implique une foule d'intrusions. (p. 61)

[Heart transplants are just a distant metaphor for – or an outward sign of – the many intrusions involved in the 'self-being' (of a person, of a country, of a language, of a thought).]

Varela, too, describes surgical and pharmacological interventions in terms of violation and sees tissue transfer's impact as not a single event, but ongoing. While Nancy speaks of *béance*, however, Varela develops a different metaphor: the recipient's body becoming occupied by death. In the imaginative economy of Varela's essay, two kinds of death enter a receiver: their own, and the donor's. Furthermore, both are – as with Nancy's *béance* – associated with ongoing change.

Describing the night of his surgery, Varela says:

> there has been, the encounter with the radical alteration of death, which approached closely over the years, and then finally made its irruption in all the brutality of a night when my chest and abdomen were laid open. It was done; I was not there, drowned in anaesthetics (which I? Certainly there was presence, I suffered) ... Never have I felt more acutely my fragile ontology, the impossibility of grasping onto anything, a living dot suspended in a space that goes so beyond anything representable. The utter loneliness for which there is no utterance. Deprived of any intimacy, nothing left but gaping gap for intrusion ... Awakening into my new state, I see that night when death travelled through my open body is to remain indelibly. (p. 269)

It remains as a visible scar, and also as visceral sensation:

> death's trace, which never lets me slip by this memory that is not a memory, but rather a feeling of recognition of its presence, of an inevitable guest whose movements are way beyond anything within my reach. From then on the trace of death has set its own agenda, its own rhythm to my life. I have, in fact, become another never entirely re-done after being so meticulously undone. (p. 270)

Henceforth, Varela experiences his lived viscera in a way that doctors say is impossible. He should not be able to feel his new liver because there is no tissue innervating the organ, but he can feel it, and speculates:

> Maybe a dis-membered proprioception from the terminals left behind in the hole of my previous liver. And when the new one comes to lodge ... I imagine those connective tissue membranes that were left there, dangling like the veils of a mummy, senseless, sentient-less ... [T]hey will find their way into the new nooks and crannies of those new cells. (p. 264)

In this striking evocation of 'dis-membered proprioception' and the 'veils of a mummy', Varela uses a Gothic language to describe reaching towards impossible connections across severed viscera. The transferred liver *has* been 'mummified' in the sense that it is, very literally, the tissue of a dead person prevented from decaying through artificial intervention, but in Varela's formulation such metaphorical embalming is not static. The preserved tissue and the capsule around it move, the 'veils … find[ing] their way'. This is not a stasis but a changing, an encounter that simultaneously neither denies that it is dead tissue that is lodged here, nor that liver transplant surgery brings recipients to the very edge of life.

These essays, then, use a lexis of dismemberment, vivisection, and violation to describe a process, a mode of being. Both acknowledge these procedures as simultaneously life-enabling and far from emotionally uncomplicated, sometimes engendering deeply ambivalent and grief-laden states.

Similar affective and ontological complexity characterises Claire Denis's film *L'intrus* (2004), loosely inspired by Nancy's essay and also rich in images of emotional strain and physical degeneration after organ transfer. This disorienting, meandering work relies on odd juxtapositions of scenes and striking visual textures. The film describes Louis, a cold, elderly man, seemingly an ex-mercenary, living alone in a cabin in a forest near the Franco-Swiss border. He obtains a black-market heart transplant, and with his new lease of life sets off to the South Seas. He intends to reconnect with an estranged son he fathered as a sailor years before. Eventually, he suspects that his French son was killed for his transplant heart. This bald summary, however, misses the point of the film, for reality and guilt-ridden fantasy are blurred throughout. The entire film is told from Louis Trebor's perspective. Denis recalls that 'I wanted each image to convey a sense that it was generated by his mind … everything is his'.[98] As time passes, Louis's guilt makes his world fantastical. When he orders his heart by email, the black-market dealer responds, 'The surcharge is to be paid upon arrival', but he gradually becomes aware that money will never fully repay this debt. He imagines being rope-dragged behind horses through snow by his Russian organ-dealer, who tells him, 'You'll never pay enough.'

Like Nancy and Varela, Denis renders the transfer recipient's body strange. She represents transfer processes symbolically, as in a human heart on the snow, torn by dogs, a dream-refraction of a transplant heart held on ice or an organ ravaged by acute rejection. The film also uses a visual language to show Louis's body become progressively alien: initially, he blends visually into the environment of the French countryside, but as the film progresses he increasingly becomes a dark silhouette on the screen, 'a black hole on the surface of the image', itself intrusive and alien.[99] Denis makes the materiality of the film photography into a metaphor for the grafting and estrangement process in a second way, too: she incorporates clips from an incomplete 1965 film directed by Gégauff, featuring Michel Subor (who acts Louis) as a young man in Polynesia. Martine Beugnet notes that these clips 'are like pieces of tissue transplanted … [and] imperfectly integrated', and frame composition, too, communicates Louis's decline: moving '[f]rom active body in control of the space and dominating the frame' to a 'reclining figure … handled and examined by others'.[100]

The film is preoccupied by the policing of boundaries. The opening scenes depict border control guards halting smugglers, and illegal immigrants chased and killed. After Louis leaves his cabin in the woods, it continues to be a violent site. When a Bohemian girl makes it a temporary residence, she seems to be slaughtered by Louis's dogs. As the film progresses, as I will show, the boundary policing proves fragile. The film describes competing narratives, the protagonist's attempts to forge his own future narrative thwarted by multiple external and internal forces. With his new heart Louis tries to create a new life. He imagines returning to Tahiti, where he sailed as a young man, to reunite with a lost son whom he misses deeply, even while gravely neglecting a French son and grandson. The viewer receives hints of the way Louis intends this new life to play out. We are shown, in silence, a painting by Paul Gauguin of a ship sailing in the South Seas, followed by a shot from a ship moving through waters, but Louis's intended story comes under repeated pressure and ultimately it yields to a confusing, fantastical portrayal of grief and guilt. Denis deliberately resists coherence, describing the film as 'like a boat lost in the ocean drifting'.[101] First, Louis's hope of reconciliation is unfulfilled; his son has disappeared, and we have hints he may have died. Louis perseveres, staying to continue the search and rebuilding an island shack, and here he encounters a second thwarting of his hopes. He seeks to create a defensible refuge, like his earlier forest cabin. He plans to guard the shack, and, in an action reminiscent of his defence of his cabin in earlier scenes, he unearths a rifle from beneath the shack's boards, but this dilapidated dwelling is not a safe retreat. In a disturbing foreshadowing, as he rebuilds we see a small sea creature approach a rusted tin for inadequate shelter. Indeed, Louis's shack fails to protect him from his greatest threat: his own immune system. Felled by organ rejection, he returns to hospital.

In a final blow to his fantasies of a peaceful post-transplant life, Louis's guilt over the fate of his murdered donor becomes personal. After a partial recovery, a weakened Louis seems to discover his French son in a Tahitian morgue with an incision showing his heart has been removed. In this final bitter piece in his journey of guilt the quiet soundtrack, with minimal nondiegetic music, gives no cues to differentiate between real scenes and vivid fantasy. After his finding the body of the young man, we see Louis wearing a white funeral lei and overseeing a coffin carried out for burial. Denis's brutally effective filming dwells on the coffin being transported as freight, a motorised lifter grinding up to the ship alongside other lifters bearing goods. We watch the coffin lifted aboard in agonising slowness, and the ship sails into the dark for several minutes to the accompaniment of the film score's poignant musical motif for 'the intruder', denoting invader or heart transplant – music rarely used in this largely silent film. The film presents a fantastic closure in the sense that it does imagine a source of the organ, yet this narrative was far from the one Louis consciously scripted.

Both illness and medical intervention can trigger crises of narrative, a sense of being in the grip of a knowing and hostile environment that controls a story that one cannot know oneself until its bitter close. These representations are precious in that they speak to a necessary ambivalence at the heart of some recipients' experience. The protagonists in these texts traverse the carceral sterility of medical spaces, the opacity of medical discourse, and an illness and a treatment whose trajectories may resist neat prediction and whose workings within the body are a mystery. These works unsettle the language of either 'possession' or 'self-possession'. In their agonies, joys, and ambivalence, they describe something more hybrid, fractured, and real.

Notes

1 G. Tagliacozzi, *De Curtorum Chirurgia per Insiotonem* (Venice: Berolini, 1597).

2 M. Shildrick, 'Staying alive', *Body and Society*, 21:3 (2015), 20–41 (p. 25).

3 Living donation, too, can evoke fantasies of odd connection. See E. Cook, '"Off dropped the sympathetic snout"', in H. Kerr, D. Lemmings, and R. Phiddian (eds), *Passions, Sympathy, and Print Culture* (Basingstoke: Palgrave, 2016), pp. 145–64.

4 D. Punter, *Gothic Pathologies* (Basingstoke: Macmillan, 1998), p. 16.

5 R. Shaw, 'The ethical risks of curtailing emotion in social science research', *Health Sociology Review*, 20:1 (2011), 58–69 (pp. 61–2); M. Shildrick, A. Carnie, A. Wright, P. McKeever, E. Huan-Ching Jan, E. De Luca, I. Bachmann, S. Abbey, D. Dal Bo, J. Poole, T. El-Sheikh, and H. Ross, 'Messy entanglements', *Medical Humanities*, Online First (2017), 1–9 (pp. 2–3).

6 B. Murnane, 'George Best's dead livers', in J. Edwards (ed.), *Technologies of the Gothic in Literature and Culture* (London: Routledge, 2015), pp. 113–26 (p. 124).

7 M. Adler, 'Kidney transplantation and coping mechanisms', *Psychosomatics*, 13 (1972), 337–41; S. Basch, 'The intrapsychic integration of a new organ', *Psychoanalytic Quarterly*, 42 (1972), 364–84; B. Bunzel, B. Schmidl-Mohl, A. Grundbock, and G. Wolleneck. 'Does changing the heart mean changing personality?', *Quality of Life Research*, 1:4 (1992), 251–6; C. Sylvia and W. Novak, *A Change of Heart* (New York: Warner Books, 1997); P. Pearsall, G. Schwartz, and L. Russek. 'Changes in heart transplant recipients that parallel the personalities of their donors', *Journal of Near-Death Studies*, 20 (2002), 191–206; P. Castelnuovo-Tedesco, 'Transplantation', in N. Levy (ed.), *Psychonephrology* (New York: Plenum Press, 1981), pp. 219–25.

8 M. Sanner, 'Living with a stranger's organ', *Annals of Transplantation*, 10:9 (2005), 9–12 (p. 10).

9 L. Sharp, *Strange Harvest* (Berkeley: University of California Press, 2006); Sanner; M. Shildrick, P. McKeever, S. Abbey, J. Poole, and H. Ross, 'Troubling dimensions of heart transplantation', *Medical Humanities*, 35:1 (2009), 35–8 (p. 36).

10 Sharp, *Harvest*, p. 23.

11 Bunzel *et al.*, p. 252.

12 Shildrick *et al.*, 'Messy entanglements', pp. 2–3.

13 M. Almgren, A. Lennerling, M. Lundmark, and A. Forsberg, 'The meaning of being in uncertainty after heart transplantation', *European Journal of Cardiovascular Nursing*, 16:2 (2017), 167–74; J. Poole, J. Ward, E. De Luca, M. Shildrick, S. Abbey, O. Mauthner, M. Gewarges, and H. Ross, 'Getting ready and then keeping quiet', *Journal of Heart and Lung Transplantation*, 33:4 (2014), S222–S223.

14 Shaw, 'Ethical risks', pp. 61–2.

15 Shildrick *et al.*, 'Messy entanglements', p. 8.

16 T. Parsons, *The Social System* (London: Routledge, [1951] 1952); A. Clarke, L. Mamo, J. Fishman, J. Shim, and J. Fosket, 'Biomedicalisation', *American Sociological Review*, 68 (2003), 161–94.

17 S. Wasson, 'Creative manifesto', *Translating Chronic Pain*, AHRC-funded Research Network (2017), wp.lancs.ac.uk/translatingpain/creative-manifesto/ [accessed 28 March 2018]; S. L. Jain, 'Cancer butch', *Cultural Anthropology*, 22:4 (2007), 501–38; B. Ehrenreich, 'Welcome to Cancerland', *Harper's*, 303:1818 (2001), 43–53; D. Steinberg, 'Bad patient', *Body and Society*, 21:3 (2015), 115–43.

18 Sharp, *Harvest*; Shildrick, 'Staying alive'.

19 E. Cazdyn, *The Already Dead* (Durham, NC: Duke University Press, 2012), p. 4.

20 A. Frank, 'The necessity and dangers of illness narratives', in Y. Gunaratnam and D. Oliviere (eds), *Narrative and Stories in Health Care* (Oxford: Oxford University Press, 2009), pp. 161–176 (p. 170).

21 Sanner, p. 11.

22 M. Lock, *Twice Dead* (Berkeley: University of California Press, 2002), pp. 323–4; F. Varela, 'Intimate distances', *Journal of Consciousness Studies*, 8:5–7 (2001), 259–71 (p. 259). Subsequent references to the latter are within the text.

23 C. Waldby, 'Biomedicine, tissue transfer and intercorporeality', *Feminist Theory*, 3 (2002), 235–50 (p. 248).

24 J.D. Reed, 'Organ transplant', *The New Yorker* (26 September 1970), 126.

25 Waldby, 'Biomedicine', p. 245.

26 For a moving example of concorporeality, see Shaw, 'Ethical risks', pp. 63–4.

27 J. Derrida, *Aporia*, trans. T. Dutoit (Stanford: Stanford University Press, 1993), p. 34.

28 M. Shildrick, 'Hospitality and the "gift of life"', in S. Gonzalez-Arnal, G. Jagger, and K. Lennon (eds), *Embodied Selves* (London: Palgrave, 2012), pp. 196–208 (pp. 202–3).

29 J. Bennett, *Vibrant Matter* (Durham, NC: Duke University Press, 2010), pp. 23–4, xvii.

30 Shildrick, 'Staying alive', pp. 34–5.

31 Shildrick *et al.*, 'Messy entanglements', p. 8.

32 M. Mauss, *The Gift*, trans. W. Halls (New York: Norton, [1950] 1990), pp. 11–12.

33 E. Bercovitch, 'The agent in the gift', *Cultural Anthropology*, 9 (1994), 498–536.

34 G. Bataille, *Theory of Religion* (New York: Zone, 1989); J. Derrida, *Given Time: I* (Chicago: University of Chicago Press, 1994); V. Nemoianu, *A Theory of the Secondary* (Baltimore, MD: Johns Hopkins University Press, 1989); S. Wasson, 'Coven of the articulate', *Journal of Popular Culture*, 45:1 (2012), 197–213.

35 E. Malmqvist and K. Zeiler, 'Concluding reflections', in E. Malmqvist and K. Zeiler (eds), *Bodily Exchanges* (London: Routledge, 2016), pp. 197–207 (p. 205n2).

36 Sanner, pp. 9–12; Lock, *Twice Dead*; Shildrick *et al.*, 'Troubling dimensions', p. 36; L. Sharp, 'Commodified kin', *American Anthropologist*, 103:1 (2001), 112–33.

37 Shildrick *et al.*, 'Troubling dimensions'; R. Shaw, 'Perceptions of the gift relationship in organ and tissue donation', *Social Science and Medicine*, 70:4 (2010), 609–15; Shaw, 'Ethical'.

38 Lock, *Twice Dead*, p. 319; Mauss, pp. 11–12.

39 Sanner, p. 11.

40 Shildrick *et al.*, 'Messy entanglements', pp. 3–4; P. Aldhous, 'Bone marrow donors risk DNA mixup', *New Scientist* (26 October 2005), www.newscientist.com/article/mg18825234-600-bone-marrow-donors-risk-dna-identity-mix-up/ [accessed 27 September 2018].

41 S. Lederer, *Flesh and Blood* (Oxford: Oxford University Press, 2008), p. 61.

42 S. Gilbert, 'Holobiont by birth', in A. Tsing, H. Swanson, E. Gan, and N. Bubandt (eds), *Arts of Living on a Damaged Planet* (Minneapolis: University of Minnesota Press, 2017), pp. M73–M90.

43 D. Steinberg, *Genes and the Bioimaginary* (Aldershot: Ashgate, 2015).

44 N. Angier, 'Biologists seek the words in DNA's unbroken text', *The New York Times* (9 July 1991), C1; 'Breaking the code', *The Economist* (28 November 1992), 150; 'What is your DNA story?' *23andme.com*, www.23andme.com/en-gb/ [accessed 3 September 2018].

45 S. Wasson, 'Olalla's legacy: twentieth-century vampire fiction and genetic previvorship', *Journal of Stevenson Studies*, 7 (2010), 55–81.

46 R.L. Stevenson, 'Olalla', in *The Merry Men and Other Tales and Fables* (London: Chatto and Windus, [1885] 1905), pp. 143–200 (pp. 189–90).

47 E. Jentsch, 'On the psychology of the uncanny', trans. R. Sellars, *Angelaki*, 2:1 ([1906] 1996), 7–17 (p. 13).

48 S. Freud, 'The uncanny', *Penguin Freud Library*, vol. 14, trans. J. Strachey, ed. A. Richards (London: Penguin, [1919] 1985), pp. 336–76 (pp. 345–7).

49 A. Vidler, *The Architectural Uncanny* (Cambridge, MA: MIT, 1992), p. 7.

50 Freud, p. 359.

51 S. Wasson, *Urban Gothic of the Second World War* (Basingstoke: Palgrave, 2010), p. 112.

52 M. Fisher, *The Weird and the Eerie* (London: Repeater, 2016), pp. 10–11.

53 E.T.A. Hoffmann, 'The sandman', in *Weird Tales* (Virginia Beach: CreateSpace, [1817] 2016), pp. 98–115.

54 W. Hughes, 'Vampire', in M. Mulvey-Roberts (ed.), *The Handbook of the Gothic*, 2nd edn (Basingstoke: Palgrave Macmillan, 2009), pp. 252–7.

55 R. Pritchard, 'The death of Enrico Caruso', *Surgery, Gynecology and Obstetrics*, 109 (1959), 117–20.

56 Lederer, p. x.

57 *Her Surrender*, dir. by I. Abramson (Ivan Film, 1916); *A Woman Who Understood*, dir. by W. Parke (Robertson-Cole, 1920); *The Hospital Baby*, director unstated (Essanay, 1912).

58 B. Stoker, *Dracula*, ed. M. Hindle (New York: Penguin, [1897] 1993), p. 227.

59 Stoker, pp. 394–5; J. Halberstam, 'Technologies of monstrosity', *Victorian Studies*, 36:3 (1993), 333–52; S. Arata, 'The occidental tourist', *Victorian Studies*, 33:4 (1990), 621–45. Racial animus also informs fictional representations of xenotransplantation in the early twentieth century. The 1920s saw a thriving market for monkey-gland transplants and blood transfusions for restoring male virility, but, alongside this, fictions portrayed the fear of human animals changing to become less human. The silent film *Wolf Blood* (1925) describes a man gaining lupine qualities after receiving a blood transfusion from a wolf, and Arthur Conan Doyle's short story 'The adventure of the creeping man' (1923) sees a man become simian after taking monkey gland orally. *Wolf Blood*, dir. by G. Chesebro and B. Mitchell (Ryan Brothers, 1925); A. Conan Doyle, 'The adventures of the creeping man', in *Complete Sherlock Holmes* (London: Penguin, [1923] 2009), pp. 1070–82.

60 F. Kinsella, *The Degeneration of Dorothy* (Charleston: Bibliofile, [1899] 2018).

61 C. Darwin, *The Variation of Animals and Plants Under Domestication* (London: John Murray, 1875), p. 370.

62 *Mortmain* and *Orlac* inspired other texts adapting hand transfer with markers of otherness salient to particular contexts, and in Chapter 3 I discuss another, Charles Gardner Bowers's 'The black hand' (1931). Other examples include: *Mad Love*, dir. by K. Freund (Metro-Goldwyn-Mayer, 1935); *The Hands of Orlac*, dir. by E. Gréville (Pendennis, 1960); *Les mains de Roxana*, dir. by P. Setbon (Juin, 2012); *Frankenstein Chronicles*, dir. by B. Langford and B. Ross, television series (2015–); *Hands of a Stranger*, dir. by Newt Arnold (Rainmark, 1962); and N. Shusterman, *Unwind* (London: Simon and Schuster, [2007] 2008), *UnWholly* (New York: Simon and Schuster, 2012), *UnSouled* (New York: Simon and Schuster, 2013), *Undivided* (New York: Simon and Schuster, 2014). This list is far from exhaustive.

63 Other examples of self-willed hands include: W. Harvey, *The Beast with Five Fingers* (London: J.M. Dent, [1928] 1960); *The Beast with Five Fingers*, dir. by Robert Florey (Warner, 1946); *The Hand*, dir. by O. Stone (Orion, 1981); C. Miéville, *Perdido Street Station* (London: Pan, [2001] 2002).

64 H. Moawad, 'Alien hand syndrome', *Neurology Times* (17 August 2016), www. neurologytimes.com/blog/alien-hand-syndrome [accessed 22 August 2018].

65 A.C. Train, *Mortmain* (New York: Charles Scribner, 1907). Subsequent references in parenthesis.

66 Lederer, p. 75.

67 M. Renard, *The Hands of Orlac*, trans. I. White (London: Souvenir, [1920] 1981). Subsequent references in parenthesis.

68 Lederer, p. 21.

69 V. Campion-Vincent, 'Organ theft narratives as medical and social critique', *Journal of Folklore Research*, 39:1 (2002), 33–50 (p. 37).

70 *Orlacs Hände*, dir. by R. Wiene (Berolina, 1924).

71 *Das Cabinet des Dr. Caligari / Cabinet of Dr. Caligari*, dir. by R. Wiene (Decla-Bioscop, 1920).

72 A. Hans, "'These hands are not my hands'", in C. Rogowski (ed.), *The Many Faces of Weimar Cinema* (Rochester, NY: Camden House, 2010), pp. 102–15 (pp. 103, 105).

73 Whilst I offer a reading focused on transfer recipient affect, critical work also grapples with the film's gender representation, notably the way the transferred hands begin to caress the maidservant in transgression of marital fidelity, and potential symbolic violence in Paul's embrace of his wife (Hans, p. 112).

74 S. Geroulanos, 'Postwar facial reconstruction', *French Politics, Culture & Society*, 31:2 (2013), 15–33 (pp. 19–20).

75 Ibid, p. 20.

76 R. Garland-Thomson, *Extraordinary Bodies* (New York: Columbia University Press, 1997).

77 *Les yeux sans visage* (*Eyes without a Face*), dir. by G. Franju (Champs-Élysées, 1958).

78 S. Biernoff, 'Theatres of surgery', *Wellcome Open Research*, 3:54 (2018), 1–20 (p. 9).

79 A. Lowenstein, 'Films without a face', *Cinema Journal*, 37:4 (1998), 37–58 (p. 45).

80 J. Cocteau, *The Art of Cinema*, trans. R. Buss (London: Marion Boyars, 1992), p. 121.

81 I. Sinclair, 'Homeopathic horror', *Sight and Sound*, 5:4 (1995), 24–7 (p. 27). As with all works 'about' transplantation, transplant is not the only cultural referent. For example, the film can be approached in dialogue with representations of fashion and cosmetics at the period, as well as the expansion of cosmetic surgeries (Biernoff).

82 T. Milne, 'Georges Franju', *Sight and Sound*, 44:2 (1975), 68–72 (pp. 68–9).

83 Ibid, p. 70.

84 Sinclair, p. 26; Milne, p. 71.

85 Milne, p. 70.

86 J.-L. Nancy, '*L'intrus*', trans. S. Hanson, *New Centennial Review*, 2:3 ([2000] 2002), 1–14; Varela; *L'intrus*, dir. by C. Denis (Ognon, 2004) Subsequent references to the essays appear in parenthesis.

87 R. Charon, *Narrative Medicine* (Oxford: Oxford University Press, 2008), pp. 65–6; A. Hawkins, *Reconstructing Illness* (West Lafayette, IN: Purdue University Press, 1999), pp. 2–3.

88 M. Hyvärinen, L.-C. Hydén, M. Saarenheimo, and M. Tamboukou (eds), *Beyond Narrative Coherence* (Philadelphia: John Benjamins, 2010), pp. 1–15; L. Salisbury, 'Aphasic modernism', in A. Whitehead, A. Woods, S. Atkinson, *et al.* (eds), *Edinburgh Companion to the Critical Medical Humanities* (Edinburgh: Edinburgh University Press, 2016), pp. 444–62; A. Woods, 'Beyond the wounded storyteller', in H. Carel and R. Cooper (eds), *Health, Illness and Disease* (Durham: Acumen, 2013), pp. 113–28; A. Woods, 'The limits of narrative', *Medical Humanities*, 37 (2011), 91–6; S. Wasson, 'Before narrative', *Medical Humanities*, 44:2 (2018), 106–12; Wasson, 'Creative manifesto'.

89 A. Frank, 'Caring for the dead', in L.-C. Hydén and J. Brockmeier (eds), *Health, Illness and Culture* (London: Routledge, 2008), pp. 122–30 (p. 122); Frank, 'Necessity', p. 172.

90 A. Frank, *The Wounded Storyteller* (Chicago: University of Chicago Press, [1995] 1997); A. Frank, 'Afterword', *The Wounded Storyteller*, 2nd edn (Chicago: University of Chicago Press, 2013), pp. 187–221.

91 Frank, *Storyteller*, pp. 97–8.

92 B. Smith and A. Sparkes. 'Exploring multiple responses to a chaos narrative', *Health*, 15:1 (2011), 38–53; E. Uehara, M. Farris, P. Morelli, and A. Ishisaka. 'Eloquent chaos', *Culture, Medicine and Psychiatry*, 25:1 (2001), 29–61; L. Langer, *Holocaust Testimonies* (New Haven: Yale University Press, 1991).

93 Frank, *Storyteller*, pp. 110–35; Langer; Uehara *et al.*; Smith and Sparkes.

94 Wasson, 'Before narrative', p. 107.

95 Shildrick, 'Hospitality', p. 203.

96 J.-L. Nancy, *L'intrus*, nouvelle edition augmentée (Paris: Galilée, 2017), p. 51. Subsequent references in parenthesis.

97 Personal translation provided informally by Naomi Salman.

98 D. Smith, '*L'intrus*', *Senses of Cinema*, 35 (2005), sensesofcinema.com/2005/conversations-with-filmmakers/claire_denis_interview/ [accessed 30 July 2019], paras 84–6.

99 M. Beugnet, 'The practice of strangeness', *Film Philosophy*, 12:1 (2008), 31–48 (p. 37).

100 Ibid., pp. 40–5.

101 D. Smith, para. 19.

5

Scalpel and metaphor:
'machines of social death' and state-sanctioned harvest in dystopian fiction

Both immunologically and culturally, tissue transfer requires a forgetting. Immunosuppression changes the recipient's body to diminish ability to recognise tissue as alien, and, without implying that cultural responses are as predictable as immunological ones (and even the latter can be unpredictable), transfer is accompanied by cultural labour.[1] Language domesticates the radical otherness of the tissue and normalises the transfer process: metaphors reclassify tissue to enable its redeployment, to frame the process for practitioners and public and to influence how transfer is administered and understood both within and outside healthcare institutions.

Such discursive work is central to the fictions of this chapter. Whilst previous chapters imagine corporate profit gleaned from the comatose or vulnerable (Chapter 2), or clinical labour informed by long-term structural inequality and slow violence (Chapter 3), this chapter explores dystopian fictions imagining juridical state-sanctioned surgery or execution, in which an explicit hierarchy of lives prevails. In a medico-juridical nexus, hospitals become prisons and surgical theatres become places of torment or execution. David Punter has commented on the implacable quality of legal decree: 'The law is … there to will away the body; where the law is, bodies cannot exist or plead'.[2] In these dystopian fictions, discursive work performs its own violence alongside the scalpels; metaphors for transfer material are part of the discursive field that produces 'machines of social death' that effect a hierarchy of human life.[3] Whilst the fictions are fantastical, the metaphors for transfer tissue are commonplace and contemporary; similarly, hierarchies of life value are also in play today, even if not in dystopian state-sanctioned harvest schemes (though in this, too, there are terrible precedents).[4]

I analyse three works from the early days of transplantation prior to the cyclosporine era, during the establishing of transplantation and the emergence of neurological criteria for death: Cordwainer Smith's novella 'A planet called Shayol' (1961), Larry Niven's *A Gift from Earth* (1968), and Dennis Etchison's 'Calling all monsters' (1973, rev. 1982), each of which offers a vision of an unwilling body vivisected for tissue under legal rule.[5] I then consider three twenty-first century novels, Neal Shusterman's *Unwind* (2007), Kazuo Ishiguro's *Never Let Me Go* (2005), and Ninni Holmqvist's Swedish novel *Enhet* (*The Unit*) (2006, translated into English in 2010). My discussion will focus on the US and UK context (I am discussing *The Unit* in its American translation). These later texts also feature characters in the same plight, but some show a surprising degree of surrender and acceptance. This acceptance is partly mediated by these characters internalising metaphors for transfer tissue, in ways that reinforce social hierarchies of worth.[6] None the less, these later works offer glimpses of resistance, and this resistance specifically gathers around what might be called a tension between clinical time and juridical time, on the one hand, and something that might be called 'queer' time, something more askew, aslant, in which a person marked as socially non-normative dreams of interpersonal connection.

Though classified differently – Smith, Niven, and Holmqvist as science fiction, Shusterman as young adult sf/horror, Ishiguro as literary fiction – each is speculative fiction in that it imagines a future society or alternative history. Each can also be interpreted as written in the Gothic mode as defined in my introduction, in that each combines vulnerable protagonists under extreme corporeal threat, disturbing affect, claustrophobic settings, and disorienting temporalities. These fictions are not mimetic of transfer practice, but use this trope to consider hierarchies of life. In addition, they show how certain discursive moves – not least the rhetoric of organ scarcity, and contemporary metaphors of transfer material – may be bent to forms of violence.

'Machines of social death' and 'worthwhile' life

Societies render certain lives more precarious than others, and a range of critical vocabulary has been formulated to describe such precarities and their mechanisms. As discussed in my Introduction, Michel Foucault's concept of biopower explores how societies foster certain lives while neglecting others, for example fostering some life through statistical tracking and state-funded public-health measures, while others have protections removed.[7] Giorgio Agamben, in turn, identifies how some people are reduced to 'bare life' (*zoe*), stripped of social meaning and protections (*bios*).[8] Through 'states of exception' (far from rare), some are split off into occupying a death-in-life, and both neoliberal democracies and totalitarian states abound in such mechanisms of annihilation. Agamben's framework can be critiqued for grouping heterogeneous plights within the category of *homo sacer*; for erasing the particularities of marginalised experience can itself be a form of critical violence; critics have also argued that emphasising the state as vector of violence is insufficient since privatisation and profit imperatives also play into machineries of erasure.[9] The speculative fictions of this chapter recognise state power in complex relation with privatisation and profit imperatives, and describe lives in permanent precarity, 'ungrievable' because never recognised as quite alive.[10]

In this regard, Biehl draws on Gilles Deleuze and Félix Guattari's concept of assemblage to describe how tangible and intangible forces – hospitals, legislation, pharmaceutical advertising, economic inequality – combine in 'machines of social death in which the unproductive and unwanted are caught'.[11] Like any assemblage, such 'machines' comprise many forces, including the discursive, and I will now discuss two discursive constructions which dominate contemporary transfer and with which these fictions engage with: scarcity rhetoric and metaphors for transfer tissue and organs. These discursive constructions are key elements of transfer assemblages, and both may also intersect perilously, at times, with discourses of variable life worth.

The language of 'organ shortage' is widespread across the transplantation field, denoting mismatch between the number of people on waiting lists and the number of procured organs. Waiting-list numbers increase due to increases in organs that can be transplanted, need for subsequent transplants, illnesses remedied with transplant, and broadening recipient eligibility criteria. Procurement figures, by contrast, are diminished not only by reluctance to consent but also by decreases in road traffic accident deaths, gunshot injuries, or opioid overdose.[12] A *New York Times* article makes the connection clear in a reflection on the transfer context in New York state:

> In the last dozen years, there have been at least two great positive social trends in America: fewer people die on America's roadways, and fewer people die at the hands of others. But this ray of sunshine has a dark shadow. 'In my field, we make morbid jokes about repealing the seat belt laws and air bag laws and gun-control laws,' [a transplant surgeon] … said with a heavy sigh. 'I guess we're kind of the ghouls of medicine.'[13]

In turn, an increase in opiate overdose deaths can give rise to headlines like 'Organ transplants hit an all-time high'.[14] Clearly no transplant surgeon ever wants such deaths to increase. Yet, as these comments show, disparities in waiting-list and procurement numbers are products of complex circumstances, a complexity obscured by the language of organ 'scarcity'. Lesley Sharp calls for scrutinising the temporal dimension of scarcity discourse: 'The temporal framing of desired resources is not simply about anticipating a future of scarcity but should also involve probing how scarcity itself comes into being – that is, how the ideation of scarcity lays claim to certain histories while neglecting, ignoring, or erasing others'.[15] Emphasis on scarcity can risk eliding other kinds of suffering within transfer milieux.

Furthermore, some assumptions underpinning scarcity rhetoric may be challenged. Margaret Lock and Vinh-Kim Nguyen warn:

> Running through debates about an organ shortage are several assumptions. First, organs go to waste if not donated ... Second, and associated with the first assumption, is the belief that organs are simply mechanical entities whose worth is entirely without symbolic or affective meaning ... Third, is that making a diagnosis of brain death is straightforward and easily accepted as human death by everyone involved and, moreover, families should be willing to interrupt the grieving process for up to 24 hours while organs are procured. A further presumption is that donation ... [always] assist[s] families in the mourning process ... [These assumptions create] an unexamined hegemony about the value of organs and their alienability ... And from the point of view of potential recipients and their close relatives these assumptions add up for many to a sense of entitlement.[16]

Even some advocates of optimising consent to donation concede that it 'can make those involved ... feel that they are required to commoditise the patient as a community resource', and shortage rhetoric fits alongside metaphoric work that helps to conceive of scarce organs as 'community property' or 'national resource', to use terms from Renée Fox and Judith Swazey.[17] In this regard, Kristin Zeiler and Eric Malmqvist offer useful cautions about the potential risks of a 'sharing' framework for transfer: whilst usually advocating for the term as an improvement on the gift/commodity dichotomy (sharing is better than either at conveying multiple involved parties and extended duration), they also acknowledge the risks of a moral imperative to share and the way the language may obscure asymmetries.[18] These two dangers are particularly salient for the texts explored in this chapter.

Scarcity rhetoric is particularly troubling when it coincides with discourses of human worth, and I will now consider three ways in which hierarchies of life can already inadvertently manifest in contemporary transfer: unequal efforts to prevent certain kinds of death; the 'slippery slope' of broadening donor eligibility criteria; and contempt lacing some practitioner language towards certain donors.

Donation after brain death requires neurological failure in an otherwise relatively healthy body, and as such disproportionately involves sudden violent death. Precise statistics on demographics of cadaveric donation have historically often been slim, and may not be rendered visible in quite the same way as publicly lamented numbers on deaths of patients waiting for transplant.[19] The prevention of deaths from opioid addiction, gun violence, and traffic fatalities may well also not see the same level of organisational infrastructure, medical research, or government funding as goes into facilitating national organ transfer.[20] 'Letting die' includes failing to invest collective energy into fostering life under particular conditions. Not all deaths are striven against to the same degree.

Discussions of expanding donor eligibility criteria may also imply variable worth to particular kinds of life.[21] In 1971, the neurologist J.B. Brierly argued that death should be declared on the loss of higher brain functions rather than brain-stem or whole-brain definitions, and there have been other calls since then to include people with some forms of chronic disorders of consciousness (CDoCs).[22] Proposals to recognise 'higher brain death', 'cerebral death', or 'neocortical death' are controversial because the subjects can often still breathe independently. Lock comments that such patients are 'rarely on ventilators and can usually breathe without assistance. All they need is assistance with feeding – as do a great number of patients who are obviously fully alive.'[23]

Asymmetries of perceived worth are also present at moments when health-care practitioners imply transplantation may redeem a donor's less worth-while life, especially if death occurred due to a vice seen as socially deplorable. Sharp identifies a strand of rhetoric which encourages kin to agree to donation with the view that a 'wasted' life – perhaps one seen by donor kin as morally problematic – can be redeemed by the donation.[24] Early in the millennium, at the time that several of these fictions were being written, Lock observes, 'In the United States, where 58 percent of organ donors die as a result of external trauma, including gunshot wounds, a social and economic disparity is likely to exist between donor and recipient. American transplant coordinators may develop a perception they are dealing primarily with donors whose lifestyles they do not share and whom they regard as wastrels', and Véronique Campion-Vincent has made similar observations about social asymmetry between donor and recipient.[25] Since that time, numbers of deaths from opiate overdose have increased, and these deaths, too, are disproportionately characterised by socio-economic disparity.[26] Such asymmetries can influence certain problematic projections on to the value of the donor's death. Linda Hogle, for example, describes Organ Procurement Organisation (OPO) workers describing donors negatively. In one example, one indicates a dead donor and says, 'Take that kid. Now his life was really worthless. He was probably an alcoholic since he was a kid, and he just wasted his life. So he got himself shot up. Now his mother can say he donated his organs for other people. That's something she can say for the next thirty years – not "oh, he got shot".'[27]

The speculative fictions in this chapter imagine certain lives as less socially valuable than others due to criminality, choice of work, failure to reproduce, or their own reproductive origins (for example status as clone). Though not mimetic of state actions in the US or UK, these texts none the less capture the vivid reality that transfer depends on the wounding or death of another, and those deaths have causes too, some of which are affected by state decisions and insidious forms of inequality and slow violence.[28] Speculative fiction's alternative social worlds mean that economies and cultural detail are sensitised, demanding reader attention rather than fading into a mere backdrop for the actions of an individual agent. Such texts can be said to estrange the social, to invoke Bertolt Brecht's sense of the *Verfremdungseffekt*, distancing readers in order that they might reflect on their own contexts.[29] Such distancing may make it easier to notice sociocultural dimensions of biomedicalised process and the impact of contemporary metaphors for transfer tissue.

Gavin Miller and Anna McFarlane have called for medical humanities scholarship to widen its recognition of the way that science fiction 'enters into a critical dialogue with the troubling ideologies of progress offered by the technoscientific imaginary'.[30] Science fiction and biotechnological research can share a promissory orientation, a distant-future focus, and anticipatory bioethics, too, has typically taken science fiction as of value inasmuch as it allows reflection on possible forthcoming bioethical issues, approaching texts as *Gedankenexperimenten*.[31] Rather than embrace a promissory valence, however, I am interested in how these works engage with contemporary discourses at play in transfer contexts, specifically scarcity rhetoric and figurative language around transfer. I am influenced by Deborah Steinberg's observation that science fiction may not only offer thought experiments on future social possibility but may also offer a chance to think about 'feeling structures' underpinning social, biomedical, and economic forms. These fictions convey a subjective experience of 'machines of social death', including a medico-juridical nexus, metaphors for tissue, and a discourse of 'worthwhile' life.[32]

Metaphor and ceremony in tissue disentanglement

Even when tissue is not for sale, the process of marking tissue off *as* transferrable, as acceptable for transplant in legal and cultural terms, echoes many of the detachment processes that accompany commodification in late capitalism. Lock and Vinh-Kim Nguyen observe, 'In order for body parts to be made alienable, they must first be visualised as thing-like, and detachable from the body, dead or alive'.[33] Economists call the process by which an object becomes alienable 'disentanglement', and this work is fraught and fragile. '[T]o transform something into a commodity', explains Michel Callon, 'it is necessary to cut the ties between the thing and the other objects or human beings one by one. It must be decontextualised, dissociated and detached.'[34]

This language of economic transformation echoes the language of Gothic ceremony, of purification and demarcation.[35] As in literary Gothic's representations of ceremony, this economic work is anxious and the boundaries it creates unstable. Callon notes that 'this work of cleansing, of disconnection ... is never over'; even in the case of more traditional commodities, market transactions establish connections between people, a process which Arjan Appadurai analyses as 'the social life of objects', for 'the commodity is not one kind of thing rather than another, but one phase in the life of some things'.[36] Disentanglement tries to cleanse an object of the human freight of its original owner/producers, but the process is inevitably incomplete. Karl Marx's theory of commodity fetishism offers a metaphor for that incompleteness. Alienation of any object – severing it from its original context and classifying it in new ways that enable it to be transacted – leaves a remnant of 'life' in the alienated object, ghostly traces of the labour and the relations of production that enabled its manufacture.[37]

The labour of disentanglement is as much cultural as economic. Transferred tissue moves through a web of language: metaphors reclassify the tissue in ways that make its transfer more culturally acceptable. In his critique of the 'cold metaphors' dominating American legal representations of the human body, Alan Hyde argues that there has been a progression from early metaphors of 'body as machine' to 'body as property/commodity'; and that common to both metaphor clusters are notions of bodily 'fungibility, estrangement, and desentimentalization'.[38] These metaphors facilitate the work of detachment often seen as necessary for tissue transfer for all parties – donor, recipient, and transplant professionals – but Sharp warns, 'the humanity of patients is frequently lost in a morass of euphemisms, where metaphors transform the patient-as-person to a generic body likened to sophisticated machinery ... minerals, fauna, and flora'.[39] It is impossible to aspire to non-metaphoric representations, but there is value, as Hyde says, in 'recognis[ing] ... the constructed nature of ... representations of the body, and not ... inappropriately naturaliz[ing] those constructions'.[40] Such recognition requires identifying what particular discomfiting realities are characteristically elided by each metaphor cluster.[41]

Five symbolic substitutions characterise much tissue transfer, with material figured as machine parts, waste, vegetation, natural resources, and gifts. Each serves multiple rhetorical functions and I have explored many of these tropes elsewhere in this book. George Lakoff observes that the metaphors we use influence our perception, each metaphoric vehicle emphasising and downplaying certain dimensions of the metaphor's tenor, and in the process shaping how we think of that tenor.[42] In what follows, I briefly comment on how each metaphor reinforces the idea of tissue as a shared social resource, in ways that could become perilous if a society has hierarchies of life.

A machinic model of the body depersonalises transplant tissue as 'spare parts'.[43] Mechanical analogies for the body are far from modern – both Aristotle and Hippocrates, for example, compare the human body to mechanical apparatus and Thomas Aquinas spoke of living bodies in terms of clockwork – but has gained particular weight in recent centuries, particularly after William Harvey's description of the heart as a pump in 1628.[44] A crucial change in the discussion is the way that the metaphoric machines have been desacralised, no longer understood as being driven by divine energy, and the emphasis on *human* manufacture is central to the way these tropes function in transfer discourse. As 'spare parts', tissues and organs are things that can be replaced but they are also things that can be made. In terms of this how this metaphor intersects with social entitlement, then, the metaphor also invites acceptance of collective human ingenuity in manufacturing, turning raw materials to valuable ends.

Waste is often raw material for technological transformation, as well as, not coincidentally, a widespread metaphor for excised tissue. The metaphor does legal work. Converting tissue into commodity for some biotechnological purposes, for example, may require relabelling excised tissue as 'abandoned tissue', as Catherine Waldby and Robert Mitchell note, 'a third term between tissue gifts and tissue commodities ... Waste does not simply add an alternative to these forms of value [i.e. gift and commodity] but ... transforms them in complex ways ... through the circuits of technical and capital transformation.'[45] Waste can be a mediating category enabling the alienation of tissue to be rendered valuable through the operations of biotechnological capital. The tissue-as-waste trope also does powerful rhetorical work in making lack of consent seem illogical and selfish, and as mentioned earlier Lock and Nguyen critique the assumptions that underpin this view, identifying 'an unexamined hegemony about the value of organs and their alienability', in that, for example, not all cultures frame dead organs as having lost value or significance.[46]

A third common metaphor for transfer material describes it as vegetation, influenced by the sixteenth-century work of Gaspare Tagliacozzi, a pioneer of modern plastic surgical method, who used the metaphor of 'grafts'.[47] Organs are 'grafted' and surgical extraction is 'harvest', and these metaphors have become so dominant that it can be hard to find alternatives. I use them several times in this book, although always with recognition of their dehumanising valence (indeed, in the texts I scrutinise, that dehumanisation exacerbates the horror). Greening metaphors are particularly prevalent in contexts where the kin of cadaveric donors are the primary audience, during which the metaphors may also reinforce institutional anonymisation of donor identity; in response, some donor kin have created alternative memorials to celebrate the particular dead.[48] Greening metaphors naturalise the artificial process of surgical extraction, and add an extra twist to reinforcing the social right to tissue: 'harvesting' implies, after all, that the tissue or plants were 'planted' with that end in mind.

A fourth cluster of metaphors is that of organs as natural resources. The transplant nurse specialist Patricia Park uses this metaphor in her argument that organs should be rationed, rather than patients receiving repeated transplants: 'While it may make us uncomfortable to think of rationing organs like gasoline, they are, like energy resources, both limited and exceedingly valuable'.[49] Park employs the natural resources metaphor to convey finitude, but thinking of organs as 'natural resources' has multiple consequences. As ecological work has long shown, materials so designated are often represented as static, inert, to be transformed by humans, and may be taken with scant regard for the environment from which they are drawn; in contrast, speculative realist work recognises the opacity and vitality of such materials.[50] The language of 'natural resources' normalises environmental depredations required to reach oil, gas, and coal. In the context of tissue transfer, these metaphors emphasise tissue as a socially available resource and similarly obscure the retrieval techniques.[51]

Whilst these four metaphors – transfer tissue as spare machine parts, waste, greenery, or natural resources – dehumanise transfer material, the final metaphor – tissue as gift – may imply that tissue retains traces of the giver. As I discuss in Chapter 4, the language of 'gift' may be emotionally challenging for some recipients, even while there are competing understandings of whether a gift is 'no strings' or requires reciprocity.[52] None the less, the language of 'gift' may smooth the transfer process, and has become so widespread that it appears even in oxymorons such as 'paid donor' and 'rewarded gifting'.[53]

One of the most troubling consequences of these symbolic moves is that they make it easier for some recipients to avoid recognising the sacrifice made by a living donor or kin; as one recipient phrased it, '"Why should I put a family member at risk when I can just buy a kidney?"'[54] Such a statement implies that the anonymous source is not human in the same way as a family member: it does not bleed. The following fictions interrogate such mystification.

'House of Pain operating room crypt castle tower': state-sanctioned 'harvest' heterotopias

Each of these works presents surgical procurement occurring in a ceremony in a bounded space that blends hospital and prison. Michel Foucault's notion of 'heterotopia' is pertinent here, a site marked off from the everyday world where transformations can occur. Foucault mentions 'heterotopias of deviation', spaces 'in which individuals whose behaviour is deviant in relation to the required mean or norm are placed', including prisons and hospitals.[55] The surgical-legal sites of these dystopian fictions are carceral heterotopias of deviation, punitive, normative, and transformative. Time may function oddly within heterotopias, Foucault describing 'heterochrony', modes of time such as 'the heterotopias … of the eternity of accumulating time', for instance in museums and libraries.[56] One might also speak of a heterochrony of illness experience. Rita Charon notes that time may be experienced differently for patient and doctor: 'When the doctor or nurse enters the room to do something … he or she remains within vectored time, that is, a state of time in which one event leads to another and can even be conceptualized as having caused it while the patient inhabits a timeless enduring'.[57] The donor-victims in these dystopian texts inhabit exactly such a state, their agency suspended and the passage of time simultaneously a reprieve (since they are still alive) and torture (since they await vivisection). These fictions present an implacable medico–juridical fatality for bodies caught within law that has decided against their worth.

Hints of resistance emerge in tension between what might be called clinical time or juridical time, on the one hand, and a more aslant, askew, awry time on the other, a temporality that entangles fragments of past memory, impossible future, or unbearable wordless present and makes none of these subordinate to a medico-legal framing. In exploring these temporal differences, I find Elizabeth Freeman's conception of 'queer times' helpful. If 'chrononormativity' can describe 'the use of time to organize individual human bodies toward maximum productivity' and socially sanctioned forms of encounter (including, for example, encounters within legal and medical process), then 'queer times' may include 'nonsequential forms of time … [like] unconsciousness, haunting, reverie … [which] can also fold subjects into structures of belonging and duration that may be invisible to the historicist eye'.[58] I am not valorising an 'authentic', 'individual' time, am not elevating a liberal humanist subject. Rather, I want to show these askance, askew, awry fragments as also social – as relational, as *yearning*, in defiance of a social context that does not recognise a right to desire, act, or survive.

Cordwainer Smith's novella 'A planet called Shayol' (1961) describes a planet where political prisoners are sentenced to interminable vivisection. Alien creatures infect their bodies and cause human organs to grow on them for transplant elsewhere in the empire. The surgical site blends hospital and prison in a heterotopia within which each victim is dehumanised in a paradoxical blend of cruelty and clinical care. When the protagonist arrives at the planet, staff 'looked him over as if he were a rare plant or a body on the operating table. They were almost kind in the clinical deftness of their touch. They did not treat him as a criminal, but as a specimen … [C]lad in their medical smocks, they looked at him as though he were already dead' (para. 2). He is treated as 'a rare plant' or a corpse, combining the metaphors of vegetation and waste, and they tell him, 'We can hear you screaming, you know. You keep on sounding like people even after Shayol begins to work on you' (para. 9). The close third-person narration takes us into the perspective of a disorientated victim protagonist, bringing us into an experience of terrifying bodily vulnerability and intense temporal disorientation: 'we know the order in which things happen, but we have no clocks'; 'He forgot the order. He did not count time'; he 'did not scream but he lay against the wall and wept for ten thousand years; in objective time, it must have been several hours' (paras 296, 205–6, 376). The novella imagines intense human suffering under a medicalised judiciary.

Medico-juridical spaces are also central to Larry Niven's 'Known Space' series (1964–2012). This series coined the term 'organlegging', illegal organ trade, which has entered wider currency.[59] My focus here, however, is on the series's depiction of nonconsensual procurement with state sanction. In this society, tissue-matching advances have reduced rejection, and the expanded donor pool, coupled with transplantation becoming normalised for a broad range of ailments, leads to a soaring demand for tissue. In 2043 the US state of Arkansas solves the demand by making 'organ banks the official state method of execution', and the rest of the US emulates this model, voting for minor transgressions to incur death sentences because 'the citizen, who wants to live as long and as healthily as possible, will vote any crime into a capital crime if the organ banks are short of material' – even traffic offences.[60]

Niven's short story 'The jigsaw man' (1967) presents this institutional meshing of hospital and penal systems. We hear of the surgery or execution of a convicted criminal, himself an organlegger (dealer in illegal tissue). He is injected with cryogenic material and placed on a conveyor belt, and here a medical rather than legal language ensues:

> The doctor was a line of machines with a conveyor belt running through them. When ... body temperature reached a certain point, the belt started. The first machine made a series of incisions in his chest. Skillfully and mechanically, the doctor performed a cardiectomy.
>   The organlegger was officially dead.
>   His heart went into storage immediately. His skin followed, most of it in one piece, all of it still living. The doctor took him apart with exquisite care, like disassembling a flexible, fragile, tremendously complex jigsaw puzzle. (pp. 69–70)

The vivisection apparatus is repeatedly called the 'doctor'. The factory is made possible by a merging of medical and legal, in the process illuminating the carceral dimension of both domains.[61] Similar blurring occurs when he escapes and finds himself in a hospital adjacent to the jail. So perverse has the inversion of hospital become that he feels only despair when he realises he is inside one: 'A hospital. He *would* pick a hospital. And *this* hospital, the one which had been built right next to the Topeka County courthouse, for good and sufficient reason' (p. 76, emphasis in original). Medicine and law meet in a lethal nexus.

Niven's subsequent novel *A Gift from Earth* (1968) imagines a planetary colony founded three hundred years earlier by a ship that originated from that twenty-first-century earth. Descendants of the original ship's 'Crew' are aristocracy and descendants of the rest are essentially serfs who can be raided for organs. The Crew leader admits, 'We own their bodies ... We take them apart on the slightest pretext' (p. 69). Their subjects accept the status quo because a few have the opportunity to themselves benefit from the organ banks and because ethical arguments have persuaded the majority that any transgression deserves death. Even the rebels, when given the opportunity to destroy the organ banks at the end of the novel, choose to maintain them in a modified form.

Niven's text appeared in the same year as the Report of the Ad Hoc Committee of the Harvard Medical School to Examine the Definition of Brain Death.[62] Committee papers indicate that a key concern was minimising uncertainty and concealing the professional disagreements existing within the committee.[63] (To date, there continue to be variations in death definition and diagnostic protocol between nations, and variations in diagnostic protocol even between hospitals.)[64] The US and UK accepted the concept of irreversible coma rapidly, but the late 1960s and early 1970s saw anxieties about the new death play out in a range of media, as I discuss in my first two chapters. Niven's novel resists the Report's certainty, observing that each colony has a different definition of when legal death occurs and dramatising variation in practice across procurement sites (p. 92). The novel also estranges the procurement process, and it does this by using a highly Gothic register, ceremonial and elegiac. While the language of the Harvard Report was 'technical and utilitarian, rather than popular, theological, or symbolic', Niven presents the surgeries or executions in language incantatory and ceremonial.[65] The site of the tissue extraction is not a surgical theatre but a 'vivarium', and is described as silent and even sacred (pp. 90–2). Within this site, the vivisection is described in terms that evoke litany, the phrase 'in law he was still alive' repeated alongside the descriptions of the vivisection (p. 91). This language restores mystery to the process of death-by-surgery and the new categories of death, and dramatises how marking off particular bodies as harvestable is culturally mediated. Here, transgressive bodies are mortified within a medico-legal nexus.

The peril of bodies under law is evoked also in Dennis Etchison's short story 'Calling all monsters' (1973, rev. 1982), which explores legal challenges around controlling the fate of one's body after death. The protagonist has lived in dread of being misdiagnosed as dead and tissue too-hastily extracted, and had written a will insisting on an electroencephalogram (EEG) before procurement surgery commenced. In fact, as I discuss in Chapter 1, an EEG alone would not satisfy many national criteria for determination of death by neurological criteria, but none the less the flat line of electrocortical 'silence' has an iconic significance in the popular imaginary around brain death. In this short story, doctors use a syntactical quirk in the will to avoid performing such a scan (p. 97) (and also, presumably, fail to conduct the usual augmenting tests that are part of determination of neurological death today). They fail to realise that the subject is still fully conscious and conduct unanaesthetised vivisection.

The story adapts H.G. Wells's *Island of Doctor Moreau*, but with the twist that the experimental victim in the 'House of Pain' is human (p. 94).[66] His first-person, present-tense narration is interspersed with an italicised present-tense third-person narration in which a doctor tells the subject's wife that her husband is dead and refuses to perform the requested EEG. Conscious but paralysed, the protagonist is raided for tissue and used for medical experimentation, and sees other heads and bodies stored in grotesque extensions of life. Tormented beyond bearing, the first-person narrator ultimately identifies himself as monstrous, both physically and psychologically. In a futile interior scream of vengeance, he imagines a desperate connection with others who are no longer human, reaching out in his mind to the other grafts and tortured beings around him: 'at last the grafts rebel appendages reborn to murder I call you back I call you in now do not wait come as always to the laboratory House of Pain operating room crypt castle tower' (p. 98). Yet nothing can prevent the vivisection:

> O now the obscene sucking sound growing fainter even as my hearing dissolves, wet tissue pulling apart. They suction my blood, the incision clamped wide like another mouth a monstrous Caesarean and I hear the shiny scissors clipping tissues clipping fat, the automated scalpels striking tictactoe on my torso and I know they are taking me, the blood in my head tingles draining down down and I am almost gone ... (p. 97)

Appalling and lyrical, the story interweaves visceral description of the dissection of a living body with a hopeless legal appeal: 'O what is it what are they doing to me the monsters ME thy must be it can't be that other nono [*sic*] my papers they couldn't do THAT they couldn't break the terms it says blackandwhite NO' (p. 97). The present-tense, run-on sentences and incantatory rhythm all create a vivid sense of traumatic overwhelm.

All three abovementioned works from the 1960s and 1970s draw much of their effect from horror at the helplessness of bodies within a medico-legal nexus. The three millennial works which follow, however, offer something rather different. Bodies are again marked out as either worthy or expendable, but several victim characters internalise the rightness of their society's norms, and this acceptance is specifically inflected by metaphors for transfer tissue and scarcity discourse which hold sway today. These discursive constructions are as entangled with transfer process as the scalpel, and – in the case of these protagonists – cut quite as deep. Each novel foregrounds the experience of an imagined victim, either through first-person or close third-person narration, so one might expect that they will ultimately defy the dehumanising metaphors of donor-as-waste, vegetation, spare parts, natural resource, but instead the metaphors for transfer become structuring tropes through which some characters come to see themselves. There are also moments of tension between, on the one hand, clinical time or juridical time, and on the other hand other temporalities, a queer time, as described earlier, in which a life marked out by a society as unacceptable reaches none the less for fragments of remembered connection with others, imagined connection, scraps of past and future that may be fictional, must be secret, will be brief. The poignancy of these moments is all the more sharp in the context of character acceptance.

Shusterman's *Unwind* is the first of the 'Unwind Dystology', four novels and a novella, inspired by a real-life case of a Ukrainian orphanage which became a target for organ trade.[67] The novel imagines a future America in which a civil war between pro-life and pro-choice forces has transformed medical practice. Peace was reached through a 'Bill of Life' which forged a compromise on abortion. If parents choose, when their child is aged between thirteen and eighteen, the child can be 'unwound', every piece of their tissue transplanted to a different human recipient (p. 263). One character notes, '"Once the unwind orders were signed, we all became government property"' (pp. 56–7). The industry of 'unwinding' draws on government and private finance. In a triumph for the private sector, 'Harvest Camps' are privately owned, profit-making facilities, sustained by government investment (p. 263). Transplant is commercial and all unwound tissue must be paid for. When one character asks a camp counsellor what happens with organs that are not good calibre, she is told, '"a deaf ear is better than no ear at all, and sometimes it's all people can afford"' (p. 269). Healthcare privatisation shapes every element of the process.

This society identifies two categories of harvestable body. A small minority are 'Tithes', whom religious parents have chosen from birth to be unwound (pp. 31, 128). Dressed in white from birth, Tithes are kept apart from the majority of the Unwinds, those whom parents chose to unwind after they became teenagers. Juvenile delinquents or just plain unwanted, these Unwinds are seen as wasted lives to be redeemed through transfer; that discourse parallels some perspectives from today's procurement environments, as discussed above. Even some Unwinds subscribe to this view, one character saying, 'I was never going to amount to much anyway, but now, statistically speaking, there's a better chance that some part of me will go on to greatness somewhere in the world. I'd rather be partly great than entirely useless' (p. 1). In the sequel, a 'Public Service Announcement' makes a hierarchy of life clear, contrasting these teenagers with 'soldiers wounded in the field of duty, healed and restored by the precious parts they receive'.[68] The appeal to continue using the bodies of youth is bolstered by contrasting them with the bodies of soldiers and veterans. A hierarchy of lives is clear.

The society offers an ingenious rationale of the harvest process. It is held that consciousness persists even after tissue is unwound, so the vivisection does not result in true death. Unwinds are kept conscious throughout the dismemberment (locally anaesthetised), and after dismemberment and transplant are described as 'living in a divided state' (p. 263). Characters marked for Unwinding contemplate this notion with horror, one imagining being 'unwound into nothing – his bones, his flesh, his mind, shredded and recycled' (p. 148). The novel simultaneously mocks and endorses the notion of 'living in a divided state'. On the one hand, the idea seems absurd, as when one character is told by a harvest camp counsellor that she will not be 100 per cent alive, but 'actually ... 99.44 per cent, which takes into account things like the appendix' (p. 269). On the other hand, the novel presents multiple examples of an ongoing persistence of Unwind life. A trucker who received a transplant arm says, "'These fingers here knew things the rest of me didn't. Muscle memory, they call it'" (p. 14). When another character receives Unwind tissue, the nurse warns him, "'Parts often come with their own personalities'" (p. 319), and CyFi, a teenager who received Unwind brain tissue, says, "'It's like those ghosts who don't know they're dead'" (pp. 139–40). The novel culminates in a reassembling of unwound tissue where the contrite parents of one Unwind, Harlan Dunfee, gather recipients of his tissue for his twenty-sixth birthday, 'putting their son together in the only meaningful way they can' (p. 331). Harlan speaks to his parents at the end, all the recipients uniting their conversations, and his parents welcome him home. The extraordinary upshot of these moments endorsing the idea of 'living in a divided state' is that they unmask the horror of the initial alienation of the tissue. In other words, in this fictional world, disentanglement works even less well than in our own.

Simultaneously festive and carceral, the site where Unwinding occurs is a holiday camp or prison, a hybrid heterotopia embodying the ambivalence that accompanies the paradoxical construction of harvest in this society. As in Niven's work, a language of ritual and ceremony attends the process, emphasising the implacable systems of law and medicine – 'The harvesting of Unwinds is a secret medical ritual that stays within the walls of each harvesting clinic in the nation' (p. 287) – but Shusterman takes us into the ritual, using close third-person present-tense narration from the perspective of a victim. The character Roland is given local anaesthetic but remains conscious throughout, strapped to a table. He can hear people dropping instruments, but cannot see what they are doing. 'Surgeons leave, new ones arrive. The new ones take an intense interest in his abdomen. He looks towards his toes but can't see them. Instead he sees a surgical assistant cleaning the lower half of the table' (p. 290). A nurse makes statements of scripted sympathy, which interweave with the dialogue of surgeons: the nurse tells him she is sure he was a good son, while the surgeon calls 'scalpel' (p. 290). There is simultaneously a callousness and bizarre tenderness to the process. Medical staff 'wear scrubs the color of a happy-face', his arms and legs are bound, and 'A nurse blots sweat from his forehead. "Relax, I'm here to help you through this"' (p. 288). Greening metaphors soften the surgery throughout. Transplant is always called 'grafting', Unwinding is 'harvest', and one of his final sights (before they remove his eyes) is of the surgical staff as themselves a flower: 'Yellow figures lean all around him like flower petals closing in' (p. 291). Two hours and 33 minutes in, his eyes are gone and he experiences:

Not quite darkness, just an absence of light. He hears everything around him but can no longer communicate …
  'You'll feel a tingling in your scalp,' says a surgeon … It's the last time they talk to him. After that, the doctors talk like Roland is no longer there.

... 'Splitting the corpus callosum.'
'Nice technique.'
'Well, it's not brain surgery.' Laughter all around. (p. 292)

The doctors are right to say it is not brain surgery: rather than surgery for healing, this passage imagines dismemberment for profit, only possible because Unwinds are seen as waste, subhuman.

As in other texts in this chapter, Shusterman's novel estranges the process of surgical removal of tissue in ways that complicate the society's use of metaphors of spare parts, gift, waste, or greening; also as in the other works in this chapter, that estrangement hinges on offering an alternative to surgical temporalities. Throughout, we are given repeated prompts marking the clinical timespan of the procedure. An hour or so into the vivisection, for example, Roland hears 'A clanging of metal. The lower half of the table is unhooked and pulled away' (p. 290). One hour and 45 minutes in, the nurse says he won't be able to talk any more – they're taking his lungs. Two hours and 5 minutes in, he can communicate only by blinking, and 'Another section of the table is taken away' (p. 291). The narration includes a litany of the durations of surgical process. Yet there is a tension between such markers of clinical time and the rest of the narration, which interrupts that sequence with Roland's past experience and childhood trauma and moments when he was deprived of love. 'Memories tweak and spark. Faces. Dreamlike pulses of light deep in his mind ... Things he hasn't thought about in years ... then they're gone' (p. 292). A lifetime of suffering unfolds, exceeding the simple time bounded and sequential surgical process. The narration resists the metaphors of gift, waste, spare parts, and greening, opening up the frame to recognise the entanglement of networks of finance and self-interest in hierarchies of human life.

Metaphors of gift, waste, and recycled parts and a discourse of worth also intersect in Ishiguro's novel *Never Let Me Go*, an alternative history. The narrator is Kathy H., a young woman recalling her life as a 'student' at Hailsham school. Hailsham initially seems to be an orphanage under the care of 'guardians' – teachers, monitors – but the children never leave the grounds until adulthood and are subject to medical surveillance. Eventually we learn that the 'students' are clones made to be dismembered for organs, and Kathy H.'s first-person narration takes us into the position of realising one is marked for such dismemberment. Cruelly, the clones themselves are co-opted to maintain the system: before they become 'donors' they must work as 'carers' to keep others obedient.

This society's dominant metaphor superficially frames tissue as 'gift': we hear consistently of 'donor' and 'donation'. In complementary euphemisms, the hospitals where tissue extraction occurs are called 'recovery centres' and dying in donation is called 'completing'. 'Fourth Donation' has particular status, a milestone rarely reached. The gift rhetoric implies that donors are free agents, celebrated and appreciated, and never more so than on Fourth Donation. Kathy explains, 'A donor "on a fourth", even one who's been pretty unpopular up till then, is treated with special respect. Even the doctors and nurses play up to this: a donor on a fourth will go in for a check and be greeted by whitecoats smiling and shaking their hand' (p. 273). Gift rhetoric partially cushions this nonconsensual, exploitative procurement regime, and, as mentioned earlier, the language of gift can be used today, too, in contexts where the procurement is not freely voluntary ('rewarded gifting', 'paid donor').[69] In Ishiguro's novel, the gift rhetoric is wholly disingenuous, for 'donors' have no choice in harvest and no option to refuse. Their bodies, far from 'gift', are waste, disposable.

Ishiguro couples first-person narration with another formal strategy that seizes the reader and implicates us in Kathy's world and her identification with the abject. Throughout, her narration assumes her audience share this experience, that we, her readers, are also 'students', that we grew up somewhere like Hailsham, and that we have our own versions of her traumatic discoveries in our own childhood too. 'I'm sure somewhere in your childhood, you too had an experience like ours' (p. 36). Throughout the novel, she repeatedly assumes we are like her, that we know what it is to be destined for dismemberment. Against the positive language of 'donation', the novel constructs the position of both protagonist and implied audience as one of abject victim rather than respected giver, and ultimately even 'Fourth Donation' takes on a darker note:

> You'll have heard the same talk. How maybe, after the fourth donation, even if you've technically completed, you're still conscious in some sort of way; how then you find there are more donations, plenty of them, on the other side of that line; how there are no more recovery centres, no carers, no friends; how there's nothing to do except watch your remaining donations until they switch you off. It's horror movie stuff. (p. 274)

At such moments, the imagined society's protocols of neurological determination of death are explicitly questioned, and tissue extraction made a thing of horror. Yet strikingly, with one brief exception, Kathy H. and the other clones do not resist the gift rhetoric. As in *Unwind*, the dominant metaphors for transfer tissue – gift and waste – become primary tropes for characters in understanding themselves, to the extent that they ultimately identify with trash. Kathy's friend Ruth, for example, rages against their plight in terms which make a direct link between their status as waste and their fate of dismemberment: "'We're modelled from *trash*. Junkies, prostitutes, winos, tramps. Convicts, maybe ... That's what we came from. We all know it, so why don't we say it? ... If you want to look for possibles [originals] ... then you look in the gutter. You look in rubbish bins. Look down the toilet, that's where you'll find where we all came from'" (p. 164, emphasis in original). Even as children, the 'students' have a poignant affinity with rejected things, creating a frail illusion of care for themselves through their meagre possessions, broken toys and detritus from the lives of 'real' people. Ruth gets a discarded pencil case one year, Kathy gets a cassette tape, and these things become pivotal to fantasies they weave of nurturing love. They cherish these discarded things as they themselves are not cherished.

In a second concatenation of the language of waste and the language of love, the novel contains a long-running conceit of Norfolk being Britain's lost-property corner. This whimsical notion developed because Hailsham school has a 'lost corner' for lost property, and one day a guardian describes Norfolk as a 'lost corner' not on the way to anywhere else. The children joke that there must be trucks collecting lost objects and taking them there, and this fantasy is partially realised when, as adults years later, Kathy H. and her friend Tommy visit Norfolk, search for Kathy's lost cassette and actually find it. At the end of the novel, after Tommy has died in fourth donation, the stoic, self-controlled Kathy stands beside a field in Norfolk and uncharacteristically indulges a daydream.

> All along the fence, especially along the lower line of wire, all sorts of rubbish had caught and tangled … That was the only time, as I stood there, looking at that strange rubbish, feeling the wind coming across those empty fields, that I started to imagine just a little fantasy thing, because this was Norfolk after all, and it was only a couple of weeks since I'd lost him. I was thinking about the rubbish, the flapping plastic in the branches, the shore-line of odd stuff caught along the fencing, and I half-closed my eyes and imagined this was the spot where everything I'd ever lost since my childhood had washed up, and I was now standing here in front of it, and if I waited long enough, a tiny figure would appear on the horizon across the field, and gradually get larger until I'd see it was Tommy, and he'd wave, maybe even call. The fantasy never got beyond that – I didn't let it – and though the tears rolled down my face, I wasn't sobbing or out of control. I just waited a bit, then turned back to the car, to drive off to wherever it was I was supposed to be. (p. 282)

Again, breaking sequential time is the site of a brief, fleeting escape from medico-juridical horror. In this harrowing blend of grief and compliance, Kathy intuits their link with 'strange rubbish'. Gift and waste are structuring tropes for the first-person protagonist caught in that particular society's exploitative structure, and the novel's first-person narration takes us into the perspective of one who has internalised her abjection. Yet this reverie on trash simultaneously defies the dehumanisation of the trope itself: this passage makes rubbish both a thing longed for and a thing that itself yearns.

Holmqvist's *The Unit* can be seen as a variation on *Unwind*'s ideas of wasted lives redeemed and Ishiguro's entangling of gift and waste. The specific lives devalued are different: the 'worthless' lives are those of adults who have failed to make certain (largely reproductive) choices. This novel imagines a future in which certain people are classified as 'dispensable': men over 60 or women over 50 who are not 'needed people'. To be a 'needed person' you need to have young children, have elderly parents needing care, be in a caring profession, or be a role model to inspire children. Reproductivity is the measure of human value. As one fellow dispensable reminds the protagonist, "'It's only new con-stellations they approve of. People who make a home and produce new people. You know that ... everything has to move forward'" (p. 137). 'Dispensable' people are incarcerated, deprived of the right to vote or communicate with the outside world, subjected to permanent surveillance, used for medical experi-ments, and fatally raided as living organ banks. As in *Unwind*, these 'wasted' lives are figured as redeemed through state intervention, surgical procurement, and the redeployment of their body parts to help those more valued: the wel-come literature (on the novel's back cover blurb) declares: 'Welcome to the Second Reserve Bank Unit for Biological Material, where we will be glad to assist you in becoming a more productive and valuable member of society'.

As *The Unit* progresses, the boundary between 'dispensable' and 'indispen-sable' becomes increasingly unstable. The 'dispensable' people form loving bonds with each other, even taking on caring roles, and outside the Unit this could have precluded them from becoming dispensable. Even when the pro-tagonist becomes pregnant, however – this society's ultimate embodiment of a 'needed person – she is not released. As the novel progresses, we realise that outside the Unit, too, the definition of a 'dispensable' person is expanding as time progresses. Only young parents are now exempt, and 'if you were child-less, you were childless, end of story' (p. 223). The novel presents rapacious increase in scarcity rhetoric and laws being changed to accommodate that hunger. Here, too, as in Niven's, Shusterman's, and Ishiguro's texts, charac-ters internalise the social norms. The protagonist escapes the Unit but returns voluntarily, gives birth, gives up her child for adoption, and asks to be taken for organs. In one of her few moments of rebellion, the narrator thinks of the Unit as a 'luxury slaughterhouse' (p. 212), but even then she hastily distances herself from the words as those of another donor. The machines of social death, in all its discursive force, shapes subjects' internal worlds.

As in Ishiguro's novel, these horrors are mediated through a measured, controlled first-person narration. She submits to her unbearable situation and her grief emerges only in glimpses, particularly in meditations on the natural world. In the light of the widespread use of greening metaphors to simplify some of transfer's complexities, the novel's use of plant symbolism is worth comment. When Dorrit is taken away from her home to live in the Unit until her death, the sight of the first snowdrops and winter aconite inspire in her thoughts of the new beginning which she does not herself expect to ever have (ironically, she does find a rebirth of love and happiness in the Unit, only to lose all she has gained in devastating fashion). Ultimately, the imagery of plants and growth paradoxically comes to represent imprisonment rather than rebirth or naturalised harvest. The Unit contains a 'Winter Garden', inspired by Monet, and this place comes to signify the warped heterochrony of the harvest site:

> Under normal circumstances, in the real world out there, our memory can usu-
> ally support itself by the seasons: a certain event is linked with a particular time
> of year ... But when I think back over my time in the unit my memory has no
> such assistance from the seasons, because the seasons never change. In the unit
> there are only days and nights, that's the only thing that changes ... In the winter
> garden everything is in bud or flower, but nothing shrivels, withers or dies. It is
> never winter in the winter garden. (p. 160)

This winter garden is a place of verdant plenitude but rests on a denial of some-thing, just as transfer can be underpinned by scarcely visible suffering. Rather than serving to naturalise surgical extraction, this cumulative imagery oddly has the other effect: it makes the natural world strange too, and this estrange-ment finds expression specifically in a warped temporality.

As in the previous texts, time becomes a site of struggle. Dorrit's suppressed despair and grief come out in covert ways: after her lover is killed for donations and her newborn child is taken from her, she chooses to die, and the last lines of the novel describe the letter she writes to her child. The letter is calm, and describes how she met her child's father; it is a straightforward letter describ-ing a simple memory. Yet this memory is a deliberate fiction: it is the way she wishes that things had been. Her only outlet for expressing her anguish is playing with time, contradicting the past, bending time askew. In a sense, this *is* queer time, in that she is imagining a moment of connection, of desire, now impossible for her since she has been marked as non-normative. Her desire is impossible in this society, but she plays with time to, for just a moment, make that desire and connection thinkable.

These disturbing novels invite readers to imaginatively occupy abjected posi-tions, marshalling the immersive potency of coherently imagined worlds and merciless plot trajectories to bring home the horror of potential dismember-ments, cushioned though they are by metaphoric substitution. These societies are fantastical but the figurative language they adapt is not. Speculative fiction can offer a useful counterpoint to the influence of particular metaphoric discourse in emerging rhetoric around human bodies as a communal resource, particularly alongside any society's covert, but real, implicit hierarchies of life. *Which* futures do we write and see? Which futures get government policy booklets, advertis-ing campaigns, and national oversight and administrative bodies to ease their coming into being, and which do not get such help to be rendered visible? And: what sacrificial suffering underpins the futures we hope for, that we do *not* see?

Notes

1 In my Introduction to this book I reject the idea that tissue transfer is intrinsically a violation of some idealised inviolate human body. Like any other practice, transfer's meanings are historically and culturally specific.

2 D. Punter, *Gothic Pathologies* (Basingstoke: Palgrave Macmillan, 1998), pp. 2–3.

3 J. Biehl, *Vita*, 2nd edn (Berkeley: University of California Press, 2013), p. 366.

4 Evidence indicates that China, for example, has years of nonconsensual procurement from living political prisoners. D. Kilgour and D. Matas, *Bloody Harvest* (Niagara Falls: Seraphim, 2009); E. Gutmann, *The Slaughter* (Amherst, NY: Prometheus, 2014). During the 2012 US Congressional Hearings into allegations of Chinese harvest from political prisoners, Dr Damien Noto noted, 'In 2010 at a transplant conference in Madrid, Dr. Jiefu [China's Vice Minister of Health] stated that between 1997 and 2008 China had performed more than 100,000 transplantations with over 90% of the organs being from executed prisoners'. C. Smith, D. Burton, E. Gallegly, *et al.*, *Papers of the Joint Congressional Hearing* (Washington, DC: US Government Printing Office, 2012), p. 32.

5 C. Smith, 'A planet called Shayol', *Galaxy Science Fiction* (October 1961), www.wattpad.com/67345-Cordwainer-Smith-A-Planet-Named-Shayol [accessed 17 September 2009]; L. Niven, *A Gift from Earth* (London: Futura, [1968] 1982); D. Etchison, 'Calling all monsters', in *The Dark Country* (New York: Berkley, [1982] 1984), pp. 93–8. Subsequent references are in parenthesis. I have discussed other works by Etchison in Chapters 2 and 3.

6 K. Ishiguro, *Never Let Me Go* (London: Faber, 2005); N. Holmqvist, *The Unit*, trans. M. Delargy (Oxford: One World, [2006] 2010); N. Shusterman, *Unwind* (London: Simon and Schuster, [2007] 2008). Subsequent references are in parenthesis.

7 M. Foucault, 'Society must be defended', in T. Campbell and A. Sitze (eds), *Biopolitics* (Durham, NC: Duke University Press, [1976] 2013), pp. 61–81 (p. 62); M. Foucault, *History of Sexuality*, vol. 1 (London: Penguin, [1976] 1987), pp. 139–40. For a more detailed discussion, see Chapter 3.

8 G. Agamben, *Homo Sacer*, trans. D. Heller-Roazen (Stanford: Stanford University Press, [1995] 1998).

9 T. Lemke, *Biopolitics* (New York: NYU Press, 2011), pp. 61–2.

10 J. Butler, *Frames of War*, 2nd edn (New York: Verso, 2016).

11 Biehl, p. 366. For more on assemblage, see my discussion in my Introduction and Chapter 4.

12 D. Hamilton, *A History of Organ Transplantation* (Pittsburgh, PA: University of Pittsburgh Press, 2012), p. 400.

13 R. Pérez-Peña, 'Downside to fewer violent deaths', *New York Times* (19 August 2019), www.nytimes.com/2003/08/19/nyregion/downside-to-fewer-violent-deaths-transplant-organ-shortage-grows.html [accessed 2 August 2019].

14 A. Sifferlin, 'Organ transplants hit an all-time high in 2017', *Time Magazine* (10 January 2018), time.com/5097377/record-breaking-organ-transplants-2017/ [accessed 28 March 2018].

15 L. Sharp, *The Transplant Imaginary* (Berkeley: University of California Press, 2013), pp. 148–9. For further discussion of the language of scarcity, see M. Lock, *Twice Dead* (Berkeley: University of California Press, 2002); V. Campion-Vincent, 'Organ theft narratives', *Journal of Folklore Research*, 39:1 (2002), 33–50 (p. 45); S. Schicktanz and M. Schweda, '"One man's trash is another man's treasure"', *Journal of Medical Ethics*, 35:8 (2009), 473–6.

16 M. Lock and V.-K. Nguyen, *An Anthropology of Biomedicine* (Madden, MA: Wiley-Blackwell, 2010), pp. 235–6.

17 J. Bion, P. Nightingale, and B. Taylor, 'Will the UK ever reach international levels of organ donation?' *British Journal of Anaesthesia*, 108 (2012), Supplement 1, i10–i13 (p. 11); R. Fox and J. Swazey, *Spare Parts* (Oxford: Oxford University Press, 1992), p. 9.

18 K. Zeiler and E. Malmqvist, 'Bodily exchanges, bioethics, and border crossing', in E. Malmqvist and K. Zeiler (eds), *Bodily Exchanges* (London: Routledge, 2016), pp. 1–18 (p. 9); E. Malmqvist and K. Zeiler, 'Concluding reflections', in E. Malmqvist and K. Zeiler (eds), *Bodily Exchanges* (London: Routledge, 2016), pp. 197–207 (pp. 202–3).

19 Lock, *Twice Dead*, p. 86; R. Fox and J. Swazey, *Spare Parts* (Oxford: Oxford University Press, 1992), p. 206.

20 P. Byrne and R. Nilges, 'The brain stem in brain death', *Issues in Law and Medicine*, 9 (1993), 3–21 (p. 18); M. Rady and J. Verheijde, 'Advancing neuroscience research in brain death', *Journal of Critical Care*, 39 (2017), 293–4.

21 L. Sharp, *Harvest* (Berkeley: University of California Press, 2006), pp. 20, 64; Schicktanz and Schweda.

22 J. Brierley, D. Graham, J. Adams, and J. Simpson, 'Neocortical death after cardiac arrest', *The Lancet*, 298:7724 (1971), 560–5; Sharp, *Harvest*, p. 97.

23 Lock, *Twice Dead*, p. 120.

24 Sharp, *Harvest*, p. 97.

25 Lock, *Twice Dead*, p. 255n15; Campion-Vincent, p. 41.

26 Sifferlin.

27 L. Hogle, 'Standardization across non-standard domains', *Science, Technology and Human Values*, 20:4 (1995), 482–500 (p. 493).

28 I discuss Rob Nixon's concept of 'slow violence' in Chapter 3. R. Nixon, *Slow Violence and the Environmentalism of the Poor* (Cambridge, MA: Harvard University Press, 2013).

29 B. Brecht, *Brecht on Theatre*, trans. J. Willett (London: Methuen, 1964), p. 71.

30 G. Miller and A. McFarlane, 'Science fiction and the medical humanities', *Medical Humanities*, 42:4 (2016), 213–18 (p. 215).

31 Sharp, *Transplant Imaginary*; A. Schick, 'Whereto speculative bioethics?', *Medical Humanities*, 42:4 (2016), 225–31.

32 D. Steinberg, *Genes and the Bioimaginary* (Aldershot: Ashgate, 2015), p. 111. The concept of 'structures of feeling' is from R. Williams, *The Long Revolution* (Cardigan: Parthian, [1961] 2011).

33 Lock and Nguyen, p. 244.

34 M. Callon, 'The embeddedness of economic markets in economics', in M. Callon (ed.), *The Laws of the Markets* (Oxford: Blackwell, 1998), pp. 1–57 (p. 19).

35 D. Punter, 'Ceremonial gothic', in G. Byron and D. Punter (eds), *Spectral Readings* (London: Macmillan, 1999), pp. 37–53.

36 A. Appadurai, 'Introduction', in A. Appadurai (ed.), *The Social Life of Things* (Cambridge: Cambridge University Press, 1986), pp. 3–63; Callon, p. 17; C. Waldby and R. Mitchell, *Tissue Economies* (Durham, NC: Duke University Press, 2006), p. 68.

37 K. Marx, *Capital*, vol. 1 (London: Penguin [1976] 1990).

38 A. Hyde, *Bodies of Law* (Princeton, NJ: Princeton University Press, 1997), p. 47.

39 L. Sharp, 'Commodified kin', *American Anthropologist*, 103:1 (2001), 112–33 (pp. 116, 112).

40 Hyde, p. 4.

41 G. Lakoff and M. Johnson, *Metaphors We Live By* (London: University of Chicago Press, 1980).

42 Ibid.

43 M. Sanner, 'Living with a stranger's organ', *Annals of Transplantation*, 10:9 (2005), 9–12 (p. 10); M. Shildrick, P. McKeever, S. Abbey, J. Poole, and H. Ross, 'Troubling dimensions of heart transplantation', *Medical Humanities*, 35:1 (2009), 35–8.

44 J. Riskin, *The Restless Clock* (Chicago: University of Chicago Press, 2016); H. Zwart, 'Transplantation medicine', *Subjectivity*, 9:2 (2016), 151–80 (p. 157); W. Harvey, *Exercitatio Anatomica de Motu Cordis et Sanguinis in Animalibus* (Omaha: Gryphon, [1628] 1978).

45 Waldby and Mitchell, pp. 85–6.

46 Lock and Nguyen, pp. 235–6; Lock, *Twice Dead*. For an illustration of waste and recycling metaphors, see Ampla Advertising Agency, 'One of these two will get your organs', Brazilian advertisement, Manuel Cavalcanti (2008) abduzeedo. com/10-outstanding-ad-campaings-brazil#sthash.LKqEs01x.dpuf [accessed 2 April 2014], and Trillium Life Network, 'Recycle me', recycleme.org [accessed 10 October 2014].

47 G. Tagliacozzi, *De Curtorum Chirurgia per Insiotonem* (Venice: Berolini, 1597).

48 Sharp, *Harvest*, pp. 37, 77; Sharp, 'Commodified kin', pp. 115, 120–9.

49 P. Park, 'The transplant odyssey', *Second Opinion*, 12 (1989), 12–32 (p. 30).

50 R. Negarestani, *Cyclonopedia* (Melbourne: re.press, 2008).

51 For alternative ways for a recipient to relate to their donor in ways that do not dehumanise the donor, see Sharp, *Harvest*; Shildrick *et al.*, p. 37; C. Waldby, 'Biomedicine, tissue transfer and intercorporeality', *Feminist Theory*, 3 (2002), 235–50 (p. 239).

52 N. Scheper-Hughes, 'The tyranny of the gift', *American Journal of Transplantation*, 7:3 (2007), 507–11; S. Wasson, 'Recalcitrant tissue', in J. Edwards (ed.), *Technologies of the Gothic in Literature and Popular Culture* (New York: Routledge, 2015), pp. 99–112.

53 B. Fantus, 'Cook County's Blood Bank', *Modern Hospital*, 50:21 (1938), 57–8; Hamilton, p. 409; D. Joralemon, 'Organ wars', *Medical Anthropology Quarterly*, 9:3 (1995), 335–56 (p. 336).

54 L. Cohen, 'The other kidney', *Body and Society*, 7:2 (2001), 9–29 (pp. 22–3).

55	M. Foucault, 'Of other spaces', trans. J. Miskowiec (1984), *Repository of Texts Written by Michel Foucault*, foucault.info/documents/heteroTopia/foucault.hetero Topia.en.html [accessed 10 September 2007], para. 18.

56	Ibid, paras 23–5.

57	R. Charon, *Narrative Medicine* (Oxford: Oxford University Press, 2008), p. 44.

58	E. Freeman, *Time Binds* (Durham, NC: Duke University Press, 2010).

59	L. Niven, 'The patchwork girl', in *Flatlander* (New York: Ballantine, [1980] 1995); *Shadowrun: Fifth Anniversary Core Rulebook* (Seattle: Catalyst, 2013), pp. 9, 15, 404; T. Huff, *Blood Debt* (New York: Little Brown, 2004). Subsequent references in parenthesis.

60	Niven, *Gift*, p. 123.

61	Punter, *Pathologies*.

62	Ad Hoc Committee of the Harvard Medical School to Examine the Definition of Brain Death, 'A definition of irreversible coma', *Journal of the American Medical Association*, 205:6 (1968), 85–8. See Chapter 1 for discussion.

63	M. Giacomini, 'A change of heart', *Social Science of Medicine*, 44:10 (1997), 1465–82.

64	I discuss variability in definition and diagnostic practice in Chapter 1.

65	Giacomini, p. 1466.

66	H.G. Wells, *The Island of Dr Moreau* (London: Penguin, [1896] 2005).

67	N. Shusterman, *UnWind Unboxed: UnWind, UnWholly, UnSouled, UnStrung* (New York: Simon and Schuster ebook, [2007–14] 2014).

68	Shusterman, *Unboxed*, Kindle, loc. 7238.

69	Hamilton, p. 409; Joralemon, p. 336.

Coda

Writing wounds

In 1543, the Flemish anatomist Andreas Vesalius wrote *De Humani Corporis Fabrica* (*On the Fabric of the Human Body*), a meticulous record of what he had learned through human dissection, accompanied by woodcuts of bodies solely composed of nerve or bone or muscle. The work had a profound influence on medicine for centuries. This book, and works by others in the intervening centuries, also laid a crucial imaginative foundation that made transplantation eventually possible: specifically, shaping perceptions of the body's elements as discrete and interlayered and, ultimately, substitutable. As Lesley Sharp says, 'transplantation would remain impossible if ... human parts were not conceived of as interchangeable'.[1]

I invoke this work here for a second reason. His images present bodies opened, partitioned, and suspended mid-movement. These figures are reading a book, moving, walking outdoors. These are bodies in action, but bodies flayed. In this, they distil a preoccupation that has run throughout *Transplantation Gothic*: a focus on bodies opened, their incisions not closed, yet life ongoing. The heart of this book has been the image of bodies wounded in ways that are *not yet finished*. I have sought to respect stories that do not end or stories that do not end neatly: the wounds of donors that spread to include intangible wounds like reduced earning capacity, pain or stigma, and recipients' wounds that keep the body open for more changes – immunosuppressant pharmacology, the medical gaze, and other interventions.[2] I am interested in extended durations, the slow violence of legacies of health inequality and the long aftermath of care.

Elsewhere, I have suggested the concept of 'stigmaphilia in a minor key' to describe a particular creative or critical position which 'deliberately draws close to the textures of pain, shame, and wounds, both stigma and stigmata'.[3] The term 'stigmaphilia' entered queer theory and disability studies as part of a joyful, transgressive reclamation of stigmatised positions as a substratum for resistance.[4] This process is vital and defiant and necessary. At times, however, it may mean that 'painful and traumatic dimensions ... have been minimised or disavowed', as Heather Love warns, and 'makes it harder to see the persistence of the past in the present'.[5] Similarly, Sara Ahmed observes that 'Ethics cannot

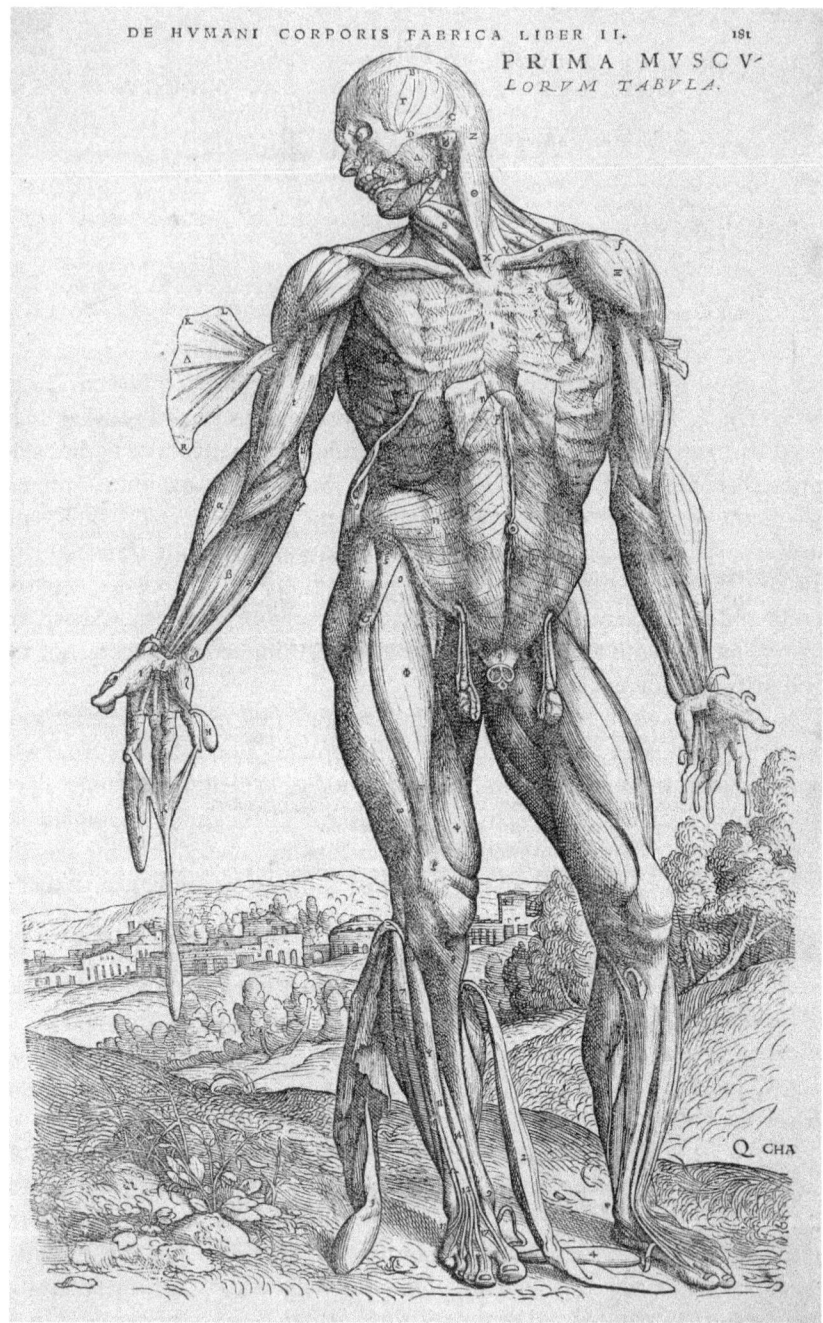

Figure 11 Andreas Vesalius, *De Humani Corporis Fabrica* (Basileæ: ex officina Joannis Oporini, 1543), p. 181. © The British Library Board, Reference Collection C.54.k.12.

be about moving beyond pain … without imposing new forms of suffering on those who do not or cannot move in this way … These histories have not gone: we would be letting go of that which persists in the present. To let go would be to keep those histories present.'[6] I use the musical metaphor of stigmaphilia in a minor key to describe a subtly different weighting in focus, less oriented towards the end-point of transformation of anguish into something positive (although that is still vital), and more towards dwelling with the initial suffering, the jagged pain and affective burden of enduring. These imaginative texts can help us recognise 'the present as not yet an event but rather a suspended impasse, a waiting and reaching, within a … particular … social and medical milieu'.[7]

The labour of enduring an ambiguous present is central to multiple chapters in this book. Chapter 1 considers the tension between death as event versus process and the way a clinical necropoetics negotiates this ambiguity in a range of contrasting ways. Chapters 2, 3, and 5 consider harvestee temporalities, including tissue transfer informed by the 'slow' violence of social, economic, and political exclusions.[8] Chapter 4 considers recipient times, the suspense of waiting, and aftermath, during which bodies are opened and never quite closed: boundaries continue to be changed surgically, pharmacologically, and imaginatively.[9] This book is concerned with extended durations of heterogeneous suffering. Yet fantastical fiction and film are also inevitably complicit in capital's processes too, and indeed, some critics have suggested that science fiction has functioned as 'ideological cyclosporine' by normalising organ transplant in ways that facilitate global inequalities in tissue transfer.[10] These polyvalent texts are also complicit in forgetting. Writing can also wound.

Literary criticism cannot emulate the specificity of ethnography, but I hope that this book can be seen as an imaginative complement to ethnographies and cultural studies of tissue transfer. Imaginative writing can offer vivid representations of both the systems around transfer and the *durée* of transfer experience. I am concerned throughout with the temporalities of transfer, not only the traumatic or catastrophic moment but also the slow, grinding experience of suffering over time – less the crisis of appalling event and more the unease of waiting, anticipation, and aftermath. Some wounds close slowly. Some wounds do not close.

Notes

1 L. Sharp, *The Transplant Imaginary* (Berkeley: University of California Press, 2013), p. 40.

2 J.-L. Nancy, '*L'intrus*', trans. S. Hanson, *New Centennial Review*, 2:3 ([2000] 2002), 1–14; M. Foucault, *The Birth of the Clinic: An Archaeology of Medical Perception*, trans. A. Sheridan (London: Routledge, [1963] 2003); M. Moniruzzaman, '"Living

cadavers" in Bangladesh', *Medical Anthropology Quarterly*, 26:1 (2012), 69–91; E. Cazdyn, *The Already Dead* (Durham, NC: Duke University Press, 2012); L. Cohen, 'Where it hurts', *Daedalus*, 128:4 (1999), 135–65.

3 S. Wasson, 'Spectrality, strangeness and stigmaphilia', in A. Hall (ed.), *Routledge Companion to Literature and Disability* (London: Routledge, in press).

4 M. Warner, *The Trouble with Normal* (New York: Free Press, 1999); E.K. Sedgwick, 'Queer performativity', in D. Hale (ed.), *The Novel* (Oxford: Blackwell, 2006), pp. 605–21; R. McRuer, *Crip Theory* (New York: NYU Press, 2006), pp. 35–6.

5 H. Love, *Feeling Backward* (Cambridge, MA: Harvard University Press, 2007), pp. 3–4, 19.

6 S. Ahmed, *The Promise of Happiness* (Durham, NC: Duke University Press, 2010), pp, 216–17.

7 S. Wasson, 'Before narrative', *Medical Humanities*, 44:2 (2018), 106–112.

8 R. Nixon, *Slow Violence and the Environmentalism of the Poor* (Cambridge, MA: Harvard University Press, 2013).

9 Nancy; F. Varela, 'Intimate distances', *Journal of Consciousness Studies*, 8:5–7 (2001), 259–71.

10 S. Squier, *Liminal Lives* (Durham, NC: Duke University Press, 2004), pp. 170, 183.

Filmography

'A question of life or death: the brain death debate', *Panorama*, BBC (19 February 1981)

'Transplants: are the donors really dead?' *Panorama*, BBC (13 October 1980)

A Woman Who Understood, dir. by W. Parke (Robertson-Cole, 1920)

The Beast with Five Fingers, dir. by R. Florey (Warner, 1946)

Coma, dir. by M. Crichton (Metro Goldwyn-Mayer, 1978)

Coma, dir. by M. Salomon (A&E TV mini-series, 3–4 September 2012)

Das Cabinet des Dr. Caligari / Cabinet of Dr Caligari, dir. by R. Wiene (Decla-Bioscop, 1920)

Dirty Pretty Things, dir. by S. Frears (BBC, Celador and Jonescompany, 2002)

Frankenstein Chronicles, dir. by B. Langford and B. Ross, television series (2015–)

Get Out, dir. by J. Peele (Universal, 2017)

The Hand, dir. by O. Stone (Orion, 1981)

Hands of a Stranger, dir. by N. Arnold (Rainmark, 1962)

The Hands of Orlac, dir. by E. Gréville (Pendennis, 1960)

Her Surrender, dir. by I. Abramson (Ivan Film, 1916)

The Hospital Baby, director unstated (Essanay, 1912)

The Island, dir. by M. Bay (Dreamworks, 2005)

L'intrus, dir. by C. Denis (Ognon, 2004)

Les mains de Roxana, dir. by P. Setbon (Juin, 2012)

Les yeux sans visage (Eyes without a Face), dir. by G. Franju (Champs-Élysées, 1958)

Mad Love, dir. by K. Freund (Metro-Goldwyn-Mayer, 1935)

Night of the Living Dead, dir. by G. Romero (Image Ten, 1968)

Orlacs Hände, dir. by R. Wiene (Berolina, 1924)

Parts: The Clonus Horror, dir. by R. Fiveson (Group 1 International Distribution Organization, 1979)

Repo! The Genetic Opera, dir. by D. Bousman (Twisted Pictures, 2008)

Turistas, dir. by J. Stockwell (2029 Entertainment, 2006)

Wolf Blood, dir. by G. Chesebro and B. Mitchell (Ryan Brothers, 1925)

Bibliography

Ad Hoc Committee of the Harvard Medical School to Examine the Definition of Brain Death, 'A definition of irreversible coma', *Journal of the American Medical Association*, 205:6 (1968), 85–8.

Adkins, L., *The Time of Money* (Stanford: Stanford University Press, 2018).

Adler, M., 'Kidney transplantation and coping mechanisms', *Psychosomatics*, 13 (1972), 337–41.

Agamben, G., *Homo Sacer*, trans. D. Heller-Roazen (Stanford: Stanford University Press, [1995] 1998).

Ahmed, S., *Cultural Politics of Emotion*, 2nd edn (Edinburgh: Edinburgh University Press, 2004).

_____, *The Promise of Happiness* (Durham, NC: Duke University Press, 2010).

Aldana Reyes, X., *Horror Film and Affect* (London: Routledge, 2016).

_____, 'What, why and when is horror fiction?', in X. Aldana Reyes (ed.), *Horror* (London: British Library, 2016), pp. 7–18.

Aldhous, P., 'Bone marrow donors risk DNA mixup', *New Scientist* (26 October 2005), www.newscientist.com/article/mg18825234-600-bone-marrow-donors-risk-dna-identity-mix-up/ [accessed 27 September 2018].

Aleccia, J., 'Wallet biopsy', *CNN.com* (24 December 2018), t.co/WXXjGkaiC3 [accessed 19 May 2019].

Alexander, M., *The New Jim Crow* (New York: New Press, 2010).

Almgren, M., A. Lennerling, M. Lundmark, and A. Forsberg, 'The meaning of being in uncertainty after heart transplantation', *European Journal of Cardiovascular Nursing*, 16:2 (2017), 167–74.

Ambagtsheer, F., D. Zaitch, and W. Weimar, 'The battle for human organs', *Global Crime*, 14:1 (2013), 1–26.

Amine, L., 'A house with two doors?', *Culture, Theory and Critique*, 48:1 (2007), 71–85.

Ampla Advertising Agency, 'One of these two will get your organs', Brazilian advertisement, Manuel Cavalcanti (2008), abduzeedo.com/10-outstanding-ad-campaings-brazil#sthash.LKqEs01x.dpuf [accessed 2 April 2014].

Ancuta, K., 'The return of the dismembered', in L. Blake and A. Soltysik Monnet (eds), *Neoliberal Gothic* (Manchester: Manchester University Press, 2017), pp. 83–103.

Andrews, L., 'My body, my property', *Hastings Center Report*, 16:5 (1986), 28–38.

Angier, N., 'Biologists seek the words in DNA's unbroken text', *The New York Times* (9 July 1991), C1.

Appadurai, A., 'Introduction', in A. Appadurai (ed.), *The Social Life of Things* (Cambridge: Cambridge University Press, 1986), pp. 3–63.

Arata, S., 'The occidental tourist', *Victorian Studies*, 33:4 (1990), 621–45.

Ariès, P., *The Hour of Our Death*, trans. H. Weaver (Harmondsworth: Penguin, [1977] 1983).

_____, *Western Attitudes Towards Death*, trans. P. Ranum (London: Marion Boyars, [1974] 1976).

Aronowitz, R., *Making Sense of Illness* (Cambridge: Cambridge University Press, 1998).

Augé, M., *Non-Places*, trans. by J. Howe (London: Verso, [1992] 1995).

Babik, J. and P. Chin-Hong, 'Transplant tourism', *Current Infectious Disease Reports*, 17:4 (2015), 1–6.

Baldick, C. (ed.), 'Introduction', *The Oxford Book of Gothic Tales* (Oxford: Oxford University Press, 1992), pp. xi–xxiii.

Baldick, C. and R. Mighall, 'Gothic criticism', in D. Punter (ed.), *A Companion to the Gothic* (Oxford: Blackwells, 2001), pp. 209–28.

Baldwin, H., 'Skin grafting', *Medical Record*, 97 (1920), 686–8.

Barkan, L., 'Cosmas and Damian', in S. Youngner, R. Fox, and L. O'Connell (eds), *Organ Transplantation* (Madison: University of Wisconsin Press, 1996), pp. 221–51.

Barrish, P., 'Health policy in dystopia', *Literature and Medicine*, 34:1 (2016), 106–31.

Baru, R. and P. Nanda, *Trading of Organs* (Delhi: Voluntary Health Association of India, 1993).

Basch, S., 'The intrapsychic integration of a new organ', *Psychoanalytic Quarterly*, 42 (1972), 364–84.

Bataille, G., *Theory of Religion* (New York: Zone, 1989).

Beidel, D., 'Psychological factors in organ transplantation', *Clinical Psychology Review*, 7:6 (2987), 677–94.

Belling, C., 'The living dead', *Perspectives in Biology and Medicine*, 53:3 (2010), 439–51.

Bennett, J., *Vibrant Matter* (Durham, NC: Duke University Press, 2010).

Bercovitch, E., 'The agent in the gift', *Cultural Anthropology*, 9 (1994), 498–536.

Bernat, J., 'The debate over death determination in DCD', *Hastings Center Report*, 40:3 (2010), 3.

_____, 'Life or death for the dead donor rule?', *New England Journal of Medicine*, 369:14 (2013), 1289–91.

Beugnet, M., 'The practice of strangeness', *Film Philosophy*, 12:1 (2008), 31–48.

Bhalla, N., 'Top Indian hospital says duped into removing kidneys for organ traffickers', *Reuters* (6 June 2016), www.reuters.com/article/us-india-trafficking-organs/top-in dian-hospital-says-duped-into-removing-kidneys-for-organ-traffickers-idUSKC N0YS1Z9 [accessed 3 February 2018].

Biehl, J., *Vita*, 2nd edn (Berkeley: University of California Press, 2013).

Biernoff, S., 'Theatres of surgery', *Wellcome Open Research*, 3:54 (2018), 1–20.

Biller-Andorno, N., 'Gender imbalance in living organ donation', *Medicine, Health Care and Philosophy*, 5:2 (2005), 199–204.

Bion, J., P. Nightingale, and B. Taylor, 'Will the UK ever reach international levels of organ donation?', British Journal of Anaesthesia, 108 (2012), Supplement 1, i10–i13.

Blake, L., 'Neoliberal adventures in neo-Victorian biopolitics', in J. Edwards (ed.), *Technologies of the Gothic in Literature and Culture* (New York: Routledge, 2015), pp. 166–78.

———, *The Wounds of Nations* (Manchester: Manchester University Press, 2008).

Blake, L. and A.S. Monnet, 'Introduction', in L. Blake and A. Soltysik Monnet (eds), *Neoliberal Gothic* (Manchester: Manchester University Press, 2017), pp. 1–18.

Bleakley, A., 'Towards a critical medical humanities', in V. Bates, A. Bleakley, and S. Goodman (eds), *Medicine, Health and the Arts* (Abingdon: Routledge, 2014), pp. 17–26.

Bolaki, S., *Illness as Many Narratives* (Edinburgh: Edinburgh University Press, 2016).

Botting, F., *Gothic* (London: Routledge, 1996).

———, *Gothic Romanced* (London: Routledge, 2008).

Bowers, C., 'The black hand', Amazing Stories, 5:10 (1931), 909–11, 923.

Boyd, J., *The Organ Bank Farm* (New York: Bantam, [1970] 1972).

Braddon, M.E., 'Good Lady Ducayne', in A. Ryan (ed.), *The Penguin Book of Vampire Stories* (London: Penguin, [1896] 1987), pp. 138–62.

Brainclinics Research Institute, 'History: from EEG to quantitative EEG (QEEG)', www.brainclinics.com/history-of-the-eeg-and-qeeg [accessed 27 May 2019].

'Breaking the code', *The Economist* (28 November 1992), 150.

Brecht, B., *Brecht on Theatre*, trans. J. Willett (London: Methuen, 1964).

Brierley, J., D. Graham, J. Adams, and J. Simpson, 'Neocortical death after cardiac arrest', *The Lancet*, 298:7724 (1971), 560–5.

Bronfen, E., *Over Her Dead Body* (Manchester: Manchester University Press, 1996).

Bruhm, S., 'Butoh', in G. Byron (ed.), *Globalgothic* (Manchester: Manchester University Press (2013), pp. 25–35.

Bryson, M. and J. Stacey, 'Cancer knowledge in the plural', *Journal of Medical Humanities*, 34:2 (2013), 197–212.

Budiana-Saberi, D. and S. Columb, 'A human rights approach to human trafficking for organ removal', *Medicine, Health Care, and Philosophy*, 16:4 (2013), 897–914.

Bunzel, B., B. Schmidl-Mohl, A. Grundbock, and G. Wolleneck. 'Does changing the heart mean changing personality?', *Quality of Life Research*, 1:4 (1992), 251–6.

Burke, E., *A Philosophical Inquiry into the Origin of Our Ideas of the Sublime and Beautiful* (Oxford: Oxford University Press, [1757] 1990).

Butler, J., *Frames of War*, 2nd edn (New York: Verso, 2016).

———, *Precarious Life* (London: Verso, 2004).

Bynum, W., *History of Medicine* (Oxford: Oxford University Press, 2008).

Byrne, P. and R. Nilges, 'The brain stem in brain death', *Issues in Law and Medicine*, 9 (1993), 3–21.

Byron, G. (ed.), *Globalgothic* (Manchester: Manchester University Press, 2013).

Callon, M., 'The embeddedness of economic markets in economics', in M. Callon (ed.), *The Laws of the Markets* (Oxford: Blackwell, 1998), pp. 1–57.

Calne, R., *Ultimate Gift* (London: Headline, 1998).

Campbell, R., 'Introduction', in D. Etchison, *The Dark Country* (New York: Berkley, [1982] 1984), pp. xi–xii.

Campion-Vincent, V., 'On organ theft narratives', *Current Anthropology*, 42:4 (2001), 555–8.

_____, 'Organ theft narratives', *Western Folklore*, 56:1 (1997), 1–37.

_____, V., 'Organ theft narratives as medical and social critique', *Journal of Folklore Research*, 39:1 (2002), 33–50.

Canavan, G., 'Fighting a war you've already lost', *Science Fiction Film and Television*, 4:2 (2011), 173–203.

_____, '"If the engine ever stops, we'd all die"', *Paradoxa*, 26 (2014), 41–66.

Cannadine, D. 'War and death, grief and mourning in modern Britain', in Joachim Whaley (ed.), *Mirrors of Mortality: Studies in the Social History of Death* (London: Europa, 1981), pp. 187–242.

Carney, S., *The Red Market* (New York: William Morrow, 2011).

Carter, A., 'Afterword', in *Fireworks* (Cambridge, MA: Harper and Row, 1974), pp. 132–3.

Castelnuovo-Tedesco, P., 'Transplantation', in N. Levy (ed.), *Psychonephrology* (New York: Plenum Press, 1981), pp. 219–25.

Castle, T., *The Female Thermometer* (Oxford: Oxford University Press, 1995).

Cazdyn, E., *The Already Dead* (Durham, NC: Duke University Press, 2012).

Cecka, M., 'Significance of histocompatibility in organ transplantation', *Current Opinion in Organ Transplantation*, 12:4 (2007), 402–8.

Charon, R., *Narrative Medicine* (Oxford: Oxford University Press, 2008).

Chaten, F., 'The dead donor rule', *Journal of Medical Ethics*, 40:7 (2014), 496–500.

Chengappa, R., 'The great organs bazaar', *India Today* (31 July 1990), 60–7.

Cherry Mark, J., *Kidney for Sale by Owner* (Washington, DC: Georgetown University Press, 2005).

Chimowitz, H. and R. Sade, 'Benefits and harms to organ donors', *The American Journal of Bioethics*, 15:8 (2015), 19–20.

Christie, J., T. O'Lenic, and R. Cane, 'Head turning in brain death', *Journal of Clinical Anesthesia*, 8:2 (1996), 141–3.

Cisney, V. and N. Morar, 'Why biopower?', in V. Cisney and N. Morar (eds), *Biopower* (Chicago: Chicago University Press, 2016), pp. 1–25.

Clarke, A., L. Mamo, J. Fishman, J. Shim, and J. Fosket, 'Biomedicalisation', *American Sociological Review*, 68 (2003), 161–94.

Clute, J., 'Fantastika in the world storm' (2007), Lecture at the American Center, Prague, www.johnclute.co.uk/word/?p=15? [accessed 23 January 2016].

Cocteau, J., *The Art of Cinema*, trans. R. Buss (London: Marion Boyars, 1992).

Cohen, L., 'A futures market in cadaveric organs', *Transplantation Proceedings*, 25 (1993), 60–1.

_____, 'Operability, bioavailability, and exception', in A. Ong and S. Collier (eds), *Global Assemblages* (Malden: Wiley-Blackwell, 2005), pp. 79–80.

_____, 'The other kidney', *Body and Society*, 7:2 (2001), 9–29.

_____, 'Where it hurts', *Daedalus*, 128:4 (1999), 135–65.

Comaroff, J. and J. Comaroff, 'Millennial capitalism', *Public Culture*, 12:2 (2000), 291–343.

Conan Doyle, A. 'The Adventures of the Creeping Man', *Complete Sherlock Holmes* (London: Penguin, [1923] 2009), pp. 1070–82.

Conrad, P., 'Medicalisation and social control', *Annual Review of Sociology*, 18 (1992), 209–32.

Cook, E., '"Off dropped the sympathetic snout"', in H. Kerr, D. Lemmings, and R. Phiddian (eds), *Passions, Sympathy, and Print Culture* (Basingstoke: Palgrave, 2016), pp. 145–64.

Cook, R., *Coma* (Boston, MA: Little Brown, 1977).

Cooper, M., *Life as Surplus* (Seattle: University of Washington Press, 2008).

Crawford, P. and C. Baker, 'Literature and madness', *Journal of Medical Humanities*, 30 (2009), 237–51.

Crow, L., 'Including all of our lives', in J. Morris (ed.), *Encounters with Strangers* (London: The Women's Press, 1996).

Crowley-Matoka, M. and M. Lock, *Domesticating Organ Transplant* (Durham, NC: Duke University Press, 2016).

———, 'Organ transplantation in a globalized world', *Mortality*, 11:2 (2006), 166–81.

Csicsery-Ronay Jr, I., *The Seven Beauties of Science Fiction* (Middletown: Wesleyan University Press, 2008).

Cushing, H., 'Some experimental and clinical observations concerning states of increased intracranial tension', *American Journal of the Medical Sciences*, 124 (1902), 377–91.

Czerwiec, M.K., I. Williams, S. Squier, M. Green, K. Myers, and S. Smith, *Graphic Medicine Manifesto* (University Park: Penn State University Press, 2015).

Dahl, G., 'Sociology and beyond', *Asian Journal of Social Science*, 37:3 (2009), 391–407.

Darwin, C., *The Variation of Animals and Plants Under Domestication* (London: John Murray, 1875), p. 370.

Das, V., 'The practice of organ transplants', in M. Lock, A. Young, and A. Cambrioso (eds), *Living and Working with the New Medical Technologies* (Cambridge: Cambridge University Press, 2000), pp. 263–87.

Daston, L. and P. Galison, *Objectivity*, 2nd edn (New York: Zone, 2010).

Davidson, H., 'Transplantation in the brave new world', *Mental Hygiene*, 5 (1968), 467–8.

Davidson, M., 'Concerto for the left hand', *PMLA*, 120:2 (2005), 615–19.

Davis, E., 'The intimacies of globalization', *Camera Obscura*, 21:62 (2006), 33–73.

Davison, C., special issue on 'Addiction', *Gothic Studies*, 11.2 (2009).

———, 'Introduction', in C. Davison (ed.), *The Gothic and Death* (Manchester: Manchester University Press, 2017).

de Boeve, A., *Narrative Care* (London: Bloomsbury, 2013).

De Lissovoy, N., 'Conceptualizing the carceral turn', *Critical Sociology*, 39:5 (2013), 739–55.

de Réaumur, R., 'Avis pour donner du secours à ceux que l'on croit noyés', in A. Louis, *Lettres Sur la Certitude des Signes de la Mort* (Paris: Michel Lambert, [1740] 1752), pp. 250–60.

Deleuze, G., *Two Regimes of Madness*, ed. by D. Lapoujade, trans. A. Hodges and M. Taormina (New York: Semiotext(e), 2007).

Delmonico, F., 'The declaration of Istanbul on organ trafficking and transplant tourism', *Indian Journal of Nephrology*, 18:3 (2008), 135–40.

Dempster, W., 'Rejection of renal homografts', *The Lancet*, 275:7123 (1960), 551.

Deomampo, D., 'Transnational surrogacy in India', *Frontiers*, 34:3 (2013), 167–88.

Derrida, J., *Aporia*, trans. T. Dutoit (Stanford: Stanford University Press, 1993).

———, *Given Time: I* (Chicago: University of Chicago Press, 1994).

———, *Specters of Marx*, trans. P. Kamuf (New York: Routledge, [1993] 2006).

Dery, M., 'Black to the future', in M. Dery (ed.), *Flame Wars* (Durham, NC: Duke University Press, 1994), pp. 179–222.

Dickason, R., V. Chauhan, A. Mor, E. Ibler, S. Kuehnle, D. Mahoney, E. Armbrecht, and P. Dalawari, 'Racial differences in opiate administration for pain relief at an academic emergency department', *Western Journal of Emergency Medicine*, 16:3 (2015), 372–80.

Diedrich, L., 'Illness as assemblage', *Body & Society*, 21:3 (2015), 66–90.

———, *Treatments* (Minneapolis: University of Minnesota Press, 2007).

Döşemeci, L., M. Cengiz, M. Yılmaz, and A. Ramazanoğlu, 'Frequency of spinal reflex movements in brain-dead patients', *Transplantation Proceedings*, 36:1 (2004), 17–19.

Dossetor, J., 'Transplantation', in P. Terasaki (ed.), *History of Transplantation* (Los Angeles: UCLA, 1971), pp. 295–306.

Duckworth, D., 'Some cases of cerebral disease', *Edinburgh Medical Journal*, 3 (1898), 145–52.

Durant, M., 'The Ethiopian's leg', *Saint Lucy*, saint-lucy.com/essays/the-ethiopians-leg/ [accessed 12 August 2018].

Egan, G., 'The extra', in J. Dann and G. Dozois (eds), *Clones* (New York: Ace, [1990] 1998), pp. 55–73.

Egan, S., *Mirror Talk* (Chapel Hill: University of North Carolina Press, 1999).

Ehrenfried, A., 'Reverdin and other methods of skin-grafting', *Boston Medical and Surgical Journal*, 161 (1909), 911–27.

Ehrenreich, B., 'Welcome to Cancerland', *Harper's*, 303:1818 (2001), 43–53.

Emanuel, L., 'Re-examining death', *Hastings Center Report*, 25:4 (1995), 27–35.

Engling, R., *Body Mortgage* (New York: Penguin, 2001).

Epstein, A., J. Ayanian, and J. Keogh, 'Racial disparities in access to renal transplantation', *New England Journal of Medicine*, 343 (2000), 1537–44.

Esposito, R., *Immunitas*, trans. Z. Hanafi (Cambridge: Polity, [2002] 2011).

Etchison, D., 'The dead line', 'Calling all monsters', and 'The machine demands a sacrifice', in *The Dark Country* (New York: Berkley, [1982] 1984), pp. 99–110, 93–8, 81–92.

Fairfield, F., *Ten Years with Spiritual Mediums* (New York: D. Appleton, 1875).

Fantus, B., 'Cook County's Blood Bank', *Modern Hospital*, 50:21 (1938), 57–8.

Fiedler, L., 'Why organ transplant programs do not succeed', in S. Youngner, R. Fox, and L. O'Connell (eds), *Organ Transplantation* (Madison: University of Wisconsin Press, 1996), pp. 56–65.

Finger, A., *Past Due* (London: Women's Press, [1990] 1991).

Fins, J., *Rights Come to Mind* (Cambridge: Cambridge University Press, 2015).

Fiser, K., *Losing and Finding* (Denton: University of North Texas Press, 2003).

Fisher, M., *Capitalist Realism* (Ropley: Zero Books, 2009).

———, *The Weird and the Eerie* (London: Repeater, 2016).

Fost, N., 'The unimportance of death', in S. Youngner, R. Arnold, and R. Schapiro (eds), *The Definition of Death* (Baltimore, MD: Johns Hopkins University Press, 1999), pp. 161–78.

Fothergill, J., *Observations on the Recovery of a Man Dead in Appearance* (San Francisco: Garth Hudson, [1745] 1980).

Foucault, M., *The Birth of the Clinic: An Archaeology of Medical Perception*, trans. A. Sheridan (London: Routledge, [1963] 2003).

———, *History of Sexuality*, vol. 1 (London: Penguin, [1976] 1987).

———, 'Of other spaces', trans. J. Miskowiec (1984), *Repository of Texts Written by Michel Foucault*, foucault.info/documents/heteroTopia/foucault.heteroTopia.en.html, para. 18 [accessed 10 September 2007].

———, 'Society must be defended', in T. Campbell and A. Sitze (eds), *Biopolitics* (Durham, NC: Duke University Press, [1976] 2013), pp. 61–81.

Foucault, M., J.-P. Barou, and M. Perrot, 'Excerpt from *The Eye of Power*', in C. Gordon (ed.), *Power/Knowledge*, trans. C. Gordon, L. Marshall, J. Mepham, and K. Soper (New York: Pantheon, [1977] 1980), pp. 146–65.

Fox, R. 'An ignoble form of cannibalism', in R. Arnold, S. Youngner, R. Schapiro, and C. Spicer (eds), *Procuring Organs for Transplant* (Baltimore, MD: Johns Hopkins University Press, 1995), pp. 155–64.

Fox, R. and J. Swazey, *The Courage to Fail* (Chicago: University of Chicago Press, 1978).

———, *Spare Parts* (Oxford: Oxford University Press, 1992).

Frank, A., 'Afterword', *The Wounded Storyteller*, 2nd edn (Chicago: University of Chicago Press, 2013), pp. 187–221.

———, 'Caring for the dead', in L.-C. Hydén and J. Brockmeier (eds), *Health, Illness and Culture* (London: Routledge, 2008), pp. 122–30.

———, 'Generosity, care, and a narrative interest in pain', in D. Carr, J. Loeser, and D. Morris (eds), *Narrative, Pain, and Suffering* (Seattle: IASP, 2005), pp. 289–300.

———, 'The necessity and dangers of illness narratives', in Y. Gunaratnam and D. Oliviere (eds), *Narrative and Stories in Health Care* (Oxford: Oxford University Press, 2009), pp. 161–76.

———, *The Wounded Storyteller* (Chicago: University of Chicago Press, [1995] 1997).

Franklin, S. and M. Lock, 'Animation and cessation', in S. Franklin and M. Lock (eds), *Remaking Life and Death* (Santa Fe, NM: School of American Research Press, 2003), pp. 3–22.

Freeman, E., *Time Binds* (Durham, NC: Duke University Press, 2010).

Freud, S., 'Mourning and melancholia', *Penguin Freud Library*, vol. 11, trans. J. Strachey, ed. A. Richards (London: Penguin, [1917] 1984), pp. 245–68.

———, 'The uncanny', *Penguin Freud Library*, vol. 14, trans. J. Strachey, ed. A. Richards (London: Penguin, [1919] 1985), pp. 336–76.

Fry, G., *Night Riders in Black Folk History* (Chapel Hill: University of North Carolina Press, [1975] 2001).

Fukunishi, I., Y. Kita, W. Paris, S. Mitchell, and B. Nour, 'Relationship between post-traumatic stress disorder and emotional conditions in families of the cadaveric donor population', *Transplantation Proceedings*, 35:1 (2014), 295.

Gardiner, D., S. Shemie, A. Manara, and H. Opdam, 'International perspective on the diagnosis of death', *British Journal of Anaesthesia*, 108 (2012), Supplement 1, i14–i28.

Gardner, L., K. Dew, M. Stubbe, T. Dowell, and L. Macdonald, 'Patchwork diagnoses', *Social Science and Medicine*, 73:6 (2011), 843–50.

Garland-Thomson, R., *Extraordinary Bodies* (New York: Columbia University Press, 1997).

Gaylin, W., 'Harvesting the dead', *Harper's* (September 1974), 23–9.

Geroulanos, S., 'Postwar facial reconstruction', *French Politics, Culture & Society*, 31:2 (2013), 15–33.

Giacomini, M., 'A change of heart', *Social Science of Medicine*, 44:10 (1997), 1465–82.

Gibson, T. and P. Medawar, 'The fate of skin homografts in man', *Journal of Anatomy*, 77:4 (1943), 299–310.

Gilbert, H., 'Manjula Padmanabhan's Harvest', *Contemporary Theatre Review*, 16:1 (2006), 123–30.

Gilbert, S., 'Holobiont by birth', in A. Tsing, H. Swanson, E. Gan, and N. Bubandt (eds), *Arts of Living on a Damaged Planet* (Minneapolis: University of Minnesota Press, 2017), pp. M73–M90.

Giroux, H., *Zombie Politics and Culture in the Age of Casino Capitalism* (New York: Peter Lang, 2011).

Goldsmith, J., 'Dirty Pretty Things', *Creative Screenwriting*, 11:1 (2004), 56.

Goodell, W., *American Slave Code in Theory and Practice* (New York: American and Foreign Anti-Slavery Society, 1853).

Goodman, C., C. Worrall, U. Chong, S. Kallinis, and M. Rockwood, *The Organ Donation Breakthrough Collaborative* (Washington, DC: US Department of Health and Human Services, 2003), docplayer.net/5153165-The-organ-donation-break-through-collaborative-best-practices-final-report.html [accessed 6 June 2018].

Goodwin, S. and E. Bronfen, 'Introduction', in S. Goodwin and E. Bronfen (eds), *Death and Representation* (Baltimore, MD: Johns Hopkins University Press, 1993), pp. 3–28.

Gordon, E., 'What race cannot tell us about access to kidney transplantation', *Cambridge Quarterly of Healthcare Ethics*, 11:2 (2002), 134–41.

Gorovitz, S. and A. MacIntyre, 'Toward a theory of medical fallibility', *Hastings Center Report*, 5:6 (1975), 13–23.

Goyal, M., R. Mehta, L. Schneiderman, and A. Sehgal, 'Economic and health consequences of selling a kidney in India', *Journal of the American Medical Association*, 288:13 (2002), 1589–93.

Graulund, R., 'Nanodead', in J. Edwards (ed.), *Technologies of the Gothic in Literature and Culture* (New York: Routledge, 2015), pp. 127–39.

Greer, D., P. Varelas, S. Haque, and E. Wijdicks, 'Variability of brain death determination guidelines in leading US neurologic institutions', *Neurology*, 70:4 (2008), 284–9.

Gross, A., J. Harmon, and M. Reidy, *Communicating Science* (New York: Oxford University Press, 2002).

'Growing shortage of organs worrying doctors', *New York Times* (5 December 1967), www.nytimes.com/1967/12/05/archives/growing-shortage-of-organs-worrying-doctors-heart-transplant.html [accessed 13 August 2018].

Gunnarson, M. and S. Lundin, 'The complexities of victimhood', *Somatechnics*, 5:1 (2015), 32–51.

Gutmann, E., *The Slaughter* (Amherst, NY: Prometheus, 2014).

Guyer, J., 'Prophecy and the near future', *American Ethnologist*, 34:2 (2007), 409–21.

Haggerty, G., *Gothic Fiction / Gothic Form* (University Park: Pennsylvania State University Press, 1989).

Halberstam, J., 'Technologies of monstrosity', *Victorian Studies*, 36:3 (1993), 333–52.

Halevy, A. and B. Brody, 'Brain death', *Annals of Internal Medicine*, 119 (1993), 519–25.

Hamburger, J. and J. Crosnier, 'Moral and ethical problems in transplantation', in F. Rapaport and J. Dausset (eds), *Human Transplantation* (New York: Grune and Stratton, 1968), pp. 37–44.

Hamdy, S., *Our Bodies Belong to God* (Berkeley: University of California Press, 2012).

Hamilton, D., *A History of Organ Transplantation* (Pittsburgh, PA: University of Pittsburgh Press, 2012).

Hans, A., '"These hands are not my hands"', in C. Rogowski (ed.), *The Many Faces of Weimar Cinema* (Rochester, NY: Camden House, 2010), pp. 102–15.

Hansmann, H., 'The economics and ethics of markets for human organs', in J. Blumstein and A. Sloan (eds), *Organ Transplantation Policy* (Durham, NC: Duke University Press, 1989), pp. 57–85.

Haraway, D., 'The biopolitics of postmodern bodies', in T. Campbell and A. Sitze (eds), *Biopolitics* (Durham, NC: Duke University Press, [1989] 2013), pp. 274–309.

_____, *Simians, Cyborgs, and Women* (London: Free Association Books, 1991).

_____, *Staying with the Trouble* (Durham, NC: Duke University Press, 2016).

Harris, R., N. Wathen, and S. Wyatt (eds), *Configuring Health Consumers* (Basingstoke: Palgrave Macmillan, 2010).

Harrison, J., *Medical Aspects of Death* (London: Longman, 1852).

Harvey, W., *Exercitatio Anatomica de Motu Cordis et Sanguinis in Animalibus* (Omaha: Gryphon, [1628] 1978).

Harvey, W., *The Beast with Five Fingers* (London: J.M. Dent, [1928] 1960).

'Have a heart', *Investor's Business Daily* (9 December 2011), A12.

Hawes, W., *An Address to the Public on Premature Death and Premature Interment* (London: Royal Humane Society, 1780), p. 40.

Hawkins, A., *Reconstructing Illness* (West Lafayette, IN: Purdue University Press, 1999).

'Heart snatch case', *Afro-American* (10 June 1972), 4.

Hejinian, J., *Extreme Remedies* (New York: Harper Collins, 1974).

Henry, T., 'Afrofuturism and the power of black imagination', *NBC News* (2 December 2015), www.nbcnews.com/news/nbcblk/power-black-imagination-can-you-dig-it-n408201 [accessed 30 June 2017].

Hernigou, P., 'Bone transplantation and tissue engineering, part I', *International Orthopaedics*, 38:12 (2014). 2631–8.

Hertz, R., *Death and the Right Hand*, trans. R. Needham and C. Needham (Oxford: Routledge, [1907] 2004).

Hill, D., 'Issues in organ donation and transplantation', *Journal of the Royal Society of Medicine*, 92:9 (1999), 493–4.

Hilts, P., 'Experiments on children', *New York Times* (15 April 1998), www.nytimes.com/1998/04/15/nyregion/experiments-on-children-are-reviewed.html [accessed 7 July 2017].

Hochschild, A., *The Managed Heart*, 3rd edn (Berkeley: University of California Press, 2012).

Hodson, N., 'The gender kidney donation gap' (18 July 2018), *Dosís*, medhum dosis.com/2018/07/18/feature-the-gender-kidney-donation-gap-where-are-all-the-male-kidneys/ [accessed 19 July 2018].

Hoffmann, E.T.A., 'The sandman', in *Weird Tales* (Virginia Beach: CreateSpace, [1817] 2016), pp. 98–115.

Hogle, L., *Recovering the Nation's Body* (New Brunswick: Rutgers University Press, 1999).

_____, 'Standardization across non-standard domains', *Science, Technology and Human Values*, 20:4 (1995), 482–500.

Holmqvist, N., *The Unit*, trans. M. Delargy (Oxford: One World, [2006] 2010).

hooks, b., 'Postmodern blackness', *Postmodern Culture*, 1:1 (1990), www.africa.upenn.edu/Articles_Gen/Postmodern_Blackness_18270.html, para. 12.

Hopkinson, N., *Brown Girl in the Ring* (New York: Grand Central, [1998] 2012).

_____, 'Introduction', in N. Hopkinson (ed.), *So Long Been Dreaming* (Vancouver: Arsenal, 2004), pp. 7–9.

Howells, C., 'The Gothic way of death in English fiction, 1790–1820', *Journal for Eighteenth-Century Studies*, 5:2 (1982), 207–15.

Huff, T., *Blood Debt* (New York: Little Brown, 2004).

Hughes, B., 'Fear, pity and disgust', in N. Watson, A. Roulstone, and C. Thomas (eds), *Routledge Handbook of Disability Studies* (London: Routledge, 2012), pp. 67–77.

Hughes, R. and G. McGuire, 'Neurologic disease and the determination of brain death', *Critical Care Medicine*, 25 (1997), 1923–4.

Hughes, W., 'Gothic medicine', in M. Mulvey-Roberts (ed.), *The Handbook of the Gothic*, 2nd edn (Basingstoke: Palgrave Macmillan, 2009), pp. 144–5.

_____, 'Vampire', in M. Mulvey-Roberts (ed.), *The Handbook of the Gothic*, 2nd edn (Basingstoke: Palgrave Macmillan, 2009), pp. 252–7.

Hunter, K.M, 'Toward the cultural interpretation of medicine', *Literature and Medicine*, 10 (1991), 1–17.

Hurley, K., *The Gothic Body* (Cambridge: Cambridge University Press, 1996).

Hurst, S. and B. Ricou, 'Death at the door of the operating room', *American Journal of Bioethics*, 15:8 (2015), 31–3.

Hurwitz, B., 'Narrative constructs in modern clinical case reporting', *Studies in History and Philosophy of Science*, 62 (2017), 65–73.

Hyde, A., *Bodies of Law* (Princeton, NJ: Princeton University Press, 1997).

Hyvärinen, M., L.-C. Hydén, M. Saarenheimo, and M. Tamboukou (eds), *Beyond Narrative Coherence* (Philadelphia: John Benjamins, 2010), pp. 1–15.

'ICU', *Webster's New World Medical Dictionary*, 3rd edn (Boston, MA: Houghton Mifflin, 2008), online [accessed 29 June 2019].

Imarisha, W. and a.m. brown (eds), *Octavia's Brood* (Oakland: AK Press, 2015), pp. 3–6.

Ishiguro, K., *Never Let Me Go* (London: Faber, 2005).

Jacobs, J., *Edge of Empire* (London: Routledge, 1996).

Jain, S.L., 'Cancer butch', *Cultural Anthropology*, 22:4 (2007), 501–38.

Jameson, F., 'Postmodernism, or the cultural logic of late capitalism', *New Left Review*, 146 (1984), 53–92.

Jarvis, B., 'Fall of the hou$e of finance', in B. Cherry, P. Howell, and C. Riddell (eds), *Twenty-First Century Gothic* (Cambridge: Cambridge Scholars' Publishing, 2010), pp. 19–38.

Jellinek, S., *Dying, Apparent-Death, and Resuscitation* (London: Baillière, Tindall and Cox, 1947).

Jentsch, E., 'On the psychology of the uncanny', trans. R. Sellars, *Angelaki*, 2:1 ([1906] 1996), 7–17.

Joffe, A., J. Carcillo, N. Anton *et al.*, 'Donation after cardiocirculatory death', *Philosophy, Ethics, and Humanities in Medicine*, 6:1 (2011), 1–20.

Johnson, R., S. Fuggle, L. Mumford, J. Bradley, J. Forsythe, C. Rudge, *et al.*, 'A new UK 2006 national kidney allocation scheme for deceased heart-beating donor kidneys', *Transplantation*, 89:4 (2010), 387–94.

Jones, E., *Medicine and Ethics in Black Women's Speculative Fiction* (Basingstoke: Palgrave, 2015).

Jones, Therese, D. Wear, and L. Friedman (eds), 'Introduction', *Health Humanities Reader* (New Brunswick: Rutgers University Press, 2014), pp. 1–9.

Jones, Tim, *The Gothic and the Carnivalesque in American Culture* (Cardiff: University of Wales Press, 2015).

Joralemon, D., 'Organ wars', *Medical Anthropology Quarterly*, 9:3 (1995), 335–56.

Jutel, A., *Putting a Name to It* (Baltimore, MD: Johns Hopkins University Press, 2011).

Kanar, S., *The J Factor* (New York: Bantam, 2000).

Kaufman, S., *And a Time to Die* (Chicago: University of Chicago Press, 2005).

Kayler, L., C. Rasmussen, D. Dykstra, A. Ojo, F. Port, R. Wolfe, and R. Merion, 'Gender imbalance and outcomes in living donor renal transplantation in the United States', *American Journal of Transplantation*, 3:4 (2003), 452.

Kennedy, M., 'The ghost in the clinic', *Victorian Literature and Culture*, 32:2 (2004), 327–51.

———, '"Let me die in your house"', *Literature and Medicine*, 32:1 (2014), 105–32.

Khajehdehi, P., 'Living non-related versus related renal transplantation', *Nephrology Dialysis Transplantation*, 14:11 (1999), 2621–4.

'Kidney theft', *Snopes*, www.snopes.com/fact-check/youve-got-to-be-kidneying/ [accessed 13 August 2018].

Kierans, C., 'Biopolitics and capital', *Body and Society*, 21:3 (2015), 42–65.

Kierans, C. and J. Cooper, 'Organ donation, genetics, race and culture', *Anthropology Today*, 27:6 (2011), 21–4.

Kilgour, D. and D. Matas, *Bloody Harvest* (Niagara Falls: Seraphim, 2009).

Kinsella, F., *The Degeneration of Dorothy* (Charleston: Bibliofile, [1899] 2018).

Kite, C., *An Essay on the Recovery of the Apparently Dead* (London: Dilly, 1788).

Knellwolff, C. and J. Goodall, 'Introduction', in C. Knellwolff and J. Goodall (eds), *Frankenstein's Science* (London: Routledge, 2016).

Korein, J., 'Terminology, definitions and usage', in J. Korein (ed.), *Brain Death* (New York: New York Academy of Science, 1978), pp. 6–10.

Kristeva, J., *Powers of Horror*, trans. L. Roudiez (New York: Columbia University Press, [1980] 1982).

Küss, R., 'Human renal transplantation memories, 1955 to 1981', in P. Terasaki (ed.), *History of Transplantation* (Los Angeles: UCLA, 1971), pp. 37–60.

Lakoff, G. and M. Johnson, *Metaphors We Live By* (London: University of Chicago Press, 1980).

Langer, L., *Holocaust Testimonies* (New Haven: Yale University Press, 1991).

Latour, B., *We Have Never Been Modern,* trans. C. Porter (Cambridge, MA: Harvard University Press, [1991] 1993).

Laurance, J., 'Alder Hey "sold" body parts to drugs firms', *Independent* (27 January 2001), 2.

Lederer, S., *Flesh and Blood: Organ Transplantation and Blood Transfusion in Twentieth-Century America* (Oxford: Oxford University Press, 2008).

Lemke, T., *Biopolitics* (New York: NYU Press, 2011).

Liptak, G., 'In reply', *Journal of the American Medical Association*, 255 (1986), 2028.

'The living dead', *The New York Times* (12 October 1975), www.nytimes.com/1975/10/12/archives/the-living-dead.html [accessed 20 January 2019].

Lock, M., 'On making up the good-as-dead in a utilitarian world', in S. Franklin and M. Lock (eds), *Remaking Life and Death* (Santa Fe, NM: School of American Research Press, 2001), pp. 165–93.

_____, *Twice Dead: Organ Transplants and the Reinvention of Death* (Berkeley: University of California Press, 2002).

Lock, M. and V.-K. Nguyen, *An Anthropology of Biomedicine* (Malden, MA: Wiley-Blackwell, 2010).

Love, H., *Feeling Backward* (Cambridge, MA: Harvard University Press, 2007).

Lowe, L., *The Intimacies of the Four Continents* (Durham, NC: Duke University Press, 2015).

Lowenstein, A., 'Films without a face', *Cinema Journal*, 37:4 (1998), 37–58.

Lucia, C., 'The complexities of cultural change', *Cineaste*, 28:4 (2003), 8–15.

Luckhurst, R., 'Biomedical horror', in J. Edwards (ed.), *Technologies of the Gothic in Literature and Culture* (New York: Routledge, 2015), pp. 84–98.

_____, 'The contemporary London Gothic', *Textual Practice*, 16:3 (2002), 527–46.

_____, *Corridors* (London: Reaction, 2019).

Machado, C., 'The first organ transplant from a brain-dead donor', *Neurology*, 64:11 (2005), 1938–42.

Machado, C. and G. Leisman, 'Towards an effective definition of death and disorders of consciousness', *Reviews in the Neurosciences*, 20:3 (2009), 147–50.

Malchow, H., *Gothic Images of Race in Nineteenth-Century Britain* (Stanford: Stanford University Press, 1996).

Malmqvist, E. and K. Zeiler, 'Concluding reflections', in E. Malmqvist and K. Zeiler (eds), *Bodily Exchanges* (London: Routledge, 2016), pp. 197–207.

Manara, A., P. Murphy and G. O'Callaghan, 'Donation after circulatory death', *British Journal of Anaesthesia*, 108 (2012), Supplement 1, i108–i121.

Marable, M., I. Steinberg and K. Middlemass (eds), *Racializing Justice, Disenfranchising Lives* (New York: Palgrave, 2007).

Marshall, K., *Corridor* (Minneapolis: University of Minnesota Press, 2013).

Martin, G., E. Rivers, N. Paradis, M. Goetting, D. Morris, and R. Nowak, 'Emergency department cardiopulmonary bypass', *Chest*, 113:3 (1998), 743–51.

Marx, K., *Capital*, vol. 1 (London: Penguin [1976] 1990).

Massumi, B., 'The autonomy of affect', *Cultural Critique*, 31 (1995), 83–109.

Matta, B., 'The implications of anaesthetising the brainstem dead', *Anaesthesia*, 55:7 (2000), 695–6.

Mattingly, C., *The Paradox of Hope* (Berkeley: University of California Press, 2010).

Matus, J., *Shock, Memory and the Unconscious in Victorian Fiction* (New York: Cambridge University Press, 2009).

Mauss, M., *The Gift*, trans. W. Halls (New York: Norton, [1950] 1990).

May, W., 'Attitudes to the newly dead', *Hastings Center Report*, 1 (1973), 3–13.

Mbembe, A., 'Necropolitics', trans. L. Mentjes, *Public Culture*, 15:1 (2003), 11–49.

McCormack, D., 'Living with others inside the self', *Medical Humanities*, 42:4 (2016), 252–8.

McNally, D., *Monsters of the Market* (Brill: Leiden, 2011).

McRuer, R., *Crip Theory* (New York: NYU Press, 2006).

Mercy for Animals, 'Extreme confinement and abuse' (2019), mercyforanimals.org/the-problem [accessed 1 July 2019].

Miéville, C., *Perdido Street Station* (London: Pan, [2001] 2002).

Mighall, R., *A Geography of Victorian Gothic Fiction* (Oxford: Oxford University Press, 1999).

Miles, R., *Gothic Writing*, 2nd edn (London: Routledge, 1993).

Miller, G. and A. McFarlane, 'Science fiction and the medical humanities', *Medical Humanities*, 42:4 (2016), 213–18.

Mills, C., 'Biopolitics and the concept of life', in V. Cisney and N. Morar (eds), *Biopower: Foucault and Beyond* (Chicago: Chicago University Press, 2016), pp. 82–101.

Milne, T., 'Georges Franju', *Sight and Sound*, 44:2 (1975), 68–72.

Mitchell, D. and S. Snyder, *Narrative Prosthesis* (Ann Arbour: University of Michigan Press, 2000).

Moawad, H., 'Alien hand syndrome', *Neurology Times* (17 August 2016), www.neurologytimes.com/blog/alien-hand-syndrome [accessed 22 August 2018].

Mohai, P. and R. Sata, 'Racial inequality in the distribution of hazardous waste', *Social Problems*, 54:3 (2007), 343–70.

Mol, A., *The Body Multiple* (Durham, NC: Duke University Press, 2002).

Mollaret, P. and G. Goulon, 'Coma dépassé et nécroses nerveuses centrales massives', *Revue Neurologique*, 35 (1959), 211–18.

Moni, S., '"In bits and pieces"', *Journal of Postcolonial Writing*, 50:3 (2014), 316–28.

Moniruzzaman, M., '"Living cadavers" in Bangladesh', *Medical Anthropology Quarterly*, 26:1 (2012), 69–91.

Monleón, J., *A Specter Is Haunting Europe* (Princeton, NJ: Princeton University Press 1990).

Moore, J. (ed.), *Anthropocene or Capitalocene?* (Oakland: PM Press, 2016).

'Moral problems in the use of borrowed organs, artificial and transplanted', *Annals of Internal Medicine*, 60:2 (1964), 309–13.

Morgan, S., T. Harrison, S. Long, et al., 'Family discussions about organ donation', *Clinical Transplantation*, 19:5 (2005), 674–82.

Morris, P., 'Transplantation: a medical miracle of the twentieth century', *The New England Journal of Medicine*, 351:26 (2004), 2678–80.

Mosley, W., 'Whispers in the dark', in S. Thomas (ed.), *Dark Matter* (New York: Aspect, [2001] 2004), pp. 162–82.

Mulvey-Roberts, M., *Dangerous Bodies* (Manchester: Manchester University Press, 2016).

Murnane, B., 'George Best's dead livers', in J. Edwards (ed.), *Technologies of the Gothic in Literature and Culture* (New York: Routledge, 2015), pp. 113–26.

———, '*In the Flesh* and the Gothic pharmacology of everyday life', *Text Matters*, 6:6 (2016), 227–44.

Nair-Collins, M. and F. Miller, 'Is heart transplantation after circulatory death compatible with the dead donor rule?', *Journal of Medical Ethics*, 42:5 (2016), 319.

Nair-Collins, M., S. Green, and A. Sutin, 'Abandoning the dead donor rule?', *Journal of Medical Ethics*, 41:4 (2015), 297–302.

Nancy, J.-L., '*L'intrus*', trans. S. Hanson, *New Centennial Review*, 2:3 ([2000] 2002), 1–14.

———, *L'intrus*, nouvelle edition augmentée (Paris: Galilée, 2017).

Negarestani, R., *Cyclonopedia* (Melbourne: re.press, 2008).

Nemoianu, V., *A Theory of the Secondary* (Baltimore, MD: Johns Hopkins University Press, 1989).

NHS Blood & Transplant, 'Organ donation and transplantation: activity figures for the UK as at 8 April 2019', *NHS Blood & Transplant*, nhsbtdbe.blob.core.windows.net/umbraco-assets-corp/15720/annual_stats.pdf [accessed 8 June 2019].

Nikas, N., D. Bordlee, and M. Moreira, 'Determination of death', *Journal of Medicine and Philosophy*, 41:3 (2016), 237–56.

Niven, L., *A Gift from Earth* (London: Futura, [1968] 1982).

———, 'The patchwork girl', in *Flatlander* (New York: Ballantine, [1980] 1995).

Nixon, R., *Slow Violence and the Environmentalism of the Poor* (Cambridge, MA: Harvard University Press, 2013).

Ojo, A. and F. Port, 'Influence of race and gender on related donor renal transplantation rates', *American Journal of Kidney Disorders*, 22:6 (1993), 835–41.

Ong, A., *Neoliberalism as Exception* (Durham, NC: Duke University Press, 2006).

Orfila, M., *Directions for the Treatment of Persons Who Have Taken Poison*, trans. R. Black (London: Longman, 1818).

Overby, K., M. Weinstein, and A. Fiester, 'Response to open peer commentaries', *American Journal of Bioethics*, 15:9 (2015), W3–W5.

Padmanabhan, M., *Harvest* (London: Aurora Metro, [1997] 2003).

Palacio, S., G. Zeppa, and C. Lucero, 'Spontaneous movements in brain dead patients', *Journal of the Neurological Sciences*, 150 (1997), S243.

Pallis, C., 'Diagnosis of brain death', *British Medical Journal*, 281:6253 (1980), 1491–2.

Pallis, C. and D. Harley, *ABC of Brainstem Death*, 2nd edn (London: BMJ, 1996).

Park, P., 'The transplant odyssey', *Second Opinion*, 12 (1989), 12–32.

Parry, B., 'Domesticating biosurveillance', *Health and Place*, 18:4 (2012), 718–25.

Parsons, T., *The Social System* (London: Routledge, [1951] 1952).

Pasternak, J. and J. Volpe, 'Full recovery from prolonged brainstem failure following intraventricular hemorrhage', *Journal of Pediatrics*, 95:6 (1979), 1047–9.

Patterson, B., '11 more things you can't do while Black (or Brown)', *Mother Jones* (9 May 2018), www.motherjones.com/crime-justice/2018/05/11-more-things-you-cannot-do-while-black-starbucks-nordstrom-rack-1/ [accessed 11 August 2018].

Pearsall, P., G. Schwartz, and L. Russek. 'Changes in heart transplant recipients that parallel the personalities of their donors', *Journal of Near-Death Studies*, 20 (2002), 191–206.

Pérez-Peña, R., 'Downside to fewer violent deaths', *New York Times* (19 August 2019), www.nytimes.com/2003/08/19/nyregion/downside-to-fewer-violent-deaths-transplant-organ-shortage-grows.html [accessed 2 August 2019].

Pernick, M., 'Back from the grave', in R. Zaner (ed.), *Death* (Dordrecht: Kluwer, 1988), pp. 17–74.

Poe, E., 'The premature burial' (1844), *Poestories.com*, poestories.com/text.php?file=premature [accessed 7 April 2018].

Pomata, G., 'The medical case narrative', *Literature and Medicine*, 32:1 (2014), 1–23.

Poole, J., J. Ward, E. De Luca, M. Shildrick, S. Abbey, O. Mauthner, M. Gewarges, and H. Ross, 'Getting ready and then keeping quiet', *Journal of Heart and Lung Transplantation*, 33:4 (2014), S222–S223.

Porter, R., *Madness* (Oxford: Oxford University Press, 2002).

Poulton, B. and M. Garfield, 'Implications of anaesthetising the brainstem dead', *Anaesthesia*, 55:7 (2000), 695.

Poulton, T., 'Spontaneous movements in brain-dead patients', *Journal of the American Medical Association*, 255 (1986), 2028.

Povinelli, E., *Economies of Abandonment* (Durham, NC: Duke University Press, 2011).

Powell, A., *Deleuze and Horror Film* (Edinburgh: Edinburgh University Press, 2005).

Price, G. and W. Darity, 'The economics of race and eugenic sterilization in North Carolina', *Economics and Human Biology*, 8:2 (2010), 261–72.

Price-Herndl, D., 'Disease versus disability', *PMLA*, 120:2 (2005), 593–8.

Prime, R., 'Stranger than fiction', *Post Script*, 25:2 (2006), 56–66.

Pritchard, R., 'The death of Enrico Caruso', *Surgery, Gynecology and Obstetrics*, 109 (1959), 117–20.

Punter, D., 'Ceremonial gothic', in G. Byron and D. Punter (eds), *Spectral Readings* (London: Macmillan, 1999), pp. 37–53.

——, *Gothic Pathologies* (Basingstoke: Palgrave Macmillan, 1998).

_____, *Literature of Terror*, vol. 2 (Edinburgh: Pearson Education, 1996).

Radcliffe-Richards, J., *The Ethics of Transplants* (Oxford: Oxford University Press, 2012).

Radley, A., *Works of Illness* (Harrow: InkerMan, 2009).

Rady, M. and J. Verheijde, 'Advancing neuroscience research in brain death', *Journal of Critical Care*, 39 (2017), 293–4.

_____, 'Lazarus phenomenon', *Resuscitation*, 85:4 (2014), 63.

Rady, M., J. Verheijde, and J. McGregor, '"Non-heart-beating," or "cardiac death" organ donation', *Journal of Hospital Medicine*, 2:5 (2007), 324–34.

_____, 'Organ donation after circulatory death', *Critical Care*, 10:5 (2006), ccforum. com/content/10/5/166, 2–3.

Ragosta, K., 'Miller Fisher Syndrome', *Clinical Pediatrics*, 32:11 (1993), 685–7.

Ramachandran, A., 'New world, no world', *Theatre Research International*, 30:2 (2005), 161–74.

Rankine, C., 'The condition of Black life is one of mourning', *The New York Times* (22 June 2015), www.nytimes.com/2015/06/22/magazine/the-condition-of-black-life-is-one-of-mourning,.htm [accessed 12 January 2018].

'Reanimate, v.' *OED Online*, Oxford University Press (March 2019), www.oed.com/view/Entry/158980 [accessed 31 May 2019].

Reed, J.D., 'Organ transplant', *The New Yorker* (26 September 1970), 126.

Renard, M., *The Hands of Orlac*, trans. I. White (London: Souvenir, [1920] 1981).

'Resuscitate, v.', *OED Online*, Oxford University Press (March 2019) www.oed.com/view/Entry/164120 [accessed 31 May 2019].

Reverby, S., 'Rethinking the Tuskegee Syphilis Study', *Nursing History Review*, 7 (1999), 3–28.

Richardson, B., 'Suspended animation', *Living Age*, 142 (1879), 99–103.

Richardson, R., *Death, Dissection and the Destitute* (London: Penguin, 1989).

_____, 'Fearful symmetry', in R. Fox, L. O'Connell, and S. Youngner (eds), *Organ Transplantation* (Madison: University of Wisconsin Press, 1996), pp. 66–100.

Riskin, J., *The Restless Clock* (Chicago: University of Chicago Press, 2016).

_____, *Science in the Age of Sensibility* (Chicago: University of Chicago Press, 2002).

Robertson, J., 'The dead donor rule', *Hastings Center Report*, 29 (1999), 6–14.

Robinson, R., 'We can't trust police to protect us from racist violence', *The Guardian* (21 August 2019), www.theguardian.com/commentisfree/2019/aug/21/police-white-nationalists-racist-violence [accessed 21 August 2019].

Rodríguez-Arias, D., M. Smith, and N. Lazar, 'Donation after circulatory death', *American Journal of Bioethics*, 11:8 (2011), 36–43.

Rollin, B., *The Frankenstein Syndrome* (Cambridge: Cambridge University Press, 1995).

Rothberg, M., *Traumatic Realism* (Minneapolis: University of Minnesota Press, 2000).

Rothman, D., E. Rose, T. Awaya, B. Cohen, A. Daar, S. Dzemeshkevich, C. Lee, R. Munro, H. Reyes, S. Rothman, K. Schoen, N. Scheper-Hughes, Z. Shapira, and H. Smit, 'The Bellagio Task Force report', *Transplantation Proceedings*, 29:6 (1997), 2739–45.

Rouse, C., *Uncertain Suffering* (Berkeley: University of California Press, 2009).

Rubenstein, A., E. Cohen, and E. Jackson, 'The definition of death and the ethics of organ procurement from the deceased', *The President's Council on Bioethics* (2006), bioethicsarchive.georgetown.edu/pcbe/background/rubenstein.html [accessed 4 May 2017].

Rylance, R., 'The theatre and the granary', *Literature and Medicine*, 25:2 (2006), 255–76.

Sage, V., *Horror Fiction in the Protestant Tradition* (New York: St Martin's, 1988).

Salisbury, L., 'Aphasic modernism', in A. Whitehead, A. Woods, S. Atkinson, *et al.* (eds), *Edinburgh Companion to the Critical Medical Humanities* (Edinburgh: Edinburgh University Press, 2016), pp. 444–62.

Sanal, A., *New Organs within Us* (Durham, NC: Duke University Press, 2011).

Sanner, M., 'Living with a stranger's organ', *Annals of Transplantation*, 10:9 (2005), 9–12.

Santner, E., 'History beyond the pleasure principle', in S. Friedlander (ed.), *Probing the Limits of Representation* (Cambridge, MA: Harvard University Press, 1992), pp. 143–54.

Santner, E., 'Terri Schiavo and the state of exception', *University of Chicago Press Blog* (29 March 2005), www.press.uchicago.edu/Misc/Chicago/05april_santner.html [accessed 27 May 2018].

Schanbacher, K., 'India's gestational surrogacy market', *Hastings Women's Law Journal*, 25:2 (2014), 201–20.

Scheper-Hughes, N., 'Bodies for sale', in N. Scheper-Hughes and L. Wacquant (eds), *Commodifying Bodies* (London: Sage, 2002), pp. 1–8.

——, 'Commodity fetishism in organs trafficking', in N. Scheper-Hughes and L. Wacquant (eds), *Commodifying Bodies* (London: Sage, 2002), pp. 31–62.

——, 'The global traffic in human organs', *Current Anthropology*, 41:2 (2000), 191–224.

——, 'The tyranny of the gift', *American Journal of Transplantation*, 7:3 (2007), 507–11.

Schick, A., 'Whereto speculative bioethics?', *Medical Humanities*, 42:4 (2016), 225–31.

Schicktanz, S. and M. Schweda, '"One man's trash is another man's treasure"', *Journal of Medical Ethics*, 35:8 (2009), 473–6.

Schlozman, S., 'Preface', in L. Servitje, and S. Vint (eds), *The Walking Med* (University Park: Pennsylvania State University Press, 2016), pp. vii–x.

Schuman, A., 'Review of Barbara-Anne Wren, *True Tales*', *BMJ Blogs* (6 February 2017), blogs.bmj.com/medical-humanities/2017/02/06/book-review-true-tales-of-organisational-life/ [accessed 10 January 2019].

Sedgwick, E.K., *The Coherence of Gothic Conventions* (New York: Methuen, [1980] 1986).

——, 'Queer performativity', in D. Hale (ed.), *The Novel* (Oxford: Blackwell, 2006), pp. 605–21.

Semprun, J., *Literature or Life*, trans. L. Coverdale (New York: Viking, [1994] 1997).

Servitje, L. and S. Vint (eds), *The Walking Med* (University Park: Penn State University Press, 2016).

Shadowrun: Fifth Anniversary Core Rulebook (Seattle: Catalyst, 2013).

Shaefer, H. and A. Ochoa, 'How blood-plasma companies target the poorest Americans', *The Atlantic* (15 March 2018), www.theatlantic.com/business/archive/2018/03/plasma-donations/555599/ [accessed 10 August 2018].

Shah, S. and F. Miller, 'Can we handle the truth?', *American Journal of Law and Medicine*, 36:4 (2010), 540–85.

Shapiro, S., 'Material Gothic', *Gothic Studies*, 10:1 (2008), 1–3.

_____, 'Transvaal, Transylvania', *Gothic Studies*, 10:1 (2008), 29–47.

Shappell, C., J. Frank, K. Husari, M. Sanchez, F. Goldenberg, and A. Ardelt, 'Practice variability in brain death determination', *Neurology*, 81:23 (2013), 2009–14.

Sharif, A., 'Directed altruistic kidney donors from overseas mask transplant tourism', *The Lancet*, 385:9973 (21 March 2015), 1074.

Sharp, L., 'Commodified kin', *American Anthropologist*, 103:1 (2001), 112–33.

_____, 'Monkey business', *Social Text*, 29:1 (2011), 43–69.

_____, *Strange Harvest: Organ Transplants, Denatured Bodies and the Transformed Self* (Berkeley: University of California Press, 2006).

_____, *The Transplant Imaginary* (Berkeley: University of California Press, 2013).

Sharpe, C., *In the Wake* (Durham, NC: Duke University Press, 2016).

_____, *Monstrous Intimacies* (Durham, NC: Duke University Press, 2010).

Shaviro, S., 'Capitalist monsters', *Historical Materialism*, 10:4 (2002), 281–90.

Shaw, R., 'The ethical risks of curtailing emotion in social science research', *Health Sociology Review*, 20:1 (2011), 58–69.

_____, 'Perceptions of the gift relationship in organ and tissue donation', *Social Science and Medicine*, 70:4 (2010), 609–15.

Shelley, M., *Frankenstein* (New York: Norton, [1818, 1823] 2012).

Shildrick, M., 'The biopolitics of heart transplant and microchimerism', *Medical Humanities Futures*, 2nd Congress, Leeds University, October 2018.

_____, *Embodying the Monster* (London: Sage, 2002).

_____, 'Hospitality and the "gift of life"', in S. Gonzalez-Arnal, G. Jagger, and K. Lennon (eds), *Embodied Selves* (London: Palgrave, 2012), pp. 196–208.

_____, 'Staying alive', *Body and Society*, 21:3 (2015), 20–41.

Shildrick, M. and D. Steinberg, 'Estranged bodies', *Body and Society*, 21:3 (2015), 3–19.

Shildrick, M., A. Carnie, A. Wright, P. McKeever, E. Huan-Ching Jan, E. De Luca, I. Bachmann, S. Abbey, D. Dal Bo, J. Poole, T. El-Sheikh, and H. Ross, 'Messy entanglements', *Medical Humanities*, Online First (2017), 1–9.

Shildrick, M., P. McKeever, S. Abbey, J. Poole, and H. Ross, 'Troubling dimensions of heart transplantation', *Medical Humanities*, 35:1 (2009), 35–8.

Shusterman, N., *Unwind* (London: Simon and Shuster, [2007] 2008).

_____, *UnWind Unboxed: UnWind, UnWholly, UnSouled, UnStrung* (New York: Simon and Schuster ebook, [2007–14] 2014).

Siemionow, M., 'The miracle of face transplantation after 10 years', *British Medical Bulletin*, 120:1 (2016), 5–14.

Sifferlin, A. 'Organ transplants hit an all-time high in 2017', *Time Magazine* (10 January 2018), time.com/5097377/record-breaking-organ-transplants-2017/ [accessed 28 March 2018].

Silver, M., *Preparedness 101*, US Centers for Disease Control and Prevention, www. cdc.gov/phpr/documents/zombie_gn_final.pdf [accessed 11 July 2016].

Simpson, P., 'What are the issues in organ donation in 2012?', *British Journal of Anaesthesia*, 108 (2012), Supplement 1: i3–i6.

Sinclair, I., 'Homeopathic horror', *Sight and Sound*, 5:4 (1995), 24–7.

Skloot, R., *The Immortal Life of Henrietta Lacks* (London: Macmillan, 2010), 'The Lacks Family', *TheLacksFamily.net*, www.lacksfamily.net/ [accessed 26 July 2017].

Smith, A., *Gothic Death* (Manchester: Manchester University Press, 2016).

———, 'Rethinking the Gothic', *Gothic Studies*, 4:1 (2002), 79–85 (p. 84).

———, *Victorian Demons* (Manchester: Manchester University Press, 2004).

Smith, A. and J. Wallace, 'Introduction', in A. Smith and J. Wallace (eds), *Gothic Modernisms* (Basingstoke: Palgrave, 2001), pp. 1–10.

Smith, B. and A. Sparkes. 'Exploring multiple responses to a chaos narrative', *Health*, 15:1 (2011), 38–53.

Smith, Cardinale. and O. Brawley, 'Disparities in access to palliative care', *Health Affairs Blog* (30 July 2014) healthaffairs.org/blog/2014/07/30/disparities-in-access-to-palliative-care/ [accessed 17 August 2019].

Smith, Chris, D. Burton, E. Gallegly, *et al.*, *Papers of the Joint Congressional Hearing* (Washington, DC: US Government Printing Office, 2012).

Smith, Cordwainer, 'A planet called Shayol', *Galaxy Science Fiction* (October 1961), www.wattpad.com/67345-Cordwainer-Smith-A-Planet-Named-Shayol [accessed 17 September 2009].

Smith, Damon, '*L'intrus*', *Senses of Cinema*, 35 (2005), sensesofcinema.com/2005/conversations-with-filmmakers/claire_denis_interview/ [accessed 30 July 2019], paras 84–6.

Smith, David, 'Hospitals in South Africa charged over kidney transplant trafficking', *The Guardian* (16 September 2010), www.theguardian.com/world/2010/sep/16/hospitals-south-africa-kidney-transplant-scam-charged [accessed 20 October 2018].

Smith, M., 'Brain death', *British Journal of Anaesthesia*, 108 (2012), Supplement 1, i6–i9.

Smith, M.M., *Spares* (London: Harper Collins, [1996] 1998).

Solomon, M., 'Maximizing benefits, minimizing harms', in Institute of Medicine (ed.), *Non-Heart-Beating Organ Transplantation* (Washington, DC: National Academy Press, 2000), pp. 67–86.

Sparks, T., *The Doctor in the Victorian Novel* (Farnham: Ashgate, 2009).

Spooner, C., *Contemporary Gothic* (London: Bloomsbury, 2017).

———, *Postmillennial Gothic* (London: Bloomsbury, 2017).

Squier, S., *Liminal Lives* (Durham, NC: Duke University Press, 2004).

Stacey Taylor, J., *Stakes and Kidneys* (Aldershot: Ashgate, 2005).

Starzl, T., *The Puzzle People* (Pittsburgh, PA: University of Pittsburgh Press, [1993] 2003).

Starzl, T. and C. Barker, 'Foreword' to D. Hamilton, *A History of Organ Transplantation* (Pittsburgh, PA: University of Pittsburgh Press, 2012), pp. vii–ix.

Steinberg, D., 'Bad patient', *Body and Society*, 21:3 (2015), 115–43.

———, *Genes and the Bioimaginary* (Aldershot: Ashgate, 2015).

Stephanou, A., *Reading Vampire Gothic through Blood* (Basingstoke: Palgrave Macmillan, 2014).

Stevenson, R.L., 'Olalla', in *The Merry Men and Other Tales and Fables* (London: Chatto and Windus, [1885] 1905), pp. 143–200.

_____, *Strange Case of Dr Jekyll and Mr Hyde* (London: Penguin [1886] 2002).

Stoker, B. *Dracula*, ed. by M. Hindle (New York: Penguin, [1897] 1993).

Stoler, A., 'Imperial debris', *Cultural Anthropology*, 23:2 (2008), 191–219.

Su, X., S. Zenios, H. Chakkera, E. Milford, and G. Chertow, 'Diminishing significance of HLA matching in kidney transplantation', *American Journal of Transplantation*, 4:9 (2004), 1501–8.

Sunder Rajan, K., *Biocapital* (Durham, NC: Duke University Press, 2006).

Sylvia, C. and W. Novak, *A Change of Heart* (New York: Warner Books, 1997).

Szurhaj, W., M. Lamblin, A. Kaminska, and H. Sediri, 'EEG guidelines in the diagnosis of brain death', *Neurophysiologie Clinique*, 45:1 (2015), 97–110.

Tagliacozzi, G., *De Curtorum Chirurgia per Insiotonem* (Venice: Berolini, 1597).

Tait, R., J. Chibnall, and J. Anderson, 'Racial/ethnic disparities in the assessment and treatment of pain', *American Psychologist*, 69:2 (2014) 131–41.

Talairach-Vielmas, L., *Wilkie Collins, Medicine and the Gothic* (Cardiff: University of Wales Press, 2009).

Telischi, M., 'The evolution of Cook County Hospital Blood Bank', *Modern Hospital*, 50 (1938), 57–8.

'The telltale heart', *Ebony* (March 1968), 118–19.

Tepper, S., *Sideshow* (Gollancz, [1988] 1992]).

Terasaki, P. (ed.), *History of Transplantation* (Los Angeles: UCLA, 1971).

Teucher, U., 'The incomprehensible density of being', in V. Raoul, C. Canam, A. Henderson, and C. Paterson (eds), *Unfitting Stories* (Waterloo, Ontario: Wilfrid Laurier University Press, 2007), pp. 71–8.

Thrailkill, J., 'Killing them softly', *American Literature*, 71:4 (1999), 679–707.

Titmuss, R., *The Gift Relationship* (New York: Vintage, [1971] 1972).

Townshend, D., 'Gothic and the ghost of Hamlet', in D. Townshend and J. Drakakis (eds), *Gothic Shakespeares* (Abingdon: Routledge, 2008), pp. 60–97.

_____, 'Gothic panoptics and the persistence of torturous enjoyment, 1764–1820', *Genre*, 37:3–4 (2004), 395–432.

_____, *The Orders of Gothic* (New York: AMS Press, 2007).

Train, A.C., *Mortmain* (New York: Charles Scribner, 1907).

Trautmann, J., 'The wonders of literature in medical education', in D. Self (ed.), *The Role of the Humanities in Medical Education* (Norfolk, VA: Eastern Virginia Medical, 1978), pp. 32–44.

Trethewey, N., 'Miracle of the black leg', in *Thrall* (Boston, MA: Houghton Mifflin, 2012), pp. 9–12.

Trillium Life Network, 'Recycle me', recycleme.org [accessed 10 October 2014].

Truog, R., 'The price of our illusions and myths about the dead donor rule', *Journal of Medical Ethics*, 42:5 (2016), 318.

Truog, R., F. Miller, and S. Halpern, 'The dead-donor rule and the future of organ donation', *New England Journal of Medicine*, 369:14 (2013), 1287–9.

Tzakis, A., 'The miracle of liver transplantation', *British Journal of Surgery*, 100:12 (2013), 1547–8.

Uehara, E., M. Farris, P. Morelli, and A. Ishisaka. 'Eloquent chaos', *Culture, Medicine and Psychiatry*, 25:1 (2001), 29–61.

Varela, F., 'Intimate distances', *Journal of Consciousness Studies*, 8:5–7 (2001), 259–71.

Venugopal, R., 'Neoliberalism as concept', *Economy and Society*, 44:2 (2015), 1–23.

Vernez, S. and D. Magnus, 'Can the dead donor rule be resuscitated?', *American Journal of Bioethics*, 11:8 (2011), 1.

Vidler, A., *The Architectural Uncanny* (Cambridge, MA: MIT, 1992).

Viney, W., F. Callard, and A. Woods, 'Critical medical humanities', *Medical Humanities*, 41 (2015), 2–7.

Vint, S., 'Suspending death, reinventing life', *Embodying Fantastika* Conference, 8–10 August 2019, Lancaster University.

Wacquant, L., *Punishing the Poor* (Durham, NC: Duke University Press, 2009).

Waddington, K., 'Death at St Bernard's', *Journal of Victorian Culture*, 18:2 (2013), 246–62.

Waddington, K. and M. Willis, 'Rethinking illness narratives', *Journal of Literature and Science*, 6:1 (2013), iv–v.

Wailoo, K., *Dying in the City of the Blues* (Chapel Hill: University of North Carolina Press, 2001).

Wald, P., *Contagious* (Durham, NC: Duke University Press, 2008).

Waldby, C., *AIDS and the Body Politic* (New York: Routledge, 1996).

———, 'Biomedicine, tissue transfer and intercorporeality', *Feminist Theory*, 3 (2002), 235–50.

———, *The Visible Human Project* (London: Routledge, 2000).

Waldby, C. and M. Cooper, *Clinical Labor* (Durham, NC: Duke University Press, 2014).

Waldby, C. and R. Mitchell, *Tissue Economies* (Durham, NC: Duke University Press, 2006).

Warner, M., *The Trouble with Normal* (New York: Free Press, 1999).

Washington, H., *Medical Apartheid* (New York: Harlem Moon, 2006).

Wasson, S. (ed.), special issue on 'Medical Gothic', *Gothic Studies*, 17.1 (2015).

———, 'Before narrative', *Medical Humanities*, 44:2 (2018), 106–12.

———, 'Butcher's shop', in S. Wasson and E. Alder (eds), *Gothic Science Fiction, 1980–2010* (Liverpool: Liverpool University Press, 2011), pp. 73–86.

———, 'The "coven of the articulate"', *The Journal of Popular Culture*, 45:1 (2012), 197–213.

———, 'Creative manifesto', *Translating Chronic Pain*, AHRC-funded Research Network (2017), wp.lancs.ac.uk/translatingpain/creative-manifesto/ [accessed 28 March 2018].

———, 'Gothic and the built environment', in D. Punter (ed.), *Gothic and the Arts* (Edinburgh: Edinburgh University Press, in press).

———, 'Gothic cities and suburbs, 1880–present', in G. Byron and D. Townshend (eds), *The Gothic World* (London: Routledge, 2014), pp. 132–42.

_____, 'Love in the time of cloning', *Extrapolation*, 45:2 (2004), 130–44.

_____, 'Olalla's legacy: twentieth-century vampire fiction and genetic previvorship', *Journal of Stevenson Studies*, 7 (2010), 55–81.

_____, 'Recalcitrant tissue', in J. Edwards (ed.), *Technologies of the Gothic in Literature and Culture* (New York: Routledge, 2015), pp. 99–112.

_____, 'Spectrality, strangeness and stigmaphilia: Gothic and disability studies', in A. Hall (ed.), *Routledge Companion to Literature and Disability* (London: Routledge, in press).

_____, 'Useful darkness', *Gothic Studies*, 17:1 (2015), 1–12.

_____, *Urban Gothic of the Second World War* (Basingstoke: Palgrave, 2010).

Wasson, S. and E. Alder (eds), *Gothic Science Fiction* (Liverpool: Liverpool University Press, 2011).

Weisbard, A., 'A polemic on principles', in S. Youngner, R. Arnold, and R. Schapiro (eds), *The Definition of Death* (Baltimore, MD: Johns Hopkins University Press, 1999), pp. 141–54.

Wells, H.G., *The Island of Dr Moreau* (London: Penguin, [1896] 2005).

Wendell, S., 'Unhealthy disabled', *Hypatia*, 16:4 (2001), 17–33.

West, C., 'Strength in the blues', *The Monarch Review* (9 September 2012), www.themonarchreview.org/cornel-west-strength-in-the-blues/ [accessed 15 August 2018].

Wester, M., *African-American Gothic* (Basingstoke: Palgrave, 2012).

Whaley, J., 'Introduction', in J. Whaley (ed.), *Mirrors of Mortality* (London: Europa, 1981), pp. 1–14.

'What is your DNA story?', *23andme.com*, www.23andme.com/en-gb/ [accessed 3 September 2018].

'When are you really dead?' *Newsweek* (18 December 1967), 87.

Whitehead, A., 'A literary perspective', in V. Bates, A. Bleakley, and S. Goodman (eds), *Medicine, Health and the Arts* (Abingdon: Routledge, 2014), pp. 107–27.

Wijdicks, E., 'The transatlantic divide over brain death determination', *Brain*, 135 (2012), 1321–31.

Williams. R., *The Long Revolution* (Cardigan: Parthian, [1961] 2011).

Willis, M., K. Waddington, and R. Marsden, 'Imaginary investments', *Journal of Literature and Science*, 6:1 (2013), 55–73.

Winslow, J.-B. [and Leander Paget], *An Mortis Incertae Signa Minus Incerta a Chirurgicis, Quam ab Aliis Experimentis?* (Paris: Quillau, 1740).

Winter, B., A. Odedra, and S. Green, 'A questionnaire based assessment of numbers, motivation and medical care of UK patients undergoing liver transplant abroad', *Travel Medicine and Infectious Disease*, 14:6 (2016), 599–603.

Wolstenholme, G. and M. O'Connor (eds), *Ethics in Medical Progress* (Boston, MA: Little, Brown, 1966).

Womack, Y., *Afrofuturism* (Chicago: Lawrence Hill, 2013).

Woods, A., 'Beyond the wounded storyteller', in H. Carel and R. Cooper (eds), *Health, Illness and Disease* (Durham: Acumen, 2013), pp. 113–28.

_____, 'The limits of narrative', *Medical Humanities*, 37 (2011), 91–6.

World Medical Association, 'Declaration of Sydney on the determination of death and the recovery of organs', *22nd World Medical Assembly, Sydney, Australia*

(August 1968), www.wma.net/policies-post/wma-declaration-of-sydney-on-the-de termination-of-death-and-the-recovery-of-organs/ [accessed 21 June 2019].

Yacoub, M., 'Cardiac donation after circulatory death', *The Lancet* 385:9987 (2015), 2554–6.

Yanke, G., M. Rady, and J. Verheijde, 'When brain death belies belief', *Journal of Religion and Health*, 455:6 (2016), 2199–213.

Young, P. and B. Matta, 'Anesthesia for organ donation in the brainstem dead', *Anaesthesia*, 55:2 (2000), 105–6.

Younger, S., 'The definition of death', in B. Steinbock (ed.), *Oxford Handbook of Bioethics* (Oxford: Oxford University Press, 2007), pp. 285–303.

Youngner, S., 'Organ retrieval', *Transplantation Proceedings*, 22:3 (1990), 1014–15.

Zamperetti, N., R. Bellomo, and C. Ronco, 'Defining death in non-heart beating organ donors', *Journal of Medical Ethics*, 29 (2003), 182–5.

Zeiler, K. and E. Malmqvist, 'Bodily exchanges, bioethics, and border crossing', in E. Malmqvist and K. Zeiler (eds), *Bodily Exchanges* (London: Routledge, 2016), pp. 1–18.

Zimmerman, D., S. Donnelly, J. Miller, D. Stewart, and S. Albert, 'Gender disparity in living renal transplant donation', *American Journal of Kidney Disorders*, 6 (2000), 534–40.

Zlosnik, S., 'Globalgothic at the top of the world', in G. Byron (ed.), *Globalgothic* (Manchester: Manchester University Press, 2013), pp. 65–76.

Zwart, H., 'The donor organ as "object a"', *Medicine, Health Care and Philosophy*, 17:4 (2014), 559–71.

———, 'Transplantation medicine', *Subjectivity*, 9:2 (2016), 151–80.

Index

Literary works can be found under authors' surnames. Films can be found under directors' surnames.

Lightning Source UK Ltd.
Milton Keynes UK
UKHW052242160522
402789UK00007BA/37